THE DEVELOPMENT OF ANOREXIA NERVOSA

THE HUNGER ARTISTS

"This remarkably fruitful work by Sylvia Brody unites the best of longterm direct child observation with the wisdom of psychoanalytic experience. The adaptive horrors of anorexia nervosa are brought to life with a richness and depth never before available." —Warren S. Poland, M.D.

"The illuminating suns of this important book on anorexia are its two central histories based on longitudinal observations of the development of anorexia in two women, around which orbit a masterful introductory historical overview of the theoretical literature and concluding with the author's use of the case histories to improve, consolidate, deepen and test the limits of our clinical understanding of anorexia."
—Charles Hanly, Ph.D.

"This book is a must for every mental health professional and physician who works with youngsters of any age, not to mention those of us with a special interest in eating disturbances. I also recommend it highly to colleagues in the social sciences. Brody places anorexia in its full historical and cultural settings, enabling us to view it in fascinating wide context." —Erna Furman

"It is a pleasure to recommend a new book by Sylvia Brody, Ph.D. The book breaks new grounds in the study of anorexia nervosa, a neglected and therefore mysterious malady seen in adolescent girls and much less frequently in boys. It is characterized by either pathological dieting or bulimia and is accompanied by mood changes and radical attempts to control the intake of their food, regardless of common sense or the entreaties of parents or doctors. All too often the result is death from willful starvation."
—Vann Spruiell, M.D.

THE DEVELOPMENT OF ANOREXIA NERVOSA

The Hunger Artists

Sylvia Brody, Ph.D.

International Universities Press, Inc.
Madison, Connecticut

Library of Congress Cataloging-in-Publication Data

Brody, Sylvia, 1914–
  The development of anorexia nervosa : the hunger artists / Sylvia Brody.
   p. cm.
  Includes bibliographical references and index.
  ISBN 0-8236-3381-0
  1. Anorexia nervosa—Etiology. I. Title.

RC552.A5 B75 2002
616.85'262071—dc21
                                                    2001039896

Copyright © 2002, International Universities Press, Inc.

INTERNATIONAL UNIVERSITIES PRESS ® AND IUP (& design) ® are registered trademarks of International Universities Press, Inc.

All rights reserved. No part of this book may be printed or reproduced or utilized in any form or by any electronic, mechanical or other means, now known or hereafter invented, including photocopying and recording, or in any information storage or retrieval system, without permission in writing from the publisher.

Manufactured in the United States of America

To Sidney Axelrad

in loving remembrance

Table of Contents

Acknowledgments ix
Foreword xi
Introduction xiii

Chapter 1. The Importance of Infancy 1
Chapter 2. The History of Anorexia: A Brief Review 19
Chapter 3. The Clinical Data: Prefatory Notes 39
Chapter 4. The History of Helen 43
Chapter 5. The History of Ariel 77
Chapter 6. Helen and Ariel: A Few Comparisons 115
Chapter 7. Mother and Infant: Four Variations in Their Quality of Engagement with Additional Notes about Both Parents 123
Chapter 8. Clinical Signs of Anorexia That Are Known 137
Chapter 9. Clinical Signs of Anorexia That Need Further Study 163
Chapter 10. A Triumph of Rage, and a Surrender 189
Chapter 11. The Present Problem 207

Afterword 215
Appendix 217
References 221
Name Index 239
Subject Index 243

Acknowledgments

My acquaintance with ideas about eating disorders began with an opportunity to attend the discussions about psychosomatic illness led by the late Philip Wilson, the late Charles Hogan, and Ira Mintz. To them I have owed much gratitude for stimulating my pursuit of the psychological sources of anorexia nervosa in two adolescent subjects who were in my longitudinal research sample. I am grateful as well to the colleagues and friends whose interest in the subject led them to offer advice to me about this text. Loretta and Felix Loeb read an initial draft, offered ideas for textual clarifications, and from time to time sent me new information about eating disorders as they appeared in current psychiatric literature. Marshall Greene, on reading the first version of the book, alerted me to certain unintended omissions about parental understanding that can protect a child from neurotic disturbance, and parents from undue self-blame. Patricia Nachman checked my remarks about some of the psychological publications related to infant development that I had not described with sufficent clarity. Judith Geizhals, by recounting to me the history of an adult of advanced years who had suffered from anorexia in adolescence, threw light on its often lifelong sequelae. Lillian Feder helped me find words to express a psychoanalytic understanding of maternal behavior; she also translated precisely for me a word that

Ernest Jones had adapted from the Greek to name the condition of a deeply sad infant. Judith Deutsch read the final manuscript with care, and reminded me to refer to several psychoanalytic publications concerned with early emotional development, so saving me from an embarrassing neglect of those works. Anna Simon, who also took the time to read the full manuscript, insisted that I emphasize more firmly than I yet had, certain of my essential ideas about long-term parental contributions to the mental health of infants and children. Ludmila McKannay, through her artistic and psychological insight into determinants of self-starvation, enriched my appreciation of the unconscious conflicts it harbors. And Judith Kurtz is the someone who has watched over me, unfailingly, as I plodded on with my task.

Irene Guttman, formerly of International Universities Press, was the first to read the manuscript, to catch the many small errors that had crept into it, and to call my attention to ambiguous statements that had escaped me. Margaret Emery, the main editor of International Universities Press, took charge of the series of emendations I had to make, and along with Martin Azarian, cheered me as she sent it on its way to publication. To all these persons whom I have fortunately been able to call upon, I owe glad thanks for their patience in listening to my writer's worries and helping me to find my way past them.

Foreword

At one time the whole town took a lively interest in the hunger artist; from day to day of his fast the excitement mounted . . . there were people who bought season tickets . . . and sat from morning till night in front of the small barred cage; there were also . . . permanent watchers . . . in case he should have some secret recourse to nourishment. . . . So he lived for many years . . . honored by the world, yet in spite of that troubled in spirit because no one would take his trouble seriously. . . . He might fast as much as he could, and he did so, but nothing could save him now. . . . Many more days went by. . . . An overseer's eye fell on the cage one day and he asked the attendants why this perfectly good cage should be left standing there unused with dirty straw inside it; nobody knew, until one man . . . remembered about the hunger artist. They poked in the straw with sticks and found him in it. "Are you still fasting?" asked the overseer, "when on earth do you mean to stop?" "Forgive me, everybody," whispered the hunger artist; only the overseer, who had his ear to the bars, understood him. "Of course," said the overseer, "we forgive you." "I always wanted you to admire my fasting," said the hunger artist. "We do admire it," said the overseer, affably. "But you shouldn't admire it," said the hunger artist. "Well then we don't admire it," said the overseer, "but why shouldn't we admire it?" "Because I have to fast, I can't help it," said the hunger artist. "What a fellow you are," said the overseer, "and why can't you help it?" "Because," said the hunger artist, lifting his head a little and speaking, with his lips pursed, as if for a kiss right into the overseer's ear, so that no syllable might be lost, "because I couldn't find the food I liked. If I had found it, believe me, I should have made no fuss and stuffed myself like you or anyone else." These were his last words, but in his dimming eyes remained the firm though no longer proud persuasion that he was still continuing to fast [*A Hunger Artist;* Franz Kafka, 1924].

Introduction

The story of how psychopathology gets its start in infancy or childhood may be told in a few paragraphs or in many pages. I have chosen the longer way in order throw direct light on experiential events that appear to have brought on the eating disorder of anorexia in two adolescents. Histories of infancy and childhood told by parents or other caregivers are subject to their capacities for sensitive observation and objective thinking. In spite of their best intentions to provide significant anamnestic data, they may be able to provide only minimal information about events that may have interfered with the infant's or child's mental health. The reason lies in our generally poor education about the needs and capacities of infants and children.

This book is a byproduct of a longitudinal research effort that began with a pilot study of data selected randomly from a larger Infancy Research Project that was carried out in Topeka, Kansas, and supported by The Menninger Foundation and The National Institute of Mental Health between 1948 and 1952 (Escalona and Leitch, 1952). I was an assistant investigator in that project from 1949 to 1950. My first exploratory study was concerned with relations between the mother's behavior with her infant, her attitude toward her infant, and the psychological health of the infant ($N = 32$;

see Appendix). It was followed by a larger direct observational study of interrelations among the behaviors and attitudes of mothers, qualities of the infants' development at intervals during the infants' first year (N = 131),[1] their familial conditions, and developmental test results. A central theme in that study came to be the relation between anxiety and ego formation in infancy (Brody and Axelrad, 1970a). The richness of the data led us to continue the study of the mothers and infants, later including the fathers as well, until the children reached the age of 7 (N = 121).[2] That first follow-up study explored connections between development in infancy and early childhood and character formation up to age 7 (Brody and Axelrad, 1978). A third follow-up study of the original subjects as they neared age 18 allowed us to study the formation of character from infancy to late adolescence (N = 91; Brody and Siegel, 1992). From the collected direct observations, films of mother–infant behavior, interviews with the mothers, and diagnostic psychological tests we learned about many aspects of the subjects' emotional states, social and cognitive development in infancy and early childhood, and at age 18, their enlarging object relations, compromise formations, character development, and capacities for sublimation in late adolescence.

Two of the female subjects, at age 18, told me they had been anorexic a few years before. We had previously published accounts of the psychological disturbances of both subjects, among others, that were observed from their births to age 7 (Brody and Axelrad, 1978). Given the further information about them, I turned back to our records to find out what personal–historical events might be understood as

---

[1] Funded by The National Institute of Mental Health, M1429, and administered by The Lenox Hill Hospital, New York City.
[2] Funded by the William T. Grant Foundation, and administered by The City University of New York.

having produced their eating disorder. The histories I present here do not derive from any form of psychological treatment or behavior inventory. The single aim of this book has been to trace the psychogenic sources of anorexia, as far as could be determined from study of the available information on two research subjects from birth to age 30.[3]

The considerations I have to offer about the development of their illness have included many more details than are usually available about the early life of anorexic patients. For some readers such details may appear to be excessive, as usually the experiences of infancy have not aroused particular interest in the general public unless psychologically adverse events have been known to occur during the first year or two. In the midtwentieth century the important issues of infancy, other than physical health and nutrition, had to do with the achievement of developmental milestones such as teething, creeping, walking, beginning speech, imitation of gestures, and forms of play. Anamneses dealt with pediatric issues, rarely with emotional or cognitive growth, or the development of object relations during infancy. In recent decades we have learned about infant states, affective needs, and early experiences that influence development in a large variety of ways. Now it is evident that serious interruptions of mental and emotional development can arise in the first years of life, although to an uninformed observer they may not be recognized as such. The influences of Hartmann and Winnicott that in the past few decades have captured the attention of workers in the field of infancy and early childhood, brought Baumrind (1993) to remind us that "the average expectable environment[4] is not good enough."[5] Were

[3]Interviews with 76 of the subjects at age 30 have been carried out by Henry N. Massie, M.D., Clinical Associate Professor, University of California School of Medicine, San Francisco.

[4]A concept adopted from the sociologist Max Weber (1921). See Hartmann (1939, pp. 23, 35).

[5]Winnicott (1962, p. 5).

we to be satisfied with what is just good enough, we should not need to study the events of infancy and childhood that have connections to later psychological dilemmas. I am addressing the problem inherent in those connections from the vantage point of classical psychoanalytic theory and practice. Other explanations about anorexia that may come from the practice of internal medicine, psychiatry, developmental psychology, and related fields may yield knowledge of other etiological factors that contribute to the syndrome of anorexia. The propositions I shall bring forward emerged from a unique opportunity to study data about a large number of subjects from birth to late adolescence, supplemented by further data about them up to age 30. My first aim was to study my data for premonitory signs of their eating disorder during infancy—approximately the first 15 months of life.

I shall begin with comments on the importance of infancy, and shall then briefly review the psychoanalytic literature about anorexia, as most of the pediatric literature has left the subject in obscurity. I shall then follow with an account of the two research subjects who developed the disorder. I shall say most about their relations with their mothers and fathers during infancy and early childhood, the qualities of their parents, and the behaviors that differentiated the two female anorexic subjects from the other 41 female subjects in the sample available for study up to age 18. I shall then discuss the dynamic conflicts found to be present as their psychopathology evolved, and submit my thoughts about the main psychological determinants of anorexia discerned in their clinical histories. Finally, I shall offer some thoughts about the apparent willingness of most severely ill anorexic patients to risk chronic illness or death.

The experiences of infancy and early childhood may appear to be too remote to explain the advent of anorexia in adolescence, but most investigators have emphasized the probability that predisposing elements are hard to isolate as being prognostic. Therefore a search for specific causative factors, especially those that show continuity from the first years of life, should in time provide for the generation of testable hypotheses that may lead to an understanding of the development of anorexia.

Chapter 1

The Importance of Infancy

This book rests on the principle that the day-to-day experiences of the infant have a continuity that binds the infant and then the young child to movement along certain psychological paths that have variable degrees of permanence, always depending on the social environment in which he or she grows. For better or worse, the paths that infants take determine the quality of their childhood and adolescent preoccupations and their adult aims. The way we live, from infancy onward, in spite of innumerable vicissitudes, carries us along with something germinal, something that harks back to first impressions. This means that an infant who lives with too little grace and hope, and with too much pain that is poorly responded to during infancy and childhood, is likely to move into adolescence with diminished resilience and with weakened ability to seek for more than mundane gratifications in his or her life. It does not mean that the experiences of infancy forecast the future, or that I am pathologizing infancy. Our beginnings can inspire us or they can haunt us. Sometimes we know them and take pleasure in knowing them; many times we dare not know them.

Everyday events that affect an infant's well-being were rarely a subject of systematic psychoanalytic study until the second third of the twentieth century. Up to then we had Freud's outlines of infantile sexuality (1905); Von Hug-Hellmuth's (1919) descriptions of the sensory and mental life of the infant that characterize the oral phase; Ferenczi's (1913) ideas about infantile thought; and the descriptions by Bernfeld (1929) of the physical and mental capacities of infants, the instinctual gratifications that accompany body functions, and the pleasure of mastery. Many of Bernfeld's contributions have been absorbed in our views of infant experience; some have faded from sight because in the first decades of the century those studying the general psychology of infants turned, for good reason, to studying their physical, sensory, and cognitive development (e.g., Gesell, 1928; Carmichael, 1946) in the first half of the century, previously reviewed (see Brody, 1956). Another stream of theory had entered the field, in the work of Klein. Her ideas would have been more welcome to mainstream psychoanalysts and psychologists had she not described sadistic fantasies arising during the first months of life (1928) and oedipal fantasies as well as persecutory and depressive states by the end of the first year (1935). Klein (1936) was the first psychoanalyst to discuss weaning as a critical experience of infancy, but she became overly occupied with infant fantasies about the breast that she believed aroused processes of projection and introjection and a sense of guilt (1937, 1940). Later Furman (1982) provided clinical observations, with an enlightened discussion of emotional problems related to weaning, for both mothers and infants. Klein followed with a set of propositions (1952a,b) about the feelings and fantasies of young infants based on secondary observations, anecdotal data, and symbolic interpretations of infant behaviors. She disregarded the value of empirical data. "The *fact*" (italics added), she wrote, "that at the beginning of postnatal life an unconscious knowledge of the breast exists and that feelings toward the breast are experienced can only be conceived of as a phylogenetic inheritance" (1952b, p. 117). In view of the actual immaturity of infant mentation, her ideas remain open to question, although they have been taken up by many in branches of psychiatry, especially by practitioners concerned with psychosis. The psychoanalytic study of the real experiences of infancy was derailed by her ideas about the content of unconscious fantasies of infants which in the present are beyond disproof. Nevertheless, she did alert psychoanalysts to the dark continent of the mental life of the infant.

Before Klein, psychoanalysts interested in infancy had given most attention to themes of oral gratification or deprivation, fear of object loss, and fear of loss of the object's love, as originally expressed by Freud (1905). As far as I know, there has been no organized investigation of specific salient experiences of infants, such as the frustrations that accompany weaning, teething, and being alone, or the effects of prolonged dependence on pacifiers and transitional objects. For better or worse, the psychological aspects of these issues have been left to pediatricians who, by and large, and in accordance with their medical education, have limited their attention to the infant's physical condition.

The principal behaviors of the oral phase enunciated by Freud (1905), sucking and biting, were recognized as givens, with fluctuations taken for granted as long as there were clinical reports of connections between oral-phase experiences and later clinical symptoms. Up to the middle 1940s the main current in observations of infant experience lay in the general quality of the infant's relation to the mother who was presumed to be the person who satisfies the infant's oral needs. But as the psychoanalytic method depended on speech, and infants do not yet speak, a way to learn about their inner psychological states was at that time hardly conceivable. A change came with Winnicott's publications (1936, 1941, 1945) and his BBC radio talks about the mutual needs of mothers and infants (1957), which brought attention to details of experience within the emotional world of mother and infant. In 1949 I had the opportunity to observe a series of about 75 infants at ages 4 to 32 weeks in the care of their mothers for a four-hour period in a standard situation (see Appendix). I was struck by the variety of activities involved in the feeding of an infant, and the oral phase took on new meaning for me. I realized that while the feeding of infants was a necessary and universal activity of every mother, accompanying behaviors like holding, gazing at, talking to, or playing with an infant, and indeed how they fed, were matters of individual convenience or chance, and largely dependent on the mother's feelings and attitudes about being a mother, and about her child. I considered that observations of maternal feeding of their infants might provide for a pilot study to identify, provisionally, types of maternal behaviors and attitudes, and any relations between any types that could be identified, and the early development of their infants. An unexpected finding (Brody, 1956) was that for the infants observed at the earliest age of 4 weeks it was the mothers' moving (handling) of her infant, which included holding and touching of the infant's body, and not her offering of food or oral gratification, that was found to be the most significant index of a mother's general maternal behavior. At succeeding infant ages, observed up to 28 weeks, it was the maternal feeding of their infants, as had been expected, that was the best index of the mothers' general maternal behavior. This implied that a mother's handling of the young infant's body might be more critical for the infant's earliest development than the oral gratification she offered. That is, the early oral phase appeared to be more complex than had been assumed since Freud had mapped out its importance. He (1905) had described sucking as the infant's first and most vital *activity*. Later (1938), he described the mouth as the first *organ* to make libidinal demands on the mind. On the basis of these statements, and my observations of neonates and young infants, I suggested:

> The skin has none of the power that the mouth has actively to respond to external stimuli. It is capable only of passive sensations. It can react with alterations in the vasomotor balance, and the skin of the infant does that quite readily, as manifested by pressure marks, flushing, paling and irritations. . . . It may be plausible to think of the infant's perception of reality as being first through the external skin of the whole body surface and then through the internal skin or membrane of the mouth cavity; and to think of gratifications as taking place primarily in the postnatal restoration of warmth and equilibrium and secondarily in the intake of milk. . . . Observation of maternal behavior showed that save under conditions of body security and comfort no infant, however hungry, appeared to enjoy his feeding [Brody, 1956, pp. 339–340].

This understanding of the primary importance of tactile and kinesthetic gratification of the very young infant preceded the findings of Harlow and Zimmerman (1959) and Harlow (1961), which had followed upon studies of imprinting (Lorenz, 1935; Tinbergen, 1951). Bowlby (1958, 1960b, 1969) welcomed the latter studies because of his earlier findings about the abiding painful experiences of early loss in his studies (1940, 1944) of juvenile thieves as "affectionless characters." This may in part explain why he set aside the psychoanalytic proposition that the infant is from the beginning endowed with an oral instinctual drive. He placed an alternative emphasis on a primary biological need for proximity to the mother, a behavior activated by object clinging, and necessary for evolutionary adaptedness. The proximity he described encompassed five patterns of behavior—sucking, clinging, following, crying and smiling, which build "a control theory of attachment behaviour" (1969, p. 180). Although Bowlby acknowledged that the human infant may take weeks or months to acquire the mobility needed to achieve physical proximity to the mother, unlike newborn animals who do so before they suck her milk, he argued that the primary attachment-seeking of subhuman primates "is likely to be truly homologous with what obtains in man" (p. 183). My observation (1956), that the young infant's need for physical intimacy and body safety appeared to precede the need for food, did not obviate the infant's libidinal drive. It rather indicated that the infant's instinctual need for physical intimacy and body safety just preceded the immediate need for food; when those physical needs are unfulfilled, oral sucking may be impeded. That is to say, the earliest instinctual needs for body and mouth satisfactions followed so soon upon each other that they were close to being a twinship. Bowlby argued in favor of a behavioral system, in which the infant's primary need was for proximity to the mother. Oral instinctual needs represented a secondary drive. He knew of the neonate's immediate need for physical security, but not for the almost simultaneous instinctual *pleasure* of sucking milk and satisfying hunger. He (1958, 1960a) wished to highlight the cardinal importance of separation anxiety in order to construct an empirical method by which to learn about the origin of anxiety in the infant.

We may one day be able to determine whether an infant's need to follow visually, to cling, to cry, and other innate acts that bring help from mother, as outlined by Bowlby (1958, 1960a, 1969), have first importance in the neonate. The maternal behaviors of touching, holding, and carrying the very young infants that I observed in mothers of 4-week-olds may be regarded as parallel evidence of an elemental need for whole-body safety (Brody, 1956, pp. 339-340). Even so, the needs for sucking and nutriment come so fast upon the need for physical security that neither exists first for more than a very brief time.[1] To posit a primary and then a secondary drive in earliest infancy seems to me redundant, at least until we have surer evidence than we now have that a biological need for social attachment precedes a need for oral and stomach satisfaction. For the present one may say that if in the first few weeks of life the infant receives satisfaction of the several needs for feeling body safety, for sensory awakening to a someone "out there" who provides those calming necessities with affection, then the infant is on the way to developing feelings of validation as a functioning being. This involves the acquisition of a primitive sense of ego, a body ego, in the sense that "the ego is first and foremost a body ego" (Freud, 1923). In time the body ego provides for the development of a body image and eventually a self-perception.

In general, separation anxiety as an inborn reaction to a rupture of attachment is a concept much more acceptable than the fear of object loss, which is so much more affect-laden. It is interesting to note that Bowlby's tacit separation from psychoanalytic theory (1969) came—with the exception of his paper (1960a) on pathological mourning in childhood—after the critical discussions of his paper (1960a) by A. Freud (1960), Schur (1960), and Spitz (1960). He may have been taken aback by their pointed statements, which in fact matched his own for conviction. Mutual withdrawals

---

[1]Considering the electronic recording devices that are becoming available, the earliest sequence of these needs may be measurable in the foreseeable future.

followed, unfortunately, and attachment theory developed as a distinctly separate way of studying infant composure or distress. This separation was evident in Bowlby's acknowledging (1969, 1973) but then bypassing the significance of Freud's seminal work (1926) on the psychological sources of anxiety. He may have been influenced to make this turn away from psychoanalytic theory not only by the new ethological studies, but by his discontent with Klein's speculations about infant mental life, and his discomfort with Winnicott's insightful but sometimes too imaginative ideas on the same subject.

A. Freud (1960) saw another aspect of the problem in discriminating sources of disturbances during infancy when she said that Bowlby dealt rightly with behavioral and biological issues, but omitted those that are metapsychological, that involve the concepts of primary process, the unconscious, and the structural point of view. "As analysts," she wrote.

> we do not deal with drive activity as such but with the mental representatives of the drives. In the case of the biological tie to the mother this representation has to be recognized ... in the infant's inborn readiness to cathect objects with libido.... We do not deal with happenings in the external world as such but with their repercussions in the mind, that is, the form in which they are registered by the child ... which are experienced as events in the pleasure-pain series [p. 54].

Hanly's (1978) discussion of Bowlby's ethological theory is straightforward:

> [The] theory of attachment, in the interest of an apparent scientific objectivity, does not provide any place for the all-important facts of libidinal and aggressive exchange between

mother and child. I say "apparent scientific objectivity" because what has actually occurred in Bowlby's theorizing is the abandonment of the psychodynamic viewpoint for the external, behavioral viewpoint when what one hopes to find is their integration. . . . The difficulty with [his] theorizing is not what it adds to our understanding of the behavior of children but what it omits and displaces [pp. 366–367].

Bowlby (1951) had opened up the subjects of maternal deprivation, and the breaking up of affective bonds between mother and infant through separation and loss (1960a,b). His subsequent theory about attachment, being behavioral, was much simpler to grasp, and incomparably easier to measure, than the fitness of a psychoanalytic theory that involved unconscious processes and libidinal and aggressive drives. It needed no inferences about psychodynamics. Ainsworth and Wittig (1969) made use of his propositions about the infant's tie to the mother (1958, 1960b) by devising the "Strange Situation" experiment, which has since become a favored instrument of developmental psychologists. Briefly described, it consists of a series of eight episodes. The mother and her 1-year-old infant are at first together in an unfamiliar room where playthings are at hand; then mother leaves, a stranger enters, the infant is left with the stranger, mother returns to the infant. The situation and its consequences have been fully described by Main (1995). The behavior of the infant when reunited with the mother is the crux of the experiment. The infant's reaction to the mother's return is described as secure, insecure, ambivalent, or avoidant. But this classification omits negative attachment, which I believe transpires well after infancy among serious delinquents and criminals, having been "implanted" very early in life as a result of a mother's firm emotional and physical detachment from her infant. I have known it to occur as an indirect consequence of desertion by the mother in the child's early years. It appears in certain adolescents and adults known for their "cold personality." Of course it is fostered by pathological narcissism. During infancy or early childhood this kind of attachment may be seen as avoidant or ambivalent. Later on it may be transformed into an almost unmixed hostility, with conscious and unconscious components. I call attention to it here because it characterized the relations of two research subjects to their parents, as I shall discuss below.

Use of the Strange Situation paradigm has provided information about the quality of the infant's attachment at age 1, seen in behavioral terms (Stayton and Ainsworth, 1973; Sroufe and Fleeson, 1986; Goldberg, Muir, and Kerr, 1995; see also Brody, 1981). Important as this live experiment may be for learning about the quality of the infant's investment in the mother at age 1, it does not deal with how that investment changes and develops during the infant's long first year, long from the infant's point of view because it includes so many first-time experiences. Clinical data have shown that the first die for the quality of attachment is cast during the infant's life before 2 months (Brody and Axelrad, 1970b, 1978; Brody and Siegel, 1992). An infant's capacity to tolerate separation from the mother at age 1 depends on when, how often, and under what circumstances, breaks in the attachment have occurred, with what effects, during the infant's whole first year. Moreover, for an adequate assessment of an infant's attachment, the affective quality of the mother-infant relationship and their mutual activities, needs to be known. Behaviors at age 1 may provide a summary picture of much that has gone before. That picture allows for approximations of behaviors that are likely to have continuity, at least as long as the infant goes on living with the same main persons, in much the same environment. But that the quality of an infant's attachment has a genesis beginning at birth seems clear to all who study early emotional development (Stern, 1971, 1974, 1985; Brazelton, Tronick, Adamson, Als, and Wise, 1975; Brazelton and Als, 1979; Emde, Gaensbauer and Harmon, 1976; Emde, 1983). To understand how attachment can be observed and measured throughout the first year of life, and under what conditions it has continuity in the next several years, is a task that eventually should lead to construction of a bridge between developmental psychology and psychoanalytic psychology.

For all the important leads to knowledge about early psychological growth that Bowlby provided, he did not take up the ways that attachments to human persons are stabilized or diversified in the first year of life. His theory related to the origin of anxiety in the infant. In it he distinguished between primary anxiety, which included fright, expectant or anticipatory anxiety, and avoidance behavior (which appear in the Strange Situation paradigm), as these occur with physical separation from the mother, and create a rupture in their attachment (1960b, p. 93). He was not concerned with connections between early anxiety and ego formation, especially the onset of defense structures such as avoidance, restriction, and regression.

As a disturbance of body image is central in anorexic patients, who maintain a feeling or a fantasy of being fat and/or a fear of getting fat (Wilson, Hogan, and Mintz, 1983), we may turn to the basic contribution of Schilder to understand the vulnerability of the body image in infancy. Schilder (1935) observed that every sensation contributes to the building of the body image, emphasizing the part played by physical security, and adding that continued activity is the base of our bodily self. Although he made no specific reference to the state of the infant, his considerations about the development of the body image encompass infant experience, and can help us to understand some of the underpinnings of anorexia. For example, he suggested that two factors play a special part in the creation of the body image: pain, which is inherent in hunger, and motor control of one's limbs (pp. 104–105). There is no question, he said, that our own activity is insufficient to build up the image of the body. "The touches of others, the interest others take in the different parts of our body, will be of enormous importance in the development of the postural model of the body" (pp. 126–127). And further, "The building-up of the body image is based not only upon the individual history of an individual, but also on his relation to others. The inner history is also the history of our relations to other human beings" (p. 138). As to the effects of two few physical and sensory contacts during early infancy, he wrote, "There are tendencies which try to make the body-image complete, but it cannot remain so without a renewed effort. There are opposite tendencies as well . . . towards the dissolution of the body-image. When we close our eyes and remain as motionless as possible, the body-image tends toward dissolution. . . . The body-image . . . is never static " (p. 287). These statements mean that the infant's acquisition of a sound body image needs early and continual reinforcement by persons in the infant's intimate environment. Schilder's observations take on importance for our understanding of the strains placed on the body image during infancy for the anorexic subjects to be described below.

On the same theme Ribble (1943) emphasized the importance of tactile and cutaneous stimulation for the infant's breathing, and indirectly, for the infant's building of a mental representation of his or her body. In my initial study of mothers and infants (N = 32) I found that the 4-week-old infants whose mothers had provided them with most positive care and stimulation were at 28 weeks most advanced in the Motor and Adaptive sectors in the Gesell Developmental Tests, while the infants of that age who had been provided with the least positive care and stimulation performed least well in the same subtests at 28 weeks. The latter were most advanced, however, in Personal–Social sector, possibly a result of high negative stimulation (Brody, 1956). This implies that the psychological investments in persons and the environment of the most advanced infants were present and positive, compared to that of the least advanced infants, whose investments were shaky. About early skin erotism A. Freud (1965) wrote, "At the beginning of life, being stroked, cuddled, and soothed by touch libidinizes the various parts of the body, helps to build up a healthy body image and body ego, increases its cathexis with [necessary] narcissistic libido, and simultaneously promotes the development of object love . . . the surface of the skin in its role as erotogenic zone fulfills a multiple function in the child's growth" (p. 199). Similarly, Montagu (1971) described the importance of gentle tactile stimulation in animals and humans: "Handling or gentling of animals in their early days results in significantly greater increases in weight, more activity, less fearfulness, and greater resistance to physiological damage" (p. 28). The significance of visual contact during a critical period of infancy for the formation of the body image has also been emphasized by many (Freud, 1914; Piaget, 1937; Werner, 1940; Greenacre, 1953; Linn, 1955; Brody, 1956, 1964; Brody and Axelrad, 1970b). Candland (1993) observed that extreme sensory deprivation of light and sound can be survived as long as the sensory experience of the skin is maintained. This happened in the cases of Helen Keller and Laura Bridgman. Although their vision and hearing were lost in their first years, they became able to communicate on a high level through the sense of touch.

Evidence that the physical handling of newborns has significant effects on their development has appeared in recent years.[2]

Regarding the young infant's need to feel body safety, Sandler (1960) wrote that perception is an act of integration, and that successful sensory integration contributes to a feeling of safety. This was nicely put, yet it appeared to me that a feeling of safety derives in the beginning less from an amalgam of sensory experiences, and more from the equilibristic security of the whole body. That security is naturally reinforced by positive sensory experiences, which in turn give form to the infant's mental representation of his or her body and nascent self. To have a clear knowledge of this mental journey, from birth to beyond the first year, we shall need physiological as well as psychological studies of relations between received sensations in the body and perceptual responses to external stimuli. All indications are that young infants need gentle and safe physical handling and consistently affectionate regard for their well-being. The days are long gone when it was assumed that adequate physical care

---

[2]Field et al. (1986) found that touching, stroking, and passive movements of the limbs of 20 preterm neonates for 15-minute periods of the day for 10 days resulted in more than average weight gain (47%), activity, and alertness, and shorter hospital stays for the stimulated infants. A similar experiment by Wheedon et al. (1993) with 15 cocaine-addicted preterm infants averaged a 28 percent greater weight gain and fewer postnatal complications. The infants were more mature at the end of the 10-day period than the control cases. Prodromidis et al. (1995) studied the maternal behavior of 31 mothers of low socioeconomic status who had extended contact with their newborns; they showed more touching of the infant's face and head and more interaction than did the control group. Palaez-Nogueras, Field, Hossain, and Pickens (1996) found that tactile stimulation by a caregiver during face-to-face interactions increased affect and attention in 3-month-old infants. When touch was used as part of the caregiver's social stimulation it affectively reinforced and maintained higher rates of infant eye contact, smiles, and vocalizations.

and feeding are all that infants need. The idea that infants of any age can be left alone as long as they are physically safe and contented with a pacifier, a stuffed animal, or television pictures, should also be long gone. Other psychoanalytic writers about aspects of infancy (Alice and Michael Balint, Anna Freud, Provence and Lipton, Mahler, Sandler, Spitz, Winnicott), some of whose contributions I have discussed before (Brody, 1980, 1982a), have provided evocative ideas, but few systematic observations of specific infant behaviors in normal settings, in the first year of life. It is to be hoped that additional findings about the everyday experience of the infant living at home will become available in the years ahead.

In the beginning the infant accepts gratification from anyone at any time. The person who takes first place in satisfying the infant's wishes, and the order in which the various needs are satisfied by familiar persons, appear to be of basic significance for the shaping of relations to persons from infancy through childhood, and beyond. We may say that a clear move from one stage in the development of object relations to the next represents a first kind of binding of energy, and that this binding occurs first with recognition of the mother qua mother, assuming that the satisfactions she provides are positive, reliable, and consistent. This means, for the very young infant, that the cognitive and the affective are inextricably intertwined. Once psychic energy is firmly invested in a human object, a first stage of socialization has taken place. This investment represents a tiny piece of abstract thinking. It permits the infant to single out the mother from all other persons, a process integrally affected by the degree of physiological anxiety present in the young infant, because that anxiety can blunt awareness of differences between the self representation and the outer world. The more slowly the infant converts physiological anxiety to signal anxiety (a mental warning of danger), the greater is the possibility that the infant's absorption with his or her own sensations and feelings will be excessive. This condition was probably present in Helen and Ariel, the research subjects described below. In an effort to escape from physiological anxiety related to hunger and the need for body safety, the infant may be impelled to rely on hallucinatory gratification, and so may be discouraged from eliciting appropriate responses from the real world.

Every psychoanalyst is trained to understand that events in the oral phase have a major influence on our psychological lives. To learn which experiences in that phase can fortify positive psychological growth in the oral phase and after, we need empirical studies based on direct observation of variations in mother–infant behavior. We also need data from psychoanalytically guided *longitudinal* studies of behavior and development, including elements of the human environment in which the child lives, from birth, and the influence of the parents' histories, the state of the infant's control of affects and impulses, and the family's socioeconomic status. When I began to observe infants in the presence of their mothers in 1949 I had only a glimmering knowledge of the importance of these factors. Otherwise, in the larger study (Brody and Axelrad, 1970b) I would have searched more carefully into the infants' experiences at the hands of the mother in their first few weeks together; that is, I would not have moved from day 3 to 6 weeks; and I would have aimed to observe the mother–infant interaction and the infant's inclinations at more frequent intervals in their first year. In addition to observing the mother's feeding behavior, I would have tried to observe her efforts regarding neatness and cleanliness during the feedings. Such observations would have afforded opportunities to learn about (1) the onset of the infant's responses to dirtiness allowed or disallowed by the mother; which might reveal (2) the transition between gratification in the oral and anal phases; and (3) the generation of defensive measures to ward off anxiety. It might not have been feasible to carry out any such plan, considering the costs, and the generally low interest in the study of mothers' relationships to their infants when I began my first study in 1950 as well as my second study in 1963.

The importance of infancy lies in its being a prologue to acquiring knowledge of earliest sources of mental peace or conflict. That knowledge should in time yield a map for early ego and superego development through the building of object relations, cognitive appetence, a capacity to wait, to be alone for short periods (Winnicott, 1958, 1963), to bear frustration, and to practice a range of expressive behaviors (Winnicott, 1963). Of course, the psychological events of infancy do not tell the whole story of the beginnings of anorexia[3]—far from it. They are of essential importance for mental health or illness, but do not by themselves explain the incidence of either. They tell only about the earliest contributions to the later development of this eating disorder. Aside from specific traumatic events, it is mainly by virtue of continuous repetition of positive or negative psychological events in various forms during infancy, and their entrenchment in childhood and preadolescence, that the influence of early experiences gathers force and shapes the adolescent's self-perception. When the maladaptive experiences are observed and respected for the influence they have all along the way, and appropriate interventions are made in good time and with good will, then the infant's, the child's, and the adolescent's mental health can be significantly safeguarded.

[3]*Nervosa* is omitted in this context because it is now generally understood that the disorder derives from a psychological rather than a neurological condition.

Chapter 2

The History of Anorexia: A Brief Review

Primitive taboos against eating have been traced to medieval beliefs in Eastern and African cultures (MacCulloch, 1912). They represented religious rites observed in food preparation, initiation ceremonies, magical purification, acts of penance and expiation of sin, and a life of asceticism. The extreme forms had been practiced by monks and anchorites between 250 and 400 CE (Bliss and Branch, 1960). Rabbinical law in the medieval period, influenced by Christian beliefs, imposed fasting as a regular spiritual discipline of asceticism: intentional self-denial at certain intervals for religious reasons was in itself believed to lead one to a higher plane of existence, the pursuit of pleasure was a waste of time and the deadliest of sins, and the pleasure to be gained through food intake had to be forsworn (Diamond, 1998). By the theology of the twelfth century, periodic fasting as a religious observance was a rite of atonement, of a restoration of friendly relations between God and sinners, and so an expiation of sin. During the next few centuries, especially among Catholics, fasting was believed to mean that the capacity to live in spite of prolonged abstinence was a miracle. It implied sainthood, especially among women, for their perfectionistic ideals, suffering, and service to others (Hildanus, 1646, cited in Skrabanek, 1983; Morton, 1689; Thomä, 1967; Bynum, 1985; Brumberg, 1988; Bemporad, 1996). Periodic fasting as a religious rite still appears in the Catholic season of Lent, the Jewish Day of Atonement, and the Moslem fasting from sunrise to sunset for thirty days during Ramadan.

In the seventeenth century, habitual abstention from food began to be related to organic causes, still with largely varying ideas about its source as put forth by religious and medical proponents. It was then called *anorexia mirabilis*, being understood as a miraculously inspired loss of appetite. The latter emphasis was partially misleading in that it simplified the phenomenon as being related only to food. Confusions continued to arise in the eighteenth and nineteenth centuries around the problem of appetite as necessary to religious practice, or to feminine decorum, or to specious forms of illness; or as a mark of psychopathology. To this day the separate meanings of fasting as a religious observance and as a compulsion to reject food have been confused (Brumberg, 1988). The two separate motives for what was long regarded as a "loss of appetite" may overlap in the patient. A distinction is to be made between fasting as a mark of religious idealism or self-starvation as a sign of psychological disorder, although the two motives are altogether different in their conscious aims. Periodic fasting is not harmful, and can signify normal or neurotic feelings of absolution. Prolonged self-starvation leads to physical and psychological disorder, and may be lethal.

In the seventeenth and eighteenth centuries, physicians at first attributed the condition to a female craving for sympathy, sometimes to female spitefulncsss. They were on the way to accepting the problem as a symptom of hysteria. Still, as numbers of adolescents and young women asserted they were staying alive without partaking of any nourishment, the aura of spirituality held until a series of such claims were found to be fraudulent. The abstention from food gradually took on a secular meaning, after Erasmus Darwin in 1796 brought scientific method to an understanding of the problem. He classified three categories of anorexia: those that occurred with fits, with insanity, and with a general aversion to food by "young ladies." Gradually the concept changed from a clerical to a scientific one (Brumberg, 1988). While medical investigators had begun to search for clues in endocrinological and metabolic disorders, hysteria remained the primary diagnosis until Gull (1873) diagnosed the refusal to eat as a nervous disease. In his time the majority of psychological disturbances were routinely attributed to problems of the nervous system, mostly in women. One might read of nervous exhaustion, nervous instability, nervous temperament, nervous prostration, neurasthenia, and the like, all understood to be related to hereditary weakness. "Psychiatry could assume the status of science only if it embraced a somatic model of mental alienation, tracing the roots of the disease to some lesion or malfunction of the body" (Oppenheim, 1991, p. 35). Gull (1873) renamed the illness *anorexia nervosa*, ruling out organic disease in the patient. He believed, however, that her refusal to eat was a sign of pathological willfulness, and that the only way to cure it was to make her submit to the more powerful will of the physician (Oppenheim, 1991, pp. 212–213).

The second important increase in diagnostic understanding of the illness was provided independently in the same year by Lasègue (1873), who was impressed by its psychological aspects. He thought it might have sociological roots because he had found that it appeared mainly in middle and upper class families. Assuming, probably correctly, that those of lower socioeconomic status could not afford to deny hunger, he suggested that the incidence of anorexia was related to a group of factors among adolescents in the rising middle class. That is, compared with those of lower socioeconomic status, they had longer periods of dependence on the family and experienced closer parental attention and more parental social ambition, especially for marriageable daughters. They lived with an emphasis on manners, daintiness of habit, especially eating habits, and other Victorian ideals of feminine delicacy, including "a physique that symbolized rejection of all carnal appetites. . . . Body image rather than body function became a paramount concern" (Brumberg, 1988, pp. 182–185). Chlorosis, another "female" illness characterized by lack of energy, poor appetite, inertia, and melancholy, was frequently diagnosed in adolescence. The diagnosis overlapped with hysteria and anorexia at the turn of the century, the period when "young ladies" went into a "decline," and lost their vigor and vitality. The cause was largely assumed to be related to the advent of menses. Once the normal menstrual cycle was understood, in 1908, the mistaken idea of chlorosis fell away, and the real cause was understood to result from an iron deficiency, a form of anemia (for a discussion of the supposed illness see Brumberg [1982]). The supposed connection between chlorosis and the onset of menstruation may have originated in prejudice against females: simply, they bleed. Taboos regarding menstruation have long existed in many cultures. Added to general anxieties related to the female genital is a primitive horror of what is seen as its bleeding. To the child or the uninformed adolescent, bleeding signifies a wound and a danger to be avoided, an issue about which much may be learned in clinical psychoanalytic studies of anorexia in adolescence.

In the last decade of the nineteenth century the advent of dynamic psychiatry and psychoanalysis brought studies of the life histories that turned attention to psychogenic factors of "nervous disease." Breuer and Freud (1893–1895) described a case in which the act of eating was connected with lingering memories of disgust (p. 89). They included anorexia as one product of hysteria, with an event in childhood as its usual source. Breuer and Freud (1893–1895) traced hysterical symptoms, such as chronic vomiting, to the same source in childhood. Theirs was a first consideration of a psychodynamic meaning of anorexia. In Draft F from the Fliess papers (1892–1899) Freud went on to suggest that the neurotic illness was brought about by states of melancholia in young women who had renounced their sexuality, their seeming loss of appetite for food signifying a hysterical loss of libido (pp. 200, 203). He raised the question of what the lack of appetite might mean, and expanded upon its source in various expressions of infantile sexuality. A year later, in Draft K from the Fliess papers, he stated that the affect of disgust had been produced by shame and morality, because "the neighborhood in which the sexual organs are naturally placed must inevitably arouse disgust along with sexual experiences" (1892–1899, pp. 221–222). By the twentieth century the concept of anorexia reflected a striving for perfection according to social ideals of physical rather than of spiritual beauty. The high value placed on slenderness and restricted food intake reigned long before the popularity of the thin "flappers" in the 1920s, and before the high style of feminine slimness in the latter half of the twentieth century. Brumberg (1982) described the concern with diet in the latter years of the nineteenth century, and specifically the fears of fatness.

The normal arousal of libidinal and aggressive excitement in adolescence was becoming less hidden than in previous years, but related fears about body integrity led young females, in particular, to a regressive displacement to, and renunciation of, food. Janet (1907, cited in Ellenberger, 1970) called attention to an obsessional preoccupation of females with shame about their bodies. He thought their fear of obesity was connected to fears of sexual development, which several investigators have related to a fear of pregnancy. Freud (1905) saw the disgust with food as a prime feature of hysterical vomiting and other eating neurotic illnesses (p. 182). In turn Janet (1907) emphasized the patient's wish to control her appetite.

> Taken together, Freud and Janet gave birth to the modern psychogenetic idea that anorexic girls refused food in order to keep their bodies small, thin, and childlike, thereby retarding normal sexual development and forestalling adult sexuality.... [Both] promoted the idea that food refusal in anorexia nervosa constituted a form of symbolic behavior that served its predominantly adolescent female clientele as a statement about sexuality. Despite the power and originality of these ideas, dynamic psychiatry did not have a demonstrable effect on the clinical treatment of anorexic patients for nearly thirty years [Brumberg, 1988, p. 217].

Abraham (1916) referred to the "lengthy and uncertain way of starvation" of depressed patients who had no desire to live and regressed to a primitive stage of development, the oral or cannibalistic stage. Accordingly, their unconscious wish to incorporate the sexual object stemmed from the more primitive unconscious wish to devour and demolish the object by eating it up (pp. 274–277)—wishes that could be learned about only in intensive psychoanalytic treatment. He (1924a) also spelled out connections between oral ambivalence and later conditions such as melancholia, impatience, restlessness, a constant urge to talk, and indifference to worldly matters. He did not link these symptoms to anorexia, but in the same year (1924b) he once more related the refusal of food in depressive states to cannibalistic guilt (p. 420), to kleptomania and to biting off body parts (pp. 485–488). The unconscious sexual aim in both, he suggested, was to deprive an object of part of its body, that is, to attack its integrity without destroying its existence. In this way Abraham made an important association between oral aggression and the formation of object relations, now considered to be obvious.

Psychoanalytic interest in the neurotic eating disorders rose in the 1940s, first in the work of Masserman (1941), who reviewed the literature about the part played by nausea and vomiting in anorexia and bulimia. Most advances in the understanding of anorexia came within the same decade. Lorand (1943) identified the comorbidity of affective disturbances in the neurosis, and was the first to identify a combination of essential causative agents: inability to express tender affect, fear of being unwanted, and feelings of revengeful hostility toward mother, with a simultaneous wish for atonement through suffering and wasting away. Eissler (1943) also found that the refusal of food represented an infantile longing for gratification from the mother, along with a sadistic distortion of the wish. He saw a mother's lack of physical affection as a cause of disturbance in the anorexic's body image. This reminds us of Schilder's (1935) comments about the part played by touch and by the interest of other persons in the infant, for the building of the body image. Rose (1943) also emphasized the importance of the mother's poorly concealed rejection of her daughter, her forceful aggression in maintaining strict feeding schedules, and her intense doubts about her maternal capacity, all clearly present in the case of Ariel, as will follow below. And Fenichel (1945), looking back to the connections Freud had articulated with regard to hysteria, melancholia, and anorexia, described oral fixation in the anorexic as "one symptom of a general disturbance of all object relationships" (pp. 175–177). Probably in line with Lorand's noting of affective neurosis in the anorexic, Fenichel suggested that anorexia may be an affect equivalent as well as an hysterical equivalent for depression. As we shall see, emphasis on depression is a red thread found in most present-day writings about anorexia. Like Eissler (1943), Fenichel (1945) perceived that the conflict between a longing for gratification from the mother and the frustration of the longing created "a disturbance in the patient's mental construction of her body image" (p. 176). As far as I can tell, Eissler (1943) was also the first to posit a theoretical connection between eating disorders and body image. Lorand, Eissler, and Fenichel made evident that anorexia is a syndrome encompassing a range of intrapsychic conflicts and neurotic compromise formations. Brenman and Knight (1945) described a severely regressed anorexic adolescent with an extreme hopping compulsion. They found its source in an infantile oral conflict with the mother, which was relieved in psychoanalytically oriented treatment.

Knowledge about psychogenic sources of anorexia has expanded in keeping with the rapid rise of its incidence during the past several decades, apparently influenced by psychosocial factors such as the post-World War II affluence in some socioeconomic groups, and the overassertion of freedom for libidinal and aggressive action. For some adolescents, the latter concept of freedom has carried with it an opposite drive toward self-denial. In 1960 Bliss and Branch considered specific behaviors of anorexic patients, and again explained why anorexia is in some cases a misnomer, as the illness is not precipitated by loss of appetite. It rather begins when patients diet, and as they lose weight they lose their appetites.

> The appetite may be present, increased, or perverted. . . . Others crave food but refuse to eat. Some eat and then vomit; whereas others surreptitiously hide or dispose of their meals. . . . There are those who fear to eat because digestion may cause fearful psychosomatic distress or lead to obesity; and there are a few who eat docilely and then purge themselves of the offensive nutriments by cathartics and enemas [pp. 40–41].

Up to about 1980, recurrent references to causative factors took another step forward in touching on the part played by childhood stress, preoedipal problems in relation to the mother, and disturbed feelings about the body (e.g., Bruch, 1965, 1973, 1978; Thomä, 1967; Sperling, 1978; Sours, 1974, 1980; Minuchin, Rosman, and Baker, 1978; Mogul, 1980). Bruch (1965, 1973) defined anorexia as a relentless pursuit of excessive thinness, along with a preoccupation with food preparation for others, a narcissistic self-absorption, and regression to infantile negativism. Underlying these behaviors was a profound sense of ineffectiveness and a conviction of being helpless to change any aspect of their lives. This conscious feeling of helplessness, according to Bruch, lies behind their expressed demand to be in control of their own bodies and their own lives. Bruch was not concerned with the part played by unconscious dynamics in the illness. Sours (1974) wrote of the presence of sadness and guilt in the anorexic patient, but not true depression, and Katz (1986) pointed out that the affect of the anorexic patient does not have the quality of a typical depression in that she shows no motor retardation, no diminished energy, and no lack of reactivity to the environment. Considering the isolation of affect in the anorexic patient, it is odd that he saw no anhedonia in the patient. The diminished libido, he suggested, may also be a result of the starvation. Both probably are present, as the starving patient does lose interest in eating. It still is correct to say that the depression of the anorexic is quite different from that of the withdrawn melancholic. It is more disguised than the depression of the dispirited or despondent patient.

Rampling (1980) may have been the first to report contemporary sources telling of the significance of abnormal mothering in the genesis of anorexia. He considered that failure of normal mother–infant bonding for children liable to develop eating disorders, has a source in ambivalent maternal attitudes in which preoccupation with feeding may be a reaction formation against unconscious infanticidal wishes; my own clinical experience bears this out. He also offered evidence of a mother's lacuna in giving the history of her child's illness to allay anxiety about her possible part in its development. Such lacunae have been known to child analysts for a long time.

Sperling (1983) also emphasized the wish to be in control of every aspect of eating, a wish to reverse the experience in early childhood when mother was in control of food and the feeding situation, and so of the patient's life. The ability to go without food, she said, is taken as proof that life is possible without mother, and the patient's compromise is to reduce food intake to a minimum, and so renounce the pleasure of instinctual gratification (p. 75). Most authors on the subject also refer to the anorexic adolescent's hyperactivity and asceticism, the latter described particularly by Mogul (1980). Sours (1974) reported that parents of anorexic patients have an idealized picture of compliance and happiness in their children. No doubt this innocuous picture, mentioned by other authors as well, has been drawn from the parents' subjective impressions, or from their unconscious denial of what may be evident to a clinician. Mushatt (1992) and others have mentioned early separation anxiety (Mahler, Pine, and Bergman, 1975) as a causative factor in anorexia, but that is too general an explanation, too readily relied on to explain many kinds of problems from infancy to adulthood. It omits the subjective quality of the experience of fear of being alone during infancy, when the difference between separation and loss is not within the infant's comprehension. I consider that the fear in the infant is not of separation, which implies a temporary absence, but of the more elementary fear of loss of the loved person, especially when the infant, who cannot yet walk, cannot be sure that a person who is gone *can* return. The impersonal concept of "separation" seems to be more easily acceptable to many because it evokes less pain, even in the adult, than the affect-laden concept of "fear of object loss" (Brody and Siegel, 1992, pp. 28–30).

More recent observations about anorexia presented by Sours (1980), Sperling (1978, 1983), and Wilson, Hogan, and Mintz (1983, 1992) have pointed to the fear of being fat as the central motive for the fixed rejection of food. They see it as a food phobia, driven in part by the patient's denial of illness, and by an indefatigable demand to achieve mastery over her[1] biological need and to proclaim health, strength, and self-control. It is more than a phobia, however, as food preparation is much enjoyed by anorexic persons; and their renunciation of the pleasure of eating goes far beyond the rejection of food. It extends to a rejection of

---

[1] As the majority of patients with anorexia are female, I use the feminine pronoun to refer to them, here and below.

libidinal pleasures inherent in intimate personal relationships, and in varieties of affect expression (no joy, no humor, no signs of tenderness). Sours (1980) observed that the child who later becomes anorexic maintains intense unconscious anger about a feeling of being owned or controlled by her parents rather than being considered by them as a valid person in her own right. This complaint against the parents, even when it has validity, also defensively reverses the patients' wishes to be managed (cared for) by their parents. From the histories I have gathered of several adolescents troubled by anorexia in their adolescent years, I have found that, as Sours indicated, their parents' care was meager and pleasureless. They discouraged their daughter's active wishes, and failed to convey to her a sense of competence and self-worth. The patients developed either an immature dependence on them or an alienation from them, with related feelings of sadness, guilt, and emptiness. Usually the parents have no recall of feeding, sleeping, or emotional problems in their daughter's early years. The absence of recall, as Sours said, probably reflects parents' selective memories that serve to absolve them of any collusion, conscious or unconscious, with their child's symptom formation. Wilson, Hogan, and Mintz (1983) found that parents of anorexic patients impose strict moral codes over the life of the child who later falls ill, place emphasis on her need to achieve, and on their (ambivalent) need to maintain control over her life, while they forsake her emotionally. They also band together against her, expect her to behave in ways that do not trouble them in any way, quarrel a lot in her presence, and are complacent and smug about their parental methods. These statements are borne out in the cases to be described. They have not applied, however, in a few cases of young children, ages 4–7 that I have known, who ate very little and very slowly.

Sperling (1978, 1983), Wilson, Hogan, and Mintz (1983), and others found the wish of the anorexic patient to be in control signifies a fear of losing impulse control, a wish to be free of parental intrusion in her life, and free to have inviolate control of her body. Or, with hidden feelings of revenge, to turn the tables and take control of her parents. This demand suggests the presence of an aggressive wish to be quit of mother's interference with the patient's (old) oral instinctual wishes. It is made with implicit bravado and defiance. Mintz's statement that "the overcontrolling mother (and at times, father) requires and elicits obedience, conformity, submission, and perfection at an early age" is confirmed in my experience, but not his further remark that "The children are described as quiet, accepting, healthy, happy, and responsive . . . and never give the parents any trouble" (1983b, p. 93). The parents of anorexic persons I have known expressed a loose and ambivalent approval of their children's behavior. They may say too readily that the adolescents, when younger, were quiet and happy, but in making such statements they appear to hide from themselves the truth of their own history of ignorance or neglect of the child's emotional needs. The adolescent in mutinous anger, and mockery of the parent's belated concern, seeks retaliation. But why the wish to be in control should take such overweening importance as to promote, in the most severe cases, emaciation and possible death, remains to be understood, for the wish contains a self-contradiction. It coincides with an *inability to control* the process of slow starvation.

Adolescent anorexic patients are commonly found to be depressed as a result of anxieties brought about by rapid body changes, sexual arousals, fantasies, and wishes, and intensely ambivalent feelings and thoughts about their parents and their own increasing responsibilities. Bruch (1973) described the depressive feelings of the anorexic that came with fear of weight gain, and Mintz (1983b) also found an inverse relationship between weight loss and depression. The connections between depression in adolescence and sadness in early life need study. Early sadness that endures may take other forms, masked in a variety of defensive conditions as the child grows older.

Psychoanalytic cases of anorexic children are few but impressive. Sterba (1941) presented what is probably the first psychoanalytic account of a sudden refusal to eat in an 8-month-old girl. She kept a lump of food in her mouth, and her refusal to swallow it was found to represent a wish to withhold her bowel movement.[2] Many years ago I saw a boy of 18 months who showed a similar displacement from below, in a normal struggle against bowel control. His refusal to eat anything that was not perfectly white represented an obedience to his mother's wish to teach him bowel control. What he took into his body was confused with what he released from it. Next, Sylvester (1945) provided a classic description of the plight of a 4-year-old whose anorexia was brought about by the child's early disappointment in the mother. Her condition was related to states of apathy which changed from time to time to hyperactivity, frustration of instinctual needs, failed attempts to master elements in the human environment, and somatic problems arising from emotional disturbance, and (an assumed) turning against the self during the oral phase. Putnam, Rank, and Kaplan (1951) described an infant who from birth ingested excessive amounts of food, and by 4 months was rocking and head banging. Before 6 months he was vomiting after eating,

---

[2]During approximately the first third of the twentieth century, toilet training was quite regularly begun much earlier than later in the century. An infant's confusion between the functions of mouth and anus was probably frequent.

when upset had rapid mood changes and very low frustration tolerance, all followed by a refusal to accept or chew solid foods, and increasing social withdrawal. They attributed his condition to *primal depression*, a name conceived by Abraham (1916) in his discussion of the first pregenital stage of the libido, amplified by Rado (1928), and later by Zetzel (1953), who provided a fitting name, "depressive vulnerability" for these conditions, frequently observable in infants and young children. Hitchcock (1992) described a young child and two of latency age who developed anorexia in the course of psychoanalytic treatment.

Ritvo (1984) wrote of eating as the infant's earliest gratifying and frustrating experience with the object. It has "the longest and most complex history as a modality for the expression of wishes, aims, and conflicts relating to the object.... The clinical problems are made subtler and more complex by the introjection and incorporation of the object, resulting in a closed system which can then be extremely difficult to influence therapeutically" (pp. 453–454). Ritvo touched on a vital defensive measure in anorexia: the introjection of the object, which I shall address later. The study by Marchi and Cohen (1990) is particularly important for its contribution to our knowledge of the onset of anorexia. By tracing maladaptive eating patterns longitudinally at three age ranges (1–10, 9–18, 12–20), they found that a group of behaviors—pickiness, does not eat enough, is choosy about food, usually eats slowly, and is usually not interested—any three of these were the most stable behaviors in their eating behavior, and as a group were strongly predictive of anorexia and of weight reduction. Steiner and Lock (1998), in an extensive survey of epidemiological studies, attributed the overt causes of anorexia in our present culture to an overconcern with body weight and shape, especially as affected by pubertal change. They found that among adolescents and adults 63 percent of all patients with eating problems had lifetime affective disorders. The need for longitudinal studies of eating disorders is beyond question.

The fullest examinations of anorexia and bulimia have appeared in two volumes, *Fear of Being Fat* (1983) and *Psychodynamic Technique in the Treatment of the Eating Disorders* (1992). Both books were edited by Wilson, Hogan, and Mintz, and both include many of their own articles on these subjects. Their contributions are essential for our understanding of psychoanalytically oriented treatment of the closely related illnesses. They have brought together a large group of clinical and theoretical works concerned with fears of loss of impulse control, disturbances of body image, oral sadism, preoedipal and oedipal conflicts, sexual identity, familial issues, personality structure, and issues of control that serve to hide overwhelming feelings of helplessness that emerge in studies of unconscious conflicts and that are essential components of the major eating disorders. Chatoor, Hirsch, Ganiban, Persinger, and Hamburg (1998) found symptoms of infantile anorexia in persistent refusal of food during transitions from spoon to self-feeding, malnutrition, parental concern over food intake, mother–infant conflict, distress during feeding, and picky eating. All of these works point to the origins in the sexual conflicts in early childhood. By what paths they come to emerge in adolescence remains shadowy, except in those cases where clinical information is available in adequate detail. These paths, or predispositions, are at the core of my deliberations about the short- and long-term effects of psychological distress that can permeate infancy and early childhood.

Hogan (1992) attributes the rise in the incidence of eating disorders in recent decades to the social pressures on all adolescents:

In a particular group of young women with a specific neurotic (or occasionally psychotic) character structure, these demands are more than they can tolerate and symptoms make an early appearance.... In the middle-class Western world, the change in attitudes and morality in the past two decades have [sic] been enormous. Outside social pressures and temptations from the media, the adult world, and the adolescent's peers are no longer under the control of the family. Conflict leading to devastating symptoms is inevitable in a group of predisposed children.... I believe that in the past, the more leisurely acknowledgment of sexual needs and opportunities led to a less acutely precocious neurotic resolution of conflicts. The neurosis was there, but the manifestations and symptoms came later and were of a less devastating character.... I also agree with her observations [Helene Deutsch, 1944, pp. 129–130], that a period of time, acclimation, fantasy, experiment, and development are a necessity for the asymptomatic evolution of adult sexuality in some groups of adolescents [p. 112].

The clinical predispositions found to be most relevant to anorexia are faults in the early mother–child relationship, fear of object loss, a disturbed body image, efforts to gain control of instinctual impulses aroused in prepuberty, depression, and rigid defenses—chiefly identification with the aggressor, isolation of affect, regression, and gross denial. None of these determinants, observed singly or in combination, is unique for anorexia (or bulimia), and none offers any explanation for its predominant occurrence in females. Its incidence in males has been assessed by various authors as one-tenth to one-twentieth of females. Bliss and Branch (1960), who documented its incidence, found that for social and psychological reasons it was considered by many physicians to be female; therefore, studies of male anorexic patients are comparatively rare. Mintz (1983a), however, presented five cases of male anorexia and bulimia in childhood, adolescence, and middle age. In his extensive accounts of their treatment, he found no essential differences in the course of their treatment from that of females.

Certain aspects of female experience in adolescence indicate their greater vulnerability for disturbances of body image. Their physical changes are more visible than the equivalent changes in males. In puberty, their breasts and hips grow larger and rounder, arousing pride or consternation, depending on their preparation for these developments; and menses arrive. The menstrual blood obliges the adolescent girl to take charge of the messiness and the odor with extra hygienic measures. She cannot but be self-conscious, even in positive ways, of her altered size and shape. Now it is not only the female genital that arouses historic unrest, but the periods of bleeding, as noted above, surely a distinction about which male adolescents may bless themselves. While the adolescent girl with a body image disturbance strives to be thin, also lithe, limber, and strong, the boy with the complementary disturbance strives to show he is virile, forceful, and impregnable. Advertisements for male body building often display grotesque chest and muscular development. Among females, those more disposed than males to develop anorexia, the complex feelings, fantasies, and anxieties aroused by menarche surely constitute primary causes of the greater immediate liability to anxiety about their unstable body image, and so of their greater vulnerability to disturbances of their body ego. Brumberg (1988) has suggested that many young women still regard their bodies as the best medium with which to make a statement about their identity:

> This is what unprotected sexual intercourse and prolonged starvation have in common . . . anorexia nervosa ultimately

expresses the predicament of a very distinct group, one that suffers from the painful ambiguities of being young and female in an affluent society set adrift by social change . . . and determined to maintain control in a world where things as basic as food and sex are increasingly out of control, the contemporary anorectic unrelentingly pursues thinness—a secular form of perfection [p. 271].

Individual psychodynamics that foster this are outside of Brumberg's concern, which may explain her not mentioning that the great majority of female adolescents do not succumb to the distortion of instinctual aims that is dramatized in anorexia. But her recognition of the female dilemma is of cardinal importance to an understanding of female anorexia. Why the anorexic's derogation of her body is so exclusively about fatness has yet to be addressed. There appears to be no comparable despair about her height, or facial features, or hair, or limbs, or sexual parts, or other physical dimensions or qualities. We have to ask why her conviction of ugliness attaches mainly to her abdomen and thighs; and why, if a part of her body is repulsive to her, she works at destroying her whole body.

Chapter 3

The Clinical Data: Prefatory Notes

The histories of the two research subjects to be described have been drawn from records of their observed behavior and development from their third day to age 7, interviews with their parents when the subjects were 3 to 7, observations of them in nursery school, diagnostic psychological tests from ages 3 to 7, extensive interviews with them and diagnostic psychological tests at age 18, and videotaped interviews with them at age 30.[1] The theory and methods of the entire study have been informed by classic psychoanalytic theory of infantile sexuality, primary-process thinking, the development of object relations, unconscious defenses, and capacities for adaptation. My purpose in this book is to bring forward the usually unseen or unrecorded experiential events that, as far as I could find out, brought the subjects to become anorexic and to remain burdened by its sequelae in

---

[1] The latter carried out by Henry N. Massie, as noted in the introduction, footnote 3.

their early adulthood. I have tried to present my data as closely as I could to the clinical model stated by Edelson (1986): "The case study captures the subject completely, presents the subject vividly, matches with fidelity the complexity of the subject, and preserves what is unique about the subject—in a way that no objective–quantitative study can" (p. 249).

The histories of Helen and Ariel from birth to age 7 and our observations of them in those years were presented 11 years before I learned about their anorexia. Helen's mother was one of nine who had agreed to ask for and/or to consider suggestions that might be helpful to them in the care of their infants (Brody and Axelrad, 1978, pp. 133–153, 203).[2] For that purpose we departed from the research stricture in the last nine cases recruited. Ariel was one of 10 subjects whose development from ages 2 to 7 as perceived by their fathers have been reported before (pp. 368–391). The parents of both girls were in their twenties when the children were born, and both were of middle socioeconomic status. Both mothers strongly wished for upward social mobility; only Ariel's parents achieved it, partially. Helen had one sibling, Harry, 23 months older than she; Ariel also had one sibling, Alex, born when she was 22 months old. In order to present the two histories as succinctly as may be useful, I shall omit incidental details about the parents' social histories, the medical histories of Helen and Ariel that had no

---

[2] By the time most of the infants in the original sample reached age 1, we had observed that a number of mothers and/or infants were having difficulties that the mothers were not aware of and that we could not address within the research program. Therefore we invited the last nine recruited mothers to visit us, with their infants if possible, at two additional infant ages, 16 and 36 weeks, in addition to the regularly scheduled visits at 6, 26, and 52 weeks (Brody and Axelrad, 1978, pp. 55–57). I conducted the extra interviews and tested the infants if mother brought them.

known pertinence to their eating problems, and information about the siblings that had no known relevance to the subjects' development. In spite of the many details that I include, I have condensed much of the available information about the two subjects in order to comprehend the cumulative impact of their psychological experiences. I have aimed to present the flow of formative events and experiences in their lives in order to uncover those that can be understood to have induced their eating disorders.

The gap in our direct observations of Helen and Ariel in their second and third years was a result of our original intention to observe the mothers and their infants only through the infants' first year. By the time new funds[3] allowed us to continue our work, only 12 of the subjects were in their second year, and all the rest in their third or fourth year. This meant that there were breaks in our direct observations of the children's speech and motor development, self-care, socialization, play, and capacities for independent action in their second and third years. Nevertheless, our continuation of the study up to the children's age 7 helped us to comprehend how their earliest experiences influenced their Weltanschauung in childhood and adolescence. Among subjects who in those years showed no organic deficit or defect, suffered no major physical illness, and no known trauma, examination of the influences on the child's continuing mental and emotional states can yield understanding of the store of historical events that came to a pathological climax during early adolescence, as it appeared in the aggravation of their eating disorders.

---

[3]Further delays in resuming the study were occasioned by a search for the families with whom our contact was supposed to end after the infants reached age 1, for new offices, and for new administrative support. The latter was provided by the City University of New York.

Chapter 4

The History of Helen

The First Year

Day 1

Apgar scores: at 1 minute, 10; at 5 minutes, 10.

Day 3

Helen was more relaxed in the prone than in the supine position. Her sensory responses were moderate. When hungry she became tense, extended her leg stiffly, and cried loudly and persistently. As soon as mother offered her breast Helen sucked spontaneously and vigorously for 15 minutes, then remained quiet and alert until she fell asleep. Mother, silent and expressionless, kept her eyes on the baby with a fixed smile, rather like a grimace.

First Interview with Mother, 3 Days Postpartum

Mother agreed immediately to the interview and at once expressed her regret that she had not been interviewed about Harry, her first child, whose problems (eating, toilet training, and fear when alone) she would have liked to discuss. She answered my questions with appropriate affect until her anxiety was aroused by topics that perplexed her. She had no experience in infant or child care before Harry was born. The maternal grandmother often baby-sat for him, and mother enjoyed having him "taken off her hands." The maternal grandfather, a physician, and the maternal grandmother, a homemaker with time to spare, visited frequently. Mother had one sibling, a brother five years younger; they were not close. The paternal grandparents were high school teachers. Father expressed no affection for them and little interest in their wishes, said mother. She believed they disapproved of father's aspirations (never made clear), and of her, so "they were a constant problem." Father had no siblings.

Mother had graduated from a first-rate college where she majored in philosophy with no idea about what to do after graduation. She did not feel drawn to any career, but believed that without college experience she "might have been satisfied with a middle-class suburban life." For a few years she worked as a programmer for a few small businesses, then had a variety of short-lived "crazy" interests, such as conversion to an Indian religion. In her midtwenties she began to worry about not finding a husband, accepted a chance friend's first recommendation of a man described favorably, and married him after a few weeks. Previously she had broken an engagement with a Greek professor whose glamorous background had impressed her. I began to suspect that in her short-lived interests in men from Eastern cultures she may have been looking for a way to bring color or drama into her life.

Father had worked toward a postgraduate degree in political science, gave it up after a problem arose about his dissertation, and turned to the study of law until that pursuit also went awry. Now he was satisfied with employment as an insurance agent. He was not shrewd or aggressive, and was sometimes passive, mother said, but helpful around the house and with children, and he was "a very good person." She admired most his very high intelligence. They had few friends, they just enjoyed being together. My impression was that they were clinging to each other for some form of security, yet were floundering, without inner direction.

Mother had stopped working when she became pregnant with Harry. Now she looked forward to finding something to do that was more interesting than housework. Apparently she envisioned child care as a part of housework. Having recently read a lot about infant rearing, she expressed firm ideas about it: she would breast-feed Helen for three months because she had enjoyed nursing Harry and didn't want to bother with bottles; and she would feed the baby on a "self-demand" schedule. She would never use a pacifier. Toilet training would begin at 18 months, later than mother had begun it with Harry because he was still rebelling against it. She thought babies should have as much attention and play as possible, but in another context expressed her belief that while they should be treated leniently, they should not be given everything they wanted, and they should be left alone for most of the day so as to learn to be by themselves. She was thus already worried about the extent to which she might have to respond to Helen's demands. She did not know when habits begin, maybe about 5 or 6 months, because at about that age Harry would not go to sleep unless mother or father sat and held him; if they put him into his crib he screamed. "Ignoring him doesn't work. He can scream for an hour if no one comes to him, and then he stops." Being lenient works out best for all in the long run, mother said, because a baby is better satisfied if not told "No" all the time. She has chosen the easiest way—being lenient—but will not "give in" to Helen easily; this contradiction escaped her. Somewhat crossly she added that Harry's waking during the night for a bottle of orange juice was just a bad habit. Her statements suggested strong ambivalence about her maternal role.

Discipline could begin at about age 1, not by spanking, never by shaming, mostly by distracting the child. Father was "violently" against spanking or slapping, though often he lost his temper and shouted at Harry—which was better, mother volunteered, than striking a child. Unhesitatingly she spoke of her anticipated discontent with the possibility of having to take care of two children "without outside stimulation." The contrast between her avowed plan to be lenient with and attentive to Helen, but not too much, and her determination to be occupied away from home and the children, was not auspicious. Asked what her greatest strength with her child might be, she said it was giving love and deferring her own desires and interests. Her greatest weakness was her impatience. She hated herself for screaming at Harry, but she "had to get her rage out," and repeated that screaming was better than striking a child—which suggested that an impulse to strike was present. She was not aware that, especially to a child, a verbal assault can be as painful as a physical blow.

Age: 6 Weeks

Gesell Developmental Schedule scores (actual age 5.3 weeks)[1]

    Motor: 8 weeks

[1] Appointments with mothers for their visits were usually arranged to take place within five days before or after the infants reached the age of 6, 26, and 52 weeks.

Adaptive: 8 weeks
Language: 8 weeks
Personal-Social: 8 weeks

Helen was advanced in all sectors of development, although in the prone position she was not at ease and did not lift her head high as she had been able to do on day 3. As she lay supine, from time to time she extended her legs upward so that her body came to be in a slightly concave position. Perhaps she was inexperienced in managing her head and limbs, as mother said she always lay on her back without moving or being moved. Mother and father believed it best for her to remain supine all of the time, except when being fed. She adapted comfortably to all of mother's procedures and my testing, accommodated excellently to my holding her, and often smiled at me. She nursed comfortably, gazing at mother's face as she played her hand on mother's breast, and making soft sounds as she looked about the room. All of her responses were smooth. Although mother did not speak to her, their reciprocal gaze conveyed a quality of peaceful communication.

Mother was unhappy, however, about having so far failed to set up a feeding schedule for Helen. Each morning she waited to nurse until Helen screamed. During the rest of the day as well, mother delayed each feeding for 15 to 20 minutes while the screaming continued, because she wanted to make sure that Helen was hungry enough to be fed. For this mother, like some others I have known, feeding "on demand" was construed to mean that the baby should not be given food until she really *demanded* it. Still mother was troubled because she never knew whether she was feeding too much or too little. Until now she had tried to solve this problem by keeping each nursing short. "With luck," she said, Helen would fall asleep again, which mother favored because that would enable her to reduce the number of feedings each day. But there was another problem: typically, after each brief feeding, she put Helen in her crib to sleep. Helen soon awoke and cried, mother picked up her up and held her "a little bit" or fed her "a little bit," and replaced her in her crib; then Helen fretted and screamed before she could fall asleep again. Did mother suppose Helen's crying might mean she was still hungry? Mother thought not. The sequences of mother's doing and undoing were repeated several times each day. At about midnight she nursed Helen again briefly, believing that then Helen would not be hungry enough next morning to need an early breakfast; and so again the next day's schedule went awry. Evidently mother was feeding Helen as little and as infrequently as she could. Two weeks ago she had also tried to persuade Helen to drink from a bottle, in vain. Possibly her screaming—mother never called it crying—was an effect not only of the too late and too brief feedings, but of mother's sparse visual, vocal, or physical contact with her, as observed and reported. Helen's states of hunger and distress had by now become habitual. Mother expressed chagrin and no pleasure in her care of Helen. Her troubled story was at odds with Helen's good condition, judging by the Gesell tests. Helen's failure to lift her head high when lying prone gave the only hint of a lag in her progress.

Age: 16 Weeks

Mother came without Helen, and gave a tangled story of her failed attempt to wean her from the breast four weeks ago (her original plan). Helen had screamed a great deal for two days, and had not gained as much weight as mother thought she should. Mother felt sure the cause was a diminished flow of her milk because Helen still fell asleep too soon while nursing. Mother was so troubled by not knowing what to do that she could not realize that her silent tension might be undermining her capacity to help Helen feed actively. It appeared to me that mother's ambivalence about breast-feeding, or feeding itself, was in her actions and attitudes conveying to Helen a restlessness that interfered with her nursing. Mother had not tried to follow my suggestion, made 10 weeks ago, as to how she might help Helen stay awake and continue nursing instead of falling asleep. I had explained that then Helen might get used to a little separation in time between the experiences of feeding and falling asleep if mother talked or played with her in between. Instead, mother persuaded her pediatrician that it was time to begin bottle-feeding. On the very next morning she gave a bottle to Helen. Helen refused it and was left to cry for about 12 hours before she took two ounces of milk, with the help of father and maternal grandmother. A few hours later she awoke hungry, screaming, accepted a little milk, slept again and screamed again. This unhappy pattern recurred for days until mother, feeling worn out, decided to wean Helen from the breast at once, though dreading failure. Slowly, in the next few days Helen began to accept the bottle. A week later mother decided that she could give Helen fruit juice in a bottle as well, whereupon Helen "screamed her worst." So mother, feeling miserable about her ineptitude in nearly every aspect of the baby's feeding, decided it would be best to set her on a schedule that fitted her own (mother's) needs. I could not tell whether she or Helen suffered the greater stress in this speeded-up weaning process in which mother seemed to be unable to take any cues from the baby's emotional state, which had grown hectic. A few days later, on the telephone, she denied concern about the feeding schedule, instead telling me with relief and pride that Helen was content to lie in her crib alone and unattended for hours at a time. If mother sometimes played little games with her or pulled her up to a sitting position she was happily excited, but mother did these things infrequently, she said as a matter of fact. Father was passionately against mother's doing them at all. I had suggested during the 6-week visit that if at times Helen were helped to lie prone when awake she might enjoy holding her head up and looking about and reaching for things close by. Father found this suggestion to be "the silliest idea," so mother acquiesced and left Helen lying on her back most of the time. Still mother felt troubled: first she had failed at breast-feeding, and now she could not understand why Helen continued to scream a great deal. Yet again at the end of this meeting mother was emphatic about what a good and happy baby Helen was. So saying, she seemed to be protecting herself from any liability for Helen's discontent. Mother's complaints, mixed with almost immediate denials of them, signified a willing suspension of realistic judgment, as well as a struggle against feeling sympathy for her baby. As for Helen, it was fair to assume that in addition to her abundant screaming since her first weeks, she had endured daily episodes of hunger and fright during hours of physical stillness and silence, interrupted only by occasional intermissions of relief or pleasure. Mother's overt fears so intruded into her infant care that she seemed to have no perception of the decline in Helen's physical and emotional states. Perhaps her anxiety stemmed in part from unconscious resentment that she harbored against the infant for restricting her freedom, mixed with a troubled conscience about wishing to avoid having to respond to Helen's needs, fear of her incompetence, and rising anger against the infant. Or her resentment hid feelings of frustration originating elsewhere—in her husband's too modest earnings, his parents' disapproval, and the burden of problems presented by Harry.

Age: 26 Weeks (actual age 25.4 weeks)

Gesell Developmental Schedule scores:

Gross Motor	16 to 26 weeks
Fine Motor:	16 to 24 weeks
Adaptive:	16 to 28+ weeks
Language:	16 to 32 weeks
Personal-Social:	16 to 32 weeks

Note the decline in development in all five sectors, 16 weeks being the base in each, yet with signs of progress in the Language and Personal–Social areas.

Helen looked healthy and strong but her investment in people and things in her near environment, sturdy at 6 weeks, now appeared only in her initial smile at me. Her physical movements were slow and restricted, her facial expression mostly immobile. When she became fussy mother picked her up, rocked her in arms briefly, and although she knew Helen was hungry and ready to be fed, asked me to first carry out the Gesell Developmental Tests. Naturally, Helen's attention to test objects was hard to elicit. She withdrew from most tasks. Given the large aluminum cup (test object), she mouthed it and suddenly broke into a loud wail. She may have been disconcerted by feeling the hard cup in her mouth instead of the food she was waiting for. Dismissively mother said Helen was always moody. An hour later Helen accepted my placing her in an upright position, just momentarily. When I helped her to put her weight on her feet to stand upright, she did so gingerly, again momentarily. Her posture was rigid, her manner vigilant. Placed by mother in the infant seat (mother's choice) to be fed, she slumped to the side and looked away from mother as she had avoided looking at me. The feeding was slow, with many pauses and little eye contact with mother, who said she didn't mind if Helen ate little of her food—Harry would gladly take the rest. Toward the end of the feeding Helen began to wag her head from side to side affectlessly. Quickly mother said this had never happened before—at least never during feeding. But yes, she had seen it during a diaper change—maybe it was getting to be a bad habit—in fact, once mother had been very annoyed by it and shouted at Helen to stop it. This set of responses was typical of mother's hedging, contingent, self-contradictory, and embarrassed way of telling her story. Her self-consciousness was sad to witness. Helen was in a brighter mood after a nap, enjoyed sucking her fingers and her dress, blowing bubbles, kicking, and smiling at me from a distance. In this shift from being impassive and cranky to being cheerful and friendly, she showed a promising capacity for resilience. I noticed that she became expansive only when not pressed to respond to any person, that is, when she was free to initiate a social contact.

She had four naps a day, to mother's regret, because they might interfere with her night sleep. "On good days" she played by herself after her naps, mother said. "On bad days" she awoke very early, fussed and screamed and was demanding all day long. She loved to be sat up or picked up, or kissed and talked to, said mother, who complied with these wishes for a minute or two. But Helen "never asked" her to do these things—which revealed mother's disinclination to initiate social play with Helen. One day recently mother left her with maternal grandmother, whereupon Helen screamed uncontrollably and vomited. Mother supposed she had swallowed so much air while screaming that she felt sick, and off-handedly added that Helen sometimes had "crying fits" one to two hours long. In another context she said that Helen sometimes "stimulated herself to vomit by pushing her finger, or the handle of a small bell back toward her throat, again adding casually that Helen vomited once a day. This mention of daily vomiting fitted mother's loose reporting. Pressing her for clearer information often produced self-conscious evasions or denials. I had to assume that Helen's general distress often interfered with her digestion.

Mother and father were still sure that Helen needed no encouragement to sit or stand. At the same time mother was afraid Helen would never creep because "she was not eager to do anything for herself." If mother felt any compunction about Helen's inactivity, she appeared to acquit herself of any concern about it. As if to close off further reference to the subject, she said, "Helen is basically good, but she's been difficult from birth, she even choked on water," clearly a false memory. Helen, at 6 months, gave evidence of troubled states in her motor restriction, high irritability, poor appetite, withdrawal from mother, and periods of crying and sadness. She showed the depressive vulnerability of infants described by Zetzel (1953).

Age: 36 Weeks

Mother again came without Helen, and as before described her as quiet and content to lie in her crib or sit on the floor alone for hours, hardly moving, and to mother's expressed relief, she still resisted putting any weight on her feet. The rest of mother's reports were brief: at meals Helen slumped in her high chair, ate little, dawdled, and wanted "more entertainment and urging" than mother was disposed to offer. She could drink from a cup, but mother found that too messy. Each day as the hours went by Helen's crankiness increased, especially after her many short naps. The crankiness may have been touched off each time Helen awoke and found herself alone. On some days, though, she just screamed and didn't nap at all. Ruefully mother told of several incidents when Helen kept fussing and screaming, whereupon mother put her on the floor with a toy and left the screaming baby to herself. So it was that the familiar screaming was both prologue and epilogue to Helen's loneliness—but she was never very angry, mother said, reassuring herself that all was well because Helen was happy as soon as she got attention from anyone. Before falling asleep, she sucked on her blanket. To keep this from becoming a habit mother occasionally exchanged one blanket for another, by which method the baby's way of comforting herself with the holding and smelling of a familiar loved object was made unreliable. No one in the family paid particular attention to her, mother said—even Harry didn't play with her enough (didn't occupy her enough). Mother's withdrawal from Helen was conspicuous.

Age: 52 Weeks

Gesell Developmental Schedule scores:

Gross Motor:	44 weeks
Fine Motor:	15 months
Adaptive:	56+ weeks
Language:	15 mos.
Personal-Social:	52 weeks

Note the contrast between Helen's Gross and Fine Motor scores, a distinct change from her abilities as observed at 6 and 26 weeks. Her advanced language score indicated the unevenness in her development.

After a responsive smile at me, Helen lay where mother placed her in the crib, lumplike and motionless though visually alert. Her lower body was like that of an 8- or 9-month-old. She could neither pull herself to a sitting position, nor creep, nor crawl. On her back she ambulated by pressing her palms on the floor and levering herself forward. From time to time she rolled over on the floor. She froze when mother moved out of her immediate range of vision. Her test performance was qualified by restraint and unsteady attention, but responses that required fine coordination were mature, and each time she accomplished a subtest she looked at me with a full smile. Suddenly, in the midst of one task that she was completing very ably, she flushed and broke into loud, miserable crying, an outburst quite like the one seen six months before. Such unexpected attacks of despair had been occurring at home, mother said, but how often or for what reason she had no idea. At the end of the visit, when I stood by the crib and spoke softly to Helen, she was pleasantly responsive, a positive alteration in her social behavior like that seen six months before. It reinforced my impression that this infant had more resources for enjoyment, activity, and responsiveness than mother could recognize or foster. Mostly she reported Helen's screaming: on one day it had been so intense that her face got bright red for at least 20 minutes. Perhaps she was dramatizing the baby's misery, as if to distance herself from it. When I asked if in the midst of Helen's screaming mother ever tried to hold her, she said Helen just pushed her away. Anyway, she believed it would be a bad habit to pick up a baby when she cried. Helen had now begun to push food away or to throw it into the air, and recently she had tried to use a spoon and a fork. "She's getting more and more independent," said mother, with more than a touch of annoyance, and no awareness that she was discouraging Helen's effort to feed herself. Her own conflict about Helen's development of self-care was striking. Well-developing 1-year-olds love to manage their feedings. For Helen it might be that the amount of tension, frustration, and fury that she had been experiencing before, during, and after her feedings, had by now led to a troubled wish to exclude mother from the feeding scene.

She no longer sucked on her blanket, said mother, but pulled it over her head when she slept. Was she enacting another form of withdrawal from mother and/or the near environment? A few times mother half-heartedly asked me for specific advice, listened thoughtfully to the suggestions I offered, for each gave reasons why it would not be useful, and finally declared that nothing would help except having someone else take care of both children. The emotional destitution that prevailed in Helen's life (and in mother's?) increasingly throughout her first year was worrisome. Mother vaguely perceived Helen's unhappinesss, but her capacity to act in favor of the baby was blunted. She might be glumly surrendering to defeat.

Age: 14 Months. Poststudy Visit[2]

Mother came with Helen supposedly for a last visit. Helen's upper body now looked like that of a sturdy child of 18 months. In sharp contrast, her lower limbs were like those of a 9- or 10-month old. She moved along on the floor at a good pace by sitting with knees apart and heels pressed to each other, hopping forward on her buttocks. When I bent

---

[2]Parents were invited for poststudy conferences after the child's ages 1 and 7, each time when the research project was expected to end after those ages of the children.

near to her gently, she pulled away. Another time when I came close fondly, she broke into wild sobbing that lasted for more than 10 minutes, such was her immediate and intense fright of the nearness of a stranger, even in the presence of her mother. Then she chugged to mother, laid her head on mother's foot and again sobbed loudly, whereupon mother asked me what to do about Helen's tantrums whenever mother tried, reluctantly, to raise her to her feet. Then she quickly withdrew her question, deciding that anyway Helen would soon walk. My impression was that she wished to avoid hearing that Helen had no organic problem (as her pediatrician had assured her) because in that case she would feel obliged to encourage Helen to stand and walk, and so might find herself cast down with yet another burden.

At 14 months, Helen's behavior was qualified by an absence of body pleasure and of function pleasure, chronic frustration, a low capacity for object cathexis, and panic attacks. Few assertive behaviors and few efforts toward body mastery were seen. Active aggressiveness appeared mainly in her screaming and her angry pushing or throwing food away. Positive aspects of her development lay in her readiness to respond to social overtures at a distance, and her skill and enjoyment of tasks requiring fine coordination. She knew many words, but pronounced well only their first syllables. Perhaps she was holding back her investment in language, as well as in gross motor and social activities.

Interviews with Helen's Parents: Second Year to Age 7[3]

Mother was next interviewed when Helen was just 3. At 20 months her low body weight and reluctance to walk had

[3]As described before (Brody and Siegel, 1992), when the first unanticipated follow-up study began, more than a year after the original 131

been diagnosed by a neurologist as hypotonia. Her parents were advised to consult an orthopedist, but did not. She began to walk at 22 months, mother said, yet now (at 3) could not walk more than one short street block. At $2^1/2$ she had begun to run. She was said never to have had much appetite, and had a habit of chewing on food and then spitting it out—perhaps a sequel to her throwing food away at 14 months; and often she played with her food instead of eating it. Now she took her food rapidly and left the table as soon as she had as much as she wanted, which mother liked—it was easier that way—an echo of her earlier saying that she did not mind when Helen did not eat her whole meal, as Harry could have the rest. At 2 Helen's reaction to any restriction was "horrible." Toilet training began when she was 2, with the use of a potty, and much protest, accompanied by violent rages and frequent temper tantrums. Mother had talked and complained about it, trying not to get angry, but she did scream at Helen a lot because of her "accidents" after waiting too long to go to the toilet. By $2^1/2$, after months of bribing and nagging, Helen "trained herself overnight." At 3 she had "fantastic control"—she could go without urinating for 11 hours, a withholding that suggested an anxious overobedience rather than mastery of sphincter control. Mother continued her complaints about Helen. Sometimes she sent the child to her room because of them, but Helen refused to stay there; she talked a great deal and resented interruptions; she had been moody since her birth—the latter remark typified mother's dismissal of Helen's behavior as being unrelated to mother's care, and

---

infants had reached age 1, only 12 children were still in their second year, 42 were in their third year, and 71 were in their fourth year. Helen and Ariel were observed and their parents were interviewed, each separately, when the children were age 3 and annually thereafter until age 7.

negligible. Helen always slept well. I suspected that her willingness to go to sleep evolved from a readiness to withdraw from her unpleasurable surroundings.

Fourth and Fifth Years

During her next two years mother's accounts were of Helen's continuing temper tantrums. She would "scream hysterically" and demand that mother stay with her. She was "horrible" about restrictions, "pestered" to do things with mother until mother screamed at her, had developed several unseemly habits, and had many urinary regressions. Her demands for mother's company and care persisted, in vain. Mother's complaints about her behavior at meals also persisted: she fidgeted, took her food half-sitting and half-standing, and demanded dessert as soon as she finished the main course. No doubt these troubling behaviors reflected the larger disorder in her feelings toward mother, as well as her poor impulse control. The high tension between mother and Helen was taking a toll on the well-being of both. A kind of civil war was in the air. There were mutual recriminations, with overtones of defiance and rage on both sides. Helen's need for her blanket was another unpleasant issue in the family life. Mother's threats to impose discipline by taking it away, and father's teasing her about it brought on the oft-mentioned screaming. She had begun to suck her hair and to masturbate openly. Just the same, mother finally described her as happy and easy to manage, and was pleased to tell me that often she (mother) was able to shut herself away from both children and go to sleep.

Father's reports echoed mother's but were more judgmental than hers: Helen slobbered over her food, needed discipline, had tantrums, and was "a general nuisance." He objected to many of her behaviors but rationalized them; for example, "She resists dressing because it's a dull procedure." Perhaps he was here projecting his own dislike of having to wear clothing. He had resisted mother's objections to his going about their apartment in the nude so Helen became used to seeing both parents unclothed, and being erotically overstimulated as a matter of course. Father affirmed his "cool detachment toward the so-called traumatic experiences of childhood." Like mother, he said he needed more time for himself away from the children, and he minimized Helen's diffidence about walking, which by now may have been aggravated by lack of energy as a result of poor nutrition. Both parents teased Helen about her constant need for her baby blanket no matter how much the teasing upset her, yet they submitted to her demand for it at inappropriate times and places. They enjoyed teasing her, they said, because she looked so cute when angry. They would have been astonished at any suggestion that their behavior had even a tinge of unkindness, so fearful were they about having room in themselves for a kindly concern about Helen's unhappy moods. Their egoistic nonchalance about her came close to a veiled sadism.

Sixth and Seventh Years

As Helen moved toward the latency period, when theoretically her impulses and affects would normally be quieter than before, the emotional noise in the family did not abate. Except for mother's pleased remarks about Helen's academic progress, both parents' accounts of life with her were consistently negative. She was picky about food and was "obnoxious persistently," said mother. She screamed and hit when she wanted anything. It might well be that by now she expressed her wants with feelings of desperation. She tired easily when walking "because of her bad feet," but as the mention of a medical examination made her "hysterical," it was avoided. (Later consultations with orthopedists showed no abnormality.) She also hated to take showers, so when it was necessary, mother regularly got into the shower stall with her, so further arousing the child's erotic wishes and fantasies. At 7 Helen still needed a scrap of her blanket to sleep with and to suck on. Father said Helen had just one fear: she would not eat chocolate figures that were hollow. I wondered if the hollow figures aroused an inchoate anxiety about a hollowness in her own body, or an unconscious fantasy of emptiness in herself.

At least up to age 7 she suffered continuous dissatisfactions with her parents and with food and endured a poverty of imaginative play and cognitive exercise. In each interview with her parents their complaints about her actions and her habits were followed by glowing comments about her sweetness and happiness. Actually, she had been dejected by an excess of the major anxieties of childhood: fear of object loss (especially of mother) and fear of loss of the object's love (both implying abandonment), castration fear (of body damage and disability), and fear of punishment (superego retribution). In view of her chronic frustrations since early infancy, and of her ensuing emotional struggles with both parents, it was inevitable that their mutual disappointments would continue during the rest of her latency years.

Ages 3 to 6: Behavior in Nursery School and Kindergarten

At $3^1/2$ Helen moved about the nursery schoolroom slowly, robotlike, until she stumbled on something to do. Or she sat still, fingering her mouth and nose. She was an aimless, joyless wanderer. Similarly, at 5 she was impassive, tense, self-conscious, and indifferent to group activities. Her only social act was to imitate another girl, and in doing so her movements were stiff and jerky, her voice high-pitched and unsteady. When called by the teacher to join a rhythmic activity she jumped and pranced in a disorganized way, occasionally giggling as well. Near age 6, in kindergarten, she was immobile and stony-faced or she stared blankly, lost in autoerotic activity. Her walk was clumsy. And as observed a year before, she attached herself to one other girl, engaging with her in being silly and cavorting about. Her affect was inappropriately labile, her social behavior markedly immature, and her cognitive activity restricted. When engaged in fine motor activity, however, she was relaxed, constructive, and looked pleased.

Ages 3 to 7: Intelligence Quotients

Age 3.0	Merrill-Palmer Preschool Scale of Intelligence	IQ:136
Age 4.0	Stanford-Binet Intelligence Scale, Revised Form L-M	IQ:135
Age 5.0	Wechsler Primary and Preschool Scale of Intelligence (WPPSI)	IQ:134
Age 6.0	Wechsler Intelligence Scale for Children (WISC)[4]	

[4]Because of objections by several parents to the annual psychological testing, a minimum number of the WISC subtests were administered at age 6. They were supplemented by projective tests and several Piaget cognitive tasks.

On the abbreviated Verbal Scale Helen reached the upper range, but not reliably. On the Performance Scale she ranked in the superior range.

Age 7.0 Wechsler Intelligence Scale for
Children (WISC) IQ: Verbal: 110
Performance: 121
Full: 123

Observed Behavior during Psychological Test Sessions Ages 3 to 7

At age 3 Helen was thin and underweight (10th percentile). Her lower limbs were disproportionately small, her walk was stiff and wobbly, and she was pigeon-toed. Probably we were seeing a disuse atrophy, a result of her impeded gross motor development. Each next year up to age 6, she approached test tasks soberly and uneasily, refused all gross motor tasks, and engaged in excessive autoreotic activity. Her physical restlessness was continuous as she rocked, squirmed, got up and down from her chair, and kicked it. Confronted with difficult or disliked subtests, she mumbled and withdrew, or verged on losing her temper. In contrast, she was perfectionistic in carrying out fine motor tasks and showed excellent ability to work alone. Perhaps her fine motor ability flourished in part because she could take up the tasks all by herself, safe from physical or visual intrusion by the examiner or by mother when mother was present. Her abstract thinking was superior. At 6 her appearance was more ungainly than before: her head was a normal size, but her hands and feet were very small, her torso very thin, and her gait still unsteady. Her body control fluctuated. She slid off her chair, fiddled with nearby objects, knocked her knees together, picked her nose, hid her face, stuck out her tongue contemptuously, and made faces. Occasionally she sighed sadly or gave way to giggling or clowning for no observable reason. The degree of tension she had to discharge uninterruptedly was extraordinary.

At age 6, Helen's Children's Apperception Test (CAT) stories were mainly restricted to her naming persons in the pictures. In the few stories she told, father is punitive, parents are missing, and the tiger (parent) catches the monkey (child). Child fears danger at night, mother spanks him because he was bad ("He hit mother or something"). Baby runs away, mother finds him. They live happily ever after. Initial avoidance is thus followed by exciting aggressiveness and punishment, and finally all oedipal conflict is denied. This resolution reminds us of her parents' numerous complaints about Helen's behavior, followed immediately by their summary statements of how good and happy she was.

At 7, tall and very slender, Helen walked somewhat like a rag doll, slowly, with her arms swinging too loosely at her sides. When standing she kept her weight on the inner side of her ankles; when sitting she wriggled her body, touched her genital, fingered her lips, moved her eyebrows, blinked, sucked her knuckles, and pulled at her lips and her clothing. It looked as if every movable part of her body had to contribute to perpetual, restive movements. To questions that were easy for her, she brightened and gave long answers; otherwise they evoked shrugs, silences, long pauses, stares, empty smiles, or an angry, "Don't ask me that!" Pressed for a response, she looked at the examiner with scorn. A drop in her IQ from very superior at earlier ages to bright average at 7 could be attributed to her marked anxiety when faced with a demand to respond verbally. Helen's resistance to the

CAT pictures was extreme. She gave innocuous stories, like the bare naming of objects the year before, and went on to stories of adult (accidental) aggressive acts against child. Father is sick or absent, parents leave child, child cannot sleep. Child does not get food because he was bad. "He might have hit mother in the face, purposely." Father finds out, slaps child. The next story tells of escape (of small monkey from big tiger), leaving tiger very angry. As the stories continue, tension and hostility mount. Child (rabbit) does not listen to parents, parents leave home, child is sad and cannot sleep. Finally mother spanks child because he was bad. She is very sad about it, but she had to spank. Child runs away because mother was mean to him. Parents and child are open to painful sadomasochistic acts against one another.

Age 7: Poststudy Conference with Parents

Mother wished to discuss Helen's awkward walking, though she and father had concluded that the problem was hereditary. They agreed with our observation that the quality of Helen's speech had declined in the past two years, but set that aside as being "just babyish and unimportant." Mother conceded that she had long made the most of Helen's placidity to avoid confrontations. Father renewed his boasts about how he teased Helen, telling her, for example, that her backside was not round but pear-shaped, and how he pursued such teasing in spite of her tearful protests. He was surprised that she was offended by these remarks because he was only speaking about her body. His hostile teasing may have been born of an unconscious fear of erotic arousal by his maturing daughter. Both parents would have preferred to talk with me about the marital troubles they had revealed in recent years, and both quickly became tense and hostile in flat rejections of each other's ideas about child-rearing. Never in our meetings with them over the years had either one been seen or heard to express affection or sympathy for Helen, except once when mother, with a slight sign of regret, said that Helen had never enjoyed feeding after being weaned from the breast.

Summary: Birth to Early Latency

At age 6 weeks Helen's condition was good, but mother worried that something was wrong with her nursing schedule. In keeping with her anxiety, her feeding method had become erratic. Helen's appearance of well-being had declined. She was screaming a great deal, and mother thought she might already be spoiled. Her sudden loss of the breast at 3 months involved as well a loss of intimate physical sensory gratifications, as she was no longer held for her feedings. Only her bottle was held. Day after day she lay alone for hours at a time, her steady states of immobility, silence, and hunger interrupted only by periods of enraged crying. Perhaps she felt the absence of gratifications at first in an oneiric way, later in a consciousness of recurrent abandonments. Her passivity may have had a constitutional root, but there was no sign of it in her first weeks, and we know that her parents made no effort to enliven her. For the most part, she missed a development of joy in the use of her body and of a capacity to reach out to persons and things in her environment. Physical inertia, together with her long-frustrated wishes to be picked up and held affectionately, can have gradually weakened her perception of her body boundaries. The fear of being held to stand can have been a result, in part, of her parents' discouragement of her gross motor activity at an age when infants normally exult in acquiring new physical skills. Her cries for food, along with her taking it into her mouth and then spitting it out, may have indicated confusion as to what she should take into her body. As an infant she had little opportunity to acquire a sense of her body shape or of an intact mental self representation. By the end of her first year this physically healthy infant was restricted in many areas of development, fearful of new experience, and habituated to periods of paroxysmal screaming and panic attacks. In her next years, quick urinary control was followed by a long period of regressions; and by ambivalent yearning for mother. At age 7 her physical agitation, continual autoerotic activity, and general inaccessibility suggested that she contained much perturbation about her body representation, and that her affects were too constricted and too labile. Comparable imbalances were seen in her oscillations between body rigidity and restlessness, between withheld speech and very rapid speech, and between sober moods and awkward hilarity, as observed in school. She was as unchangingly ill at ease in her object relations as in the use of her body. Many of her abundant autoerotic activities were also autoaggressive. As she moved toward latency, she exhibited strict defenses—avoidance, restriction, inhibition, disavowal (of affects and needs), regression, reversal (disdain covering her severe affect hunger), negativism, and turning against the self (food rejection). Inner excitement continued through childhood as she went on receiving mother's scoldings about her restlessness, father's insensitive teasing, and their common disregard of her low self-esteem. After her early childhood the worn remnant of her cherished blanket could hardly be called a transitional object. It was rather like a coveted talisman, held almost as if it were an integral part of her body. We might see it as symbolic of her own feelings of being torn by fright and rage. Mother denied that Helen had any problems; father was angry at her for having them. She carried on her daily life with masochistic submission to their implacability and with bursts of unruliness that never brought her freedom from their trivialization of her feelings. She found some refuge in achieving credit for her academic and art work, but she was overburdened by feelings of low self-worth, probably linked to her identification with both mother and father as aggressors, deniers, and rationalizers.

Interview with Helen: Age 18

Helen was tall and thin (height 5' 7", weight 104 lbs), her dress and grooming were overly casual, her posture was poor, her facial expression bland. Her smile had a mechanical quality, very like mother's frequent grimace seen in her visit when Helen was 6 weeks old. Throughout our talk of several hours she sat with her arms folded across her chest and her legs crossed tightly. She was friendly and thoughtful, also tense and humorless. Her speech was extensive and very rapid. Often, as she spoke she twisted her mouth self-consciously. She had done well in school, she said, until age 10, but in seven following years her parents made six residential moves, she had to change schools repeatedly, and her grades dropped from the superior to the average range, except in art, which she loved and in which she excelled. Her parents praised her art work ("You are already an artist," mother had said, 12 years before), but father fussed about having to take her to and from the art classes. She had enjoyed playing the violin in the school orchestra, but had to drop it for lack of time. For her sexual information, mother had given her a book to read, by which time Helen already knew the facts. Mother never talked with her about any aspect of physical development. Menstruation, at 13 or 14, did not bother her, she said.

Soon after, however, she got into the habit of having "gigantic snacks," which belied her easy acceptance of maturation. She attributed the recent change in her eating habits to an intense fear of being overweight, as her parents now were. The conscious dread of eating too much and getting fat probably was linked to a less conscious adolescent wish to distance herself from them. It may have been overdetermined by conflicts about a wish to disidentify with them, and also to repair perceived faults in her changed body image. At that time in her life, she said, mother fussed constantly about what everyone in the family was eating (worry about overweight), kept watch on the contents of the refrigerator, and scolded anyone for taking anything from it instead of waiting for mealtimes. Mother's demand to control who in the family ate what and when recalls her withholding of food from Helen as an infant. Now mother also warned Helen that if she ate freely she would get flabby arms like mother's, warnings that revived the misery Helen had felt at age 11 when a friend used to tease her about having "thunder thighs" and an expectable middle-age spread. At 15 she began to diet and lose weight and "got carried away." She would have had a slice of Melba toast for breakfast, walk five miles, swim 30 laps, have a green pepper for lunch, and a light dinner. She liked being underweight and did not mind that menses stopped when she was 16. About herself, she liked only that she had artistic talent, nothing else. Her school work had suffered. Now she had a part-time job at a food shop; it must have demanded a good deal of self-control, which probably made her proud of her capacity to not eat. Her greatest worry, she said, was that she would not succeed in whatever work she chose to do, a worry that probably encased larger fears about her future emotional, social, and sexual well-being.

At home there was no peace. Mother and father were asocial, had no friends, and just watched television a lot. Harry dropped out of school for a while and got into serious trouble with the authorities for minor thefts. Helen disapproved of his wayward behavior, but liked him. He was, after all, her only friend in the family; they had together suffered feelings of abandonment by their parents in previous years. Helen said that mother had been raised as a "princess," resented having to go to work, yelled a lot, and always wanted to have her own way. Father was smart, but a loner. He didn't care a bit what other people thought. He had severe temper tantrums during which he got red in the face, stamped his feet, hit, and broke things. Once he chased Helen and Harry out of the house and ran after them in a fury. Mother also hit her a few times. Helen hit back. In the past year or two she had had occasion to hit father back. Helen's and Harry's friends were not welcome in the home at any time because mother and father felt they had a right to their privacy; besides, they were very critical of Helen's social activity, which in fact was minimal. Mother would have liked to meet Helen's friends, but for father that was out of the question. Mother had sometimes tried to do things "as a family," in vain, because father made caustic jokes about the family's "golden moments." They had terrible arguments about money, which they handled impulsively, especially in numerous purchases of real estate for which they reaped endless debts. A certain moral promiscuity seemed to have entered the family life. All of its members were now "as far apart as one could think from being cohesive." By this account, discord was ever-present in Helen's family life. She presented these facts drily, as if she had worn out any feelings about them. "I'm fatalistic," she said.

Psychological Test Findings: Age 18[5]

Helen's intelligence test performance (WAIS-R Verbal Scale: 120; Performance Scale: 129; Full Scale: 128) indicates that extreme self-criticism impinges on her judgment and evokes depressive reactions that she wards off with hypomanic denial. She is comfortable in carrying out structured tasks, accomplishes them quickly and accurately, and in them functions at the superior level. She is less at ease when required to create a verbal response, when her thinking becomes both tangential and overinclusive. She lacks a stable representation of her environment, and has a tendency to fashion the world as she wants it to be. Her Rorschach record indicates crude oral aggression, bizarre confusion of body parts, and loss of body boundaries. Incongruous combinations represent an unstable sense of self and an extreme departure from reality testing, manifest in a massive defensive effort to ward off anxiety.

Helen's Thematic Apperception Test (TAT) stories indicate that she is confused about her future, yet maintains magical and grandiose expectations of success. Although she wishes to go forward toward independent living, fear sends her home again. She feels her parents' animosity toward her wish for autonomy, submits to their harsh demands, and is depressed. There is much rumination in her stories about

---

[5]Administered by Frances Luckom-Nurnberg. The tests administered at age 18 were the Wechsler Adult Intelligence Scale-Revised (WAIS-R), Rorschach, Thematic Apperception Test (TAT), Human Figure Drawings, Sentence Completion, and Bender-Gestalt Drawings.

her future sexual activity; a mad rapist makes all females hide, they have no way out, and sexual indulgence leads to a bad end. Sibling rivalry is overdramatic, sadomasochistic qualities are highly evident, and oedipal guilt is partly relieved by oral means but ends in death. A preoccupation with dress reappears, with worry about her appearance and denigration of her body. Rage and frustration of unfulfilled narcissistic wishes are followed by guilt.

Helen models herself on people who are outside the mainstream of society, and in a counterphobic way she stalks danger by doing outrageous things, even though this evokes inner conflict. Strong dependency needs make the world a frightening place where she feels vulnerable and inadequate to accomplish any goals in life. She has vague anticipations of catastrophe. Her functioning has an "as-if" quality. She experiences her mother as sadistic and competitive, her father as interfering with her ability to establish satisfying relations to men. Oedipal conflicts are unresolved. Men are dangerous but also ineffectual. Father neglects his daughter, she dies, he is guilty and commits suicide. Although Helen describes her parents as being in discord much of the time, she sees them as a united block against her. She maintains a heavy reliance on grandiosity and denial, but these defenses are ineffective and she remains anxious and dysphoric. She is hyperalert, guarded, and angry. She has difficulty expressing the anger and turns it inward, but when overwhelmed she becomes orally aggressive and cannot modulate her feelings. The combination of sensitivity to emotional stimuli, poorly integrated impulses, and weak defenses put her at risk for acting-out behavior. There is some indication that she may abuse drugs. Principal Diagnosis: Borderline with Anxiety, Dysphoria, and Narcissistic trends.

Clinical Impression: Age 18

Helen's self representation was poor. She gave no indication of any satisfying relationships, of optimism, or of hope. The easy air with which she tried to conduct herself during our talk had a quality of undue elation. Often in her telling of unhappy events she laughed or giggled self-consciously, making her seem more emotionally shallow than she actually was. Central to her neurosis was an early history of oral and physical unpleasure, long periods of grief from feelings of hunger and of abandonment by both parents, and a disordered and passive submission that hid rage. Her later efforts at undoing in rebellious and self-destructive behaviors were motivated by a fury turned against herself, and chronic depression. Her ego strengths appeared to be too weak to fend off the strictures of an oppressive conscience. She showed no psychotic features, but fragile ego and superego states, uneven capacities for instinctual satisfaction, and impoverished object relations. In spite of these handicaps, she was making an earnest effort toward achieving a profession as an artist.

Early Adulthood: Telephone Reports, Ages 22 to 30[6]

By the time Helen entered college she was trying to eat normally, but then she began to have "terrible stomach

---

[6]I telephoned all available subjects (N = 78) when they reached age 22, when college education was likely to have ended, for information about their academic or employment histories since age 18. I spoke with them again in following years, to ask about their general well-being and

cramps," a result, she thought, of having done foolish things, such as eating only vegetables. Menses returned when she was 20, very irregularly, and were stabilized by progesterone. Then came a period of heavy drinking, followed by a siege of mononucleosis. Helen knew she had disrupted her system, yet (like mother) loosely supposed that everything would come out all right. At present she ate no breakfast, a salad for lunch, and "a regular dinner." In recent years she often had "stomach flu"—vague pains and digestive problems. Marriage at 25 to a young man with whom she had lived in her senior year of college made no change in her life. To tell the truth, she said, she felt bored with her husband as well as her job teaching art in a small college. Several consultations about her stomach cramps had brought advice for her to seek psychiatric treatment, which she did not heed. She was very depressed, and sometimes feared she might be having a "nervous breakdown." Her parents never noticed her extreme weight loss. They continued to change their places of residence innumerable times within the city, the state, and the country. "It's a weird family," Helen said. "My mother shows no emotion. I never know how she feels. She always wants to have her own way. . . . She still is mainly concerned about her own pleasures." Helen had no memory of problems with her feet. Grandmother had told her that as a baby she pushed herself across the floor on her buttocks instead of walking, and that she was taken to many doctors but nothing was done for her. Later her parents told her that she just had flat feet. Now her ankles sometimes turned inward and caused her pain. Maybe, she thought, she had pulled tendons.

---

plans, and to enlist their participation in the follow-up study by Dr. Massie at age 30.

Age 30[7]

Helen answered all questions with much effort to show that she felt good about herself. She was aware of her parents' remissness in many areas, and with muted affect expressed full rejection of their actions and attitudes. They never should have had children, she said, because they could not love them, their own comforts always came first. Never, really never, had they shown any sympathy or offered any help when she was unhappy or ill or troubled about anything at all. They rather blamed her for any discontent she voiced, or laughed at her, or teased her about being so upset they would have to call an ambulance to take her away. She told of these events without rancor, actually with a degree of exoneration, as though the past had passed away, and she had found emotional distance from her parents. Asked why, if she quite dismissed them from her life, she went to visit them from time to time, she said drearily, "You go back to the only thing you know."

She went on to speak candidly about her phobias, compulsions, hypochondriasis, low appetite, panic attacks, nervous habits, a homosexual encounter, and social difficulties, and one minor theft about which she had no remorse, but such great fear of being caught that she would never put herself in such danger again. For a time she had engaged in perverse sexual activity. Her marriage had improved as she felt grateful to her husband for his support of her chosen career in painting. She would not have children, she said, because caring for them would interfere with her career. She described an oil painting she had done: it was huge, 17 x 3 feet, in very thick paint using dark earth colors, with

---

[7]From a videotaped interview by Dr. Massie (see footnote 3 in Introduction).

amorphous form. It weighed hundreds of pounds. The content, as she described it, seemed intended to evoke feelings of dreaminess, gloom, and a preoccupation with hidden fantasies. The gross anality in this huge, somber painting might signify the weight of dark (murderous?) emotions that oppressed her, together with profound feelings of sadness, worthlessness, and hate. She had a vague recognition that the form and content of her paintings were influenced, positively, she thought, by her sad emotional history.

A few years ago she had had a nightmare that had disturbed her very much. A big bird was *vomiting* on a train, she had to jump over the tracks to reach another platform, she jumped but fell on the tracks and was electrocuted. Then she floated upward and looked down on her body. This dream, in which she was disembodied from herself, can be assumed to have contained several unconscious wishes: to get rid, orally, of her sick inner self, to punish herself for her effort to escape to a new but still precarious way of life (a new platform), all in vain. She fails and sees the end of her life. The long-standing indignation at her parents, poorly repressed, is turned against herself. Yet the end of the dream contains another wish, to be reborn, to see herself alive all over again. These are educated guesses. Had she been a psychoanalytic patient, I might have learned much more about her choice of media for her paintings, the feelings she was trying to express in them, and the release they provided for her. It is conceivable that an identification with her parents' frustrated desires for peace and personal gratification may have indirectly inspired Helen's artistic aims, through which she was trying at long last to make up for the dearth of emotional satisfaction she had long endured. She could strive to use her fine motor skill to create a kind of companion for herself, in her paintings.

Chapter 5

The History of Ariel

The First Year

Day 1

Apgar Scores at 1 minute, 9; at five minutes, 10.

Day 3

Ariel's sensorimotor responses could not be elicited because she was too sleepy, and later access to her was limited by hospital regulations. When given the bottle, she became alert, sucked eagerly and well for 15 minutes, hiccoughed, gagged slightly, and fell asleep again.

First Interview with Mother, Three Days Postpartum

Mother was dressed carefully and well made up. Her speech was brief, restrained-pleasant, and barely informative. She had grown up in a small Midwestern town. Her parents had a high-school education and were employed in service jobs. She had an older sister to whom she was not close, because the sister was "on the selfish side." As a child mother had led "a very average existence" in the suburbs. In her teens she became distant from her parents as she met new people who were of "a better class." She had not enjoyed her two years at college, had thought of a career in singing, but found it would be too demanding. She would have preferred to be an interior decorator, but did not have the "right connections." She had also hoped one day to open a small up-scale restaurant where she could meet interesting people. She had moved away from her family and lost close ties with them as she became "more intellectual" than they (probably she meant more worldly). In this way she emphasized having outgrown her parents and having striven for upward mobility. Her father, she said, was quiet and introverted, her mother an extrovert who ruled the family. She herself was a little like her own mother in that she enjoyed entertaining people, especially preparing special dishes for them. She knew nothing about infant or child care. Father, a college graduate, used to be close to his parents and three younger siblings, but by now he (like mother?) had outgrown them. He had hoped to be a reporter, then turned to a computer business. He still sometimes thought of pursuing a career in law, but probably it was not compatible with his artistic interests (none ever reported), and he was not sure where being a lawyer would lead him. He loved participating in all kinds of sports. He and mother enjoyed taking long drives to dinner, traveling, visiting museums and art galleries. Both, mother said, had a creative bent—she had once been interested in painting, he in movie production. They had few friends. Father did not care for people to get too close to the family, even if he liked them. Mother's account suggested, for both parents, a wish to declare cultural interests, but an absence of direction, a renunciation of intimate relationships, and an endorsement of exclusiveness.

She "had no need," she said, for the experiences of natural childbirth and breast-feeding. The idea of having children had once frightened her. Now she thought she might have several, as her first pregnancy was not so bad. She spoke proudly of how easy her anesthetized delivery had been. She had laughed at the emphasis placed on breast-feeding in a pamphlet she came across in the hospital, enjoyed reading it just to see how much she knew, but it didn't change her mind about bottle-feeding. A pediatrician had assured her, she said, that breast-feeding wasn't necessary unless she felt an emotional need for it. She supposed a baby could be weaned from the bottle at about 3 months, or maybe one day the bottle would just happen not to be available, so weaning would result naturally. She would use a pacifier to avoid the baby's thumbsucking. Toilet training could begin as soon as a baby could sit without support. She was sure that babies needed firm and consistent handling, that limits against habits had to be set right away "so that the child should know where she stands," and a good spanking now and then was useful. Talking did not get you anywhere. She felt that she herself, as a child, should have been given more discipline. Having gotten her own way too much, she was now "somewhat on the selfish side" (like her sister?). She was often careless and thoughtless, lacked a sense of responsibility, and was not so sensitive as father. He would probably be too indulgent.

Age: 6 Weeks

Gesell Developmental Schedules (actual age 7.4 weeks)[1]

---

[1] See chapter 3, footnote 3. Before each visit, Ariel's mother requested a change in her appointment.

Motor	4 to 8 weeks
Adaptive:	4 to 8 weeks
Language:	4 to 8 weeks
Personal-Social:	4 to 8 weeks

Ariel was alert, engaged in a great deal of jerky hand-flailing and kicking, and performed only moderately well on most of the tests, possibly because her visual responses were delayed and short-lived, and she was cranky. She showed no mouthing or hand-to-mouth activity. When mother gave her a bottle, she sucked noisily and vigorously. Then, as she slowed down, mother kept urging her to take more and more milk, and for the last 10 minutes mother force-fed. Back in the crib the baby was fretful and soon the fretting turned to sobs. Mother picked her up, and although she kept Ariel in her lap for the rest of the visit, about another hour-and-a-half, and spoke to her softly now and then, she made no eye contact with Ariel, whose irritability and restlessness did not subside. Aside from occasional soft speech to her, mother was silent, her posture tense. Both mother and infant were emotionally still. Each remained as if alone and in a state of vague discomfort.

Every morning Ariel received her bottle in her crib, in silence, slept again until placed in the infant seat for her breakfast, and then was replaced in her crib to sleep again. Usually she soon began to fuss or cry. Mother would pick her up and hold her briefly before returning her to the crib. There were times, she explained, when she simply had to let the baby cry. She appeared to be helpless about what else she might do, and unable to say so. About the rest of the day, she offered information only about the specific hours when Ariel was fed and when she slept, as if that was all she knew or needed to know. In response to questions, she said she always waited for Ariel to cry before feeding her, then mentioned that when Ariel was so hungry that she was "pushed beyond the point of tolerance, she has a screaming, enraged cry that borders on a tantrum" (observed).

Ariel's sleep during the day was fitful. Sometimes she cried out "as if she were having a bad dream." Mother had been interrupting Ariel's evening feeding to bathe her, but as Ariel sometimes regurgitated or defecated in the bath, mother tried to bathe her just before the feeding. Ariel "howled" at that. Occasionally she was constipated and had tremendous amounts of gas. "She looks as if she's in agony quite often," mother said off-handedly. She seemed to be embarrassed about Ariel's distress, and to hide her feeling by a show of indifference. She spoke with most feeling about how fatigued she was by the physical tasks that had faced her since Ariel's birth, but she "loved having her around." (She had said exactly the same about the family dog.) As the session was ending she began to dress Ariel for the trip home, whereupon Ariel broke into tantrumlike screaming, which did not divert mother from her task.

Age: 26 Weeks

Gesell Developmental Schedules (actual age 24.3 weeks):

Gross Motor	20 to 28 weeks
Fine Motor:	12 to 16 weeks
Adaptive:	12 to 16 weeks
Language	24 weeks
Personal-Social:	20 to 32 weeks

(Note the wide span of these scores, indicating uneven development.)

Ariel was neatly dressed and looked well nourished. She responded to test objects with visual alertness but did not reach for any, so that her test performance barely reached an average level. Lying in the crib, she vocalized with good clarity and sporadic loud complaints while she kept looking up at the ceiling as if nothing in her near environment could attract her attention. When later she sat in the infant seat, she moved her arms and legs continuously and vigorously, and smiled at the observer more than at mother. Shortly she made plaintive sounds, which turned to coos when mother picked her up and cuddled her for a minute or two. One could see she was a baby who was easy to hold and comfort. As mother placed her back in the infant seat to feed her, she again mentioned Ariel's dislike of interruptions in the midst of a feeding, yet a few minutes later she stopped the feeding of one food and plied Ariel with another until Ariel began to gag. The gagging could have meant a withdrawal from the ill-timed feeding or a reflexive response to displeasure, as was observed during her forced feeding at 7 weeks. It was the same with dessert. Mother kept urging her to have just one more spoonful, speeding them up toward the end. She explained that even when Ariel "spurned" any foods, mother always insisted that Ariel eat them because she firmly believed that children should eat what they are given. Mother's strong endorsement of discipline seemed to cover a marked ignorance of how to feed a baby, as well as an imperviousness to the baby's feelings.

Each day before and after her naps Ariel lay alone for 30 to 40 minutes. She loved being picked up, talked to, kissed, or held. She smiled at anyone who approached her (observed), but made loud complaints "when bored." On inquiry, mother said that sometimes she talked or sang to Ariel, or played with her "while walking outdoors." She had tried to teach the baby to sit up, to play with toys, or to drink from a cup, so far all in vain. She spoke of these efforts in her usual dispassionate manner, and went on to tell about her own condition. Not only was she fatigued, she also suffered from giddiness and a slight anemia, complaints suggestive of her own emotional disquiet. Ariel, she said, was somewhat demanding when mother had other things to do, adding, perhaps to withdraw the grievance, "She's not that bad. I don't mind because she's not a cranky or pesty baby." She foresaw trouble, though, when Ariel would begin to crawl. "I'll have to watch her," she said. "Maybe she'll make a nuisance of herself, knocking things over." Difficulties lay ahead for an infant whose mother felt so ineffective in her infant care. Father rarely paid any attention to Ariel. Ariel's trust in her own capacities or in the capacities of her parents to answer to her needs were already in default.

Age: 52 Weeks (Actually, 55 Weeks)

Gesell Developmental Schedules:

Fine Motor:	56 weeks to 15 months
Gross Motor:	15 months+
Adaptive:	48 weeks to 15 months
Language:	56 weeks to 15 months
Personal-Social:	56 weeks to 15 months

Judging by these scores alone, Ariel had recovered from the setbacks seen at 26 weeks. She now was expansive socially, vocalized often with pleasure, and spoke several words. Responses to test objects were, on the other hand, delayed, slow, and uneven. In contrast to the withheld curiosity (Adaptive sector), she prized independent gross motor activity and showed an unusual ability to be physically active for long periods, almost too independently. She spent most of the time walking about slowly, steadily, investigating objects in the room, pulling things off surfaces, trying to open the door, throwing a ball, inspecting the wastebaskets, and bringing toys to the observer (not to mother) to play with her. Her movements were economical, her coordination excellent. These actions could have represented positive developments, except that when physically inactive she was distinctly subdued. Affect and activity were not mutually modulated. Six months before, mother had said that Ariel loved to be handled, kissed, and spoken to. Now she said Ariel did not like to sit on anyone's lap and did not like to be cuddled (observed). A degree of emotional and social withdrawal had set in.

Mother's feeding of Ariel in the infant seat was brief, silent, and rote. Shortly Ariel became restless and clearly had had enough, yet mother continued urging food upon her until Ariel became agitated, whereupon mother tried in vain to distract her with toys. The connection between mother's excessive feeding and the baby's dissatisfaction was manifest; mother seemed to have no inkling of it. Then she gave Ariel small sips of milk from a cup, although she had been advised by her pediatrician not to push cup-feeding. When later Ariel moved about the room at will, mother became physically tense, several times sprang up from her chair to see what Ariel was doing, and shouted at her not to touch things. Ariel tried to bite a ball: mother grabbed it away, admonishing her not to chew on it because it was dirty. Mother's alarm and her interference with Ariel's explorations of her surroundings were disturbing to watch. She may have felt embarrassed by Ariel's poor response to the feeding we observed, and by her own lack of composure. There were spare moments when she showed pleasure in gentle, affectionate responses to Ariel, but she could not sustain them. For the most part she scolded or restricted the child. Spontaneously but drily, she mentioned that Ariel often screamed during the whole time her diaper was changed.

Tension between them mounted through Ariel's first year. An important determinant of their discontent probably lay in the frequent absences of both parents. The first was for a few days when Ariel was 6 months old; mother and father spent a week away from her, leaving her in the care of a relative who was not intimate with the family. In her next half-year, they sometimes left her with maternal grandmother. On inquiry mother said Ariel showed no reactions to their absences. It is a fair guess that these repeated absences aroused not merely separation anxiety, which implies an understanding of a temporary absence, but acute feelings of object loss and a conviction of lost love. Ariel's excessive activity when seen at age 1 hints at the presence of an overwrought quest for someone or some way to restore a feeling of safety.

Mother's account of her daily life with Ariel indicated how meager was their affective accord. Ariel had been having her morning bottle in her crib by herself, and was left there for at least an hour while mother and father had their breakfast together in a separate room. It was as if they regarded her as being outside of their private lives. During other meals, taken in her high chair, she was usually very restless—she would run her hand on her face and through her hair, and put her head down on the tray of her high chair (as seen in Film 5; Brody and Axelrad, 1970a). Feedings at home usually lasted 15 minutes at most. "Meals are no time for play," mother declared, in a reverse of her casual statement six months earlier that she played with Ariel when feeding her. Ariel never had to wait for food and was rarely frustrated, mother said, because mother kept her on a rigid schedule. After meals and naps Ariel was always put into her playpen, always against her will. Mother's saying that Ariel no longer liked physical contact with people might be a projection of her own reluctance to hold her or a sign of Ariel's now desperate demand to be physically active—or to be caught and held close? While 1-year-olds often like to move about by themselves, they do not thereby reject affectionate physical closeness to intimate persons, as Ariel was said to do. Two weeks ago, while she was having difficulty cutting her molars, she was constipated, vomited "numbers of times," (the first reference to vomiting) and her gums bled several times. Soon after, she had a viral infection, coughed, vomited phlegm many times and often cried during the night. She slept in her parents' bedroom, was a light and restless sleeper, and always awoke when mother or father came into the room. A readiness to feel tension may have come to be present even when she slept.

For the past week mother had been placing Ariel on the regular toilet seat, although this frightened her. A few days ago she fell off the seat onto the tile floor, paled, vomited, became sleepy, and then was all right. Days later she had one bowel movement in the potty chair, so mother intended to put her on it each day for about 30 minutes after breakfast and after dinner, in spite of Ariel's angry resentment of any physical restriction. When left in her playpen she "screamed bloody murder," got red in the face, and held her breath—the latter made mother very angry, she said. These rages occurred especially when Ariel was left in the playpen too long or when something was taken from her. "She gets over it very quickly," said mother, also quickly, with the further explanation that Ariel liked to be on her own, talking and singing to herself or teasing the dog; and she could play by herself for up to an hour-and-a-half. When she was in a bad mood mother picked her up and tried to distract her, otherwise mother did not talk to her much. Again, as six months ago, mother thought that often Ariel was bored (a projection?). How did she on occasion play with Ariel? Mother mentioned peek-a-boo games and showing Ariel how to put on a scarf (this matched mother's interest in fashion, as observed in all of her meetings with us). She also left the radio on all day so that Ariel could listen and not feel alone. Stifled affect pervaded mother's report, evident in her dry speech, her shallow responses to Ariel, and her inability to find pleasure in the child's presence.

And Ariel was presenting difficulties to her parents. Each had been slapping her hands for picking up things she should not, for whining, "and other aggressive acts." Now and then the slap had been so hard that Ariel's hands got red, yet each time she just laughed. Probably the slaps, received in a stirred-up state, incited the perverse reaction. Or Ariel could have already learned that her laughter dissolved her parents' tension. Sometimes she rocked on all fours or bounced up and down. She also "played with herself" or with her navel, scratched her belly, and licked the outer parts of her lips. Mother had to be very careful when she held Ariel because Ariel grabbed at her face; she did the same with other people's faces. She had bitten mother several times, once hard enough to cause bleeding. But she was much too young for discipline, mother said, except for a few habits she had developed, like sucking her finger, biting toys, pulling the dog's hair, and "getting into things." When she "got into trouble" mother put her in the playpen in spite of the fury it aroused in her. After more remarks about Ariel's fussing, whining, and screaming, mother ended her report by declaring that Ariel was easygoing and even-tempered. Finally, as in previous meetings, she turned her attention to her own state: recently she had been troubled by gastritis, "nerves and dizzy spells," and was still anemic. Caring for Ariel was so exhausting, she said, that she was grateful when

Ariel was willing to stay in her crib alone all day. She expected that by age 5 Ariel would be "a holy terror, very outgoing, into everything," and would need to be controlled. This anticipation implied that mother's disappointment in her ability to govern Ariel was stirring up a latent sadomasochistic excitement in mother that frightened her.

Interviews with Parents: Second Year to Age 7 (see Chapter 4, Note 3)

At 15 months Ariel ran in front of a swing in the playground, was struck on her forehead, and picked up bleeding. She was first taken to her pediatrician, then to a hospital emergency room for the wound to be sutured. Mother was not allowed to be present during the procedure. The terrified child screamed and vomited. I thought it possible that the accident occurred as a result of Ariel's impulsive running about without restraint in the outdoor setting as long as she was not "getting into things."

When Ariel was 22 months old her brother Alex was born. On leaving for the hospital mother merely said goodbye to Ariel. She thought Ariel guessed that "something was happening" because mother had been irritable during her pregnancy. In the three days when mother was in the hospital, she telephoned Ariel once. Father "may have" given her more attention on those days—mother did not really know. On her return home—with a baby, a complete surprise for Ariel—she was most attentive to Ariel while a temporary nurse cared for the baby. This effort to protect Ariel after the fact actually may have aroused additional confusion for Ariel. By leaving Alex to a stranger and devoting herself mainly to Ariel, mother may have unwittingly supported a fantasy in Ariel that she still could keep mother to herself, and so stirred up Ariel's subsequent hostility to Alex, to mother, and then to other children, with increasing feelings of guilt along the way. Her parents were sure Ariel had no reaction to Alex's birth. At the time, mother explained, Christmas festivities were in preparation at home, so "not too much care was given to Ariel or other matters." Mother and father went out a good deal in the holiday season. They were sure that Ariel had no concern about their absences, but she must have seen and heard a good deal of their plans to be at parties with other people. Shortly after, she suffered a viral infection with dehydration. Unfortunately we had no opportunity during Ariel's second year to learn about her reactions to any of these events. They must have reinforced a worry about her parents' allegiance to her.

By the end of her first year Ariel had objected vehemently to any physical imposition. When not quite 2, she fiercely resisted getting into a new bed, a resistance no doubt intensified by the fact that her crib was given to Alex. Bedtime soon came to involve "raving, ranting, screaming, and vomiting." She began to leave her room each night and get into her parents' bed, or they let her stay up and watch television, with the rationale that she didn't need much sleep. Their efforts to return her to her own bed were in vain. Regularly, after a few hours, she returned to theirs. Often she cried out in her sleep, "No! Don't, Mommy!" Probably there were several determinants of her disturbance: dismay about losing her bed to Alex, fear of being alone, dread of her parents' daily scoldings, restraints, and physical punishments by mother for her "rebelliousness." When father alone was in charge of Ariel at bedtime, he tried persuasion and cajolery, and finally let her sleep on the living room couch, near him. He reasoned that if she stayed in her bed for half the night it was all right for her to be in the parents' bed for the rest of it, the only problem being that it was "unrestful" for them. When Ariel was 4 her parents gave up and let her stay in their bed for the rest of the night; when she was 5 they let her stay "only for a good reason." Their submitting to her peremptory infantile demands could only have inflated her feelings of dominance over them, bolstered her childish narcissism, and intensified her fears of punishment.

When she was 3, mother said Ariel had sucked her finger "almost since she was born" (not observed or reported at 6 weeks, seen occasionally at 26 weeks, clearly present at 1 year). Mother ignored it, but when Ariel "touched herself" mother distracted her. She also said that Ariel had begun to hold onto her blanket at 6 months (not observed or reported in her first year), needed it all of the time, at home or out, and would rather miss school than go without it. (Unfortunately for Ariel's capacity to bear frustration, the school did not object.) Habitually she also stayed in her parents' bed in the morning as long as one of them stayed there with her. Father confirmed that she was just afraid of being alone, longed to be with mother all of the time, day and night, and was sad whenever mother was angry with her.

When Ariel was a year old her toilet training was begun without success; 6 months later it was the same. When she was just 3 her training was successful after mother put a rubber mat under her wherever she sat down. Ariel objected and still needed a diaper at night for several months more. There were bowel "accidents" until she was past 4 because she was "too lazy." At that age she still was allowed to be in the bathroom whenever mother or father were there. In spite of this and of Alex's presence in the family, her parents were sure that Ariel never showed any interest in sexual differences. She was "strong-headed" and obstinate, however, defying her parents without end. Sometimes she got hold of

Alex and scratched his face to the point where it bled. Her parents were annoyed or angered by her actions, but never expressed concern about her emotional states.

When Ariel was 3 she was said to have an excellent appetite and no problem about food. She was a capricious eater, though, as she nibbled all day long, had definite ideas about what foods she would accept, and often gave mother a menu for her dinner. She still took her milk in a bottle every morning and afternoon (when Alex did). Mother delayed giving it at bedtime. Usually Ariel fell asleep without it, so mother left it at her bedside for Ariel to take it by herself in the morning, thus unwittingly reinforcing Ariel's drift toward oral regression. Ariel was not fond of sweets; if she took a piece of candy she soon spat it out. Eating chocolate, especially at bedtime, made her vomit mucus, which mother attributed to an allergy. This strong rejection of sweets by a young child is so unusual that it suggests she felt anxiety about eating them. Was she already cautious about accepting oral pleasure? Since she was 3 months old, mother now said, Ariel "upchucked" easily (our records contain no reference to this, except for the regurgitation at 6 weeks when feedings were interrupted for a bath). Some self-induced vomiting or bringing up mucus in early childhood may have continued as a learned ploy to keep mother at her side. She was "sensitive to chocolate" when she had a cold, gagged a lot, and had trouble sitting with the family for a whole meal. She began to have belly aches and to resist going to school. Anxiety about ingesting food had become somatized in disordered eating, gagging, spitting, vomiting, and general restlessness during family mealtimes.

At 4 Ariel was said to prefer quiet activities at home, but she fought against being alone in her own room. If mother tried to leave her there, she would yell, scream, and grab mother's leg to hold onto her. Sometimes she cried herself to sleep. One day, "playing house," she included in her story that the mother had died. Mother, pretending to be insulted, asked why. No reply from Ariel; she let the "insult" stand. Ariel and Alex fought a lot. She bit and scratched him, and pretended to hug him while actually choking him; father thought this was "quite clever." "She doesn't like him much," said mother, and "the best discipline was a good whack." Altogether, Ariel was obstinate, and defied her parents without end.

The next year mother reported more of Ariel's undesirable habits: needing to hold a piece of her blanket, restlessly scratching her head when angry, blinking, wiping her eyes, and biting her nails. She used to bite, slap, and scratch Alex, now she scratched other children's faces and grabbed their toys. She had "night terrors" once or twice, which mother could not or wished not to elaborate upon, and sad dreams about being lost. When reproved for any disobedience, she vomited. She fought against restrictions or punishments with violent temper tantrums—she stamped, "yelled," threw shoes, knocked over plants, and kicked anything in her way. Almost nothing around her was safe. Spanking "with her pants down" or the threat of it by mother or father stopped her briefly. At times mother ignored the tantrums, comforting herself with the idea that Ariel could accept criticism as long as it was phrased in positive terms. Actually, she spoke of Ariel's imperious ways with some amusement. She knew that Ariel was possessive and ungiving, and said wistfully that she would like to think that Ariel, in her fights with children, was not always the aggressor. Father was more lenient with Ariel than mother was. When he came home from work he always had a "treat" for her, and when he did not want Ariel to scream at him he "gave in" to her. But she really was "a deep thinker," said mother—she was sad when grandmother left, when she saw animals on television being hurt or lost, or when Alex was spanked. One might say she was flooded with anxiety, which set off her parents either to submit to her demands or to punish her for them. As she drew near to latency, her anxiety, her guilt, and her oedipal conflicts can only have been extreme.

Entrance into first grade, when Ariel was 6, brought new stresses. She gave up the scraps of her baby blanket, but for months cried about having to go to school because when there she missed mother. To avoid going, she again complained of belly aches,[2] had little breakfast, and gagged a lot. With children, she was a poor loser. At her birthday party she was angry when she did not win all the prizes, and accused mother of cheating. After school hours she was at loose ends, kept asking mother to do something with her, yet to any request mother made of her she almost at once said no. Going to bed or getting up in the morning were difficult because of her dawdling and her efforts to keep mother at her side. Each day was filled with Ariel's impatient demands, defiance, and tantrums, and ended by her running to her room, slamming her door, and sometimes trying to punch mother in anger. Their mutual resentment was pervasive and intense. Mother found it hard to keep her temper with Ariel, and spanked her about every two weeks. She had not expected her child to be so outspoken, stubborn, and rebellious, and was sure these traits were inborn. Just the same, she thought Ariel's typical mood was quiet and thoughtful, also introverted, and that she was mature beyond her years in being self-possessed, logical though not affectionate, decisive, and able to deal well with people. Mother seemed to be unaware of the contradictions that

[2]Fritz, Fritsch, and Hagino (1997) found that the most common etiology of recurrent abdominal pain in children was unknown, probably functional in origin, and related to stress or secondary gain—both present in Ariel's case.

permeated her remarks, and of the ambivalence they contained, as when she cited a recent occasion when Ariel spoke rudely to a group of adults, arousing everyone's admiring (or embarrassed) laughter.

At 7 Ariel's anxieties had intensified. The gagging at breakfast, the morning belly aches, and the wishes to play at home alone or with mother continued. Bedtime difficulties increased, as she cried for mother and took a long time to fall asleep, sometimes as much as two hours. She complained of having "bad thoughts" about monsters and robbers, and bad dreams about mother's leaving or getting hurt, and begged to sleep in Alex's bed. She renewed her nightly going to her parents' bed, with complaints about noises, loneliness, and scary things. The ban on coming to their bed was imposed and lifted time after time. A contribution to her fear of being alone especially at night can have lain, in part, in mother's response to Ariel's question as to what happened to people when they died: "People get tired, they go to sleep, and they don't wake up again." In the mornings, after much urging to dress, Ariel took her clothes to the living room and there persuaded father to put on her shoes and socks (so keeping him at her side) in spite of her fear of his short temper and loud anger. She showed him no affection at all, and whenever mother and father argued she assumed he was at fault and hit him for it. Perhaps he was bearing the brunt of her rage against mother, hidden in the intense fears and wishes about losing her. Most of her emotional states at home, as mother described them, were of a dystonic nature. She worried about homework, complained of belly aches before school, expected to be scolded by her teacher, and was sad when mother and father argued. Sometimes she told mother she was sad, liked nothing about herself, but did not know why. "She's not an incessant worrier, but things stay with her," mother said, unhappily, for the first time expressing a troubled feeling about Ariel. At our final meeting she admitted with more affect than heretofore that she was a little worried about Ariel's selfishness and disobedience. About once a month she still spanked her with a hairbrush. And then she reiterated her beliefs that Ariel was sensitive to feelings of people and animals, had respect for older people, and was honest; and that these traits were hereditary. (Ariel's positive and negative characteristics were thus attributed to heredity.) Ariel had reached latency chronologically, but her psychological growth was seriously impeded by the flood of anxieties she had met at every turn.

Although mother was always polite to the interviewer, her manner was impassive and somewhat haughty, her facial expression discontented. Toward Ariel she showed an undeviating emotional distance except in the single reference to Ariel's occasionally being worried, and in a grudging recognition of the child's superior intellectual abilities. She never expressed interest in the results of Ariel's psychological tests. Her uneasy detachment from her child may have helped her to be in command of her own disappointment in her child or in herself. Sternly and sincerely she had once declared her belief that children should be seen and not heard. Father, who was extremely ill at ease in all of his interviews, said proudly that he did not get involved in Ariel's daily life, and volunteered much criticism of professionals who try to influence parents to push a child in a particular direction. For this reason he made clear his wish not to know about any of our observations of Ariel, and he saw no point in our observing the children each year up to age 7. "There's no retention before then." His distancing himself from Ariel's problematic behaviors was more brittle than mother's, although like her he was unsure about their importance: "She has nothing against sleep, she just doesn't like going to bed," or "She's spontaneous and outgoing. . . . She's very strong in her statements. . . . You have to do what she wants," or "She has developed a feminine trait of getting sympathy by crying [but] there are no vile reactions when she is angry. . . . I try not to pit my will against hers." He believed her to be happiest when played with by adults, when given presents, and when going to a restaurant—notably all situations that fed her self-centeredness. She was all right in public, was an extrovert like him, and like mother, undemonstrative—although she treated people as if they were her servants. A mixture of admiration, helplessness, and scorn suffused these remarks. In his final interview his comments about Ariel were globally positive though he conceded that she was fresh and "had an inability to comprehend disappointment." He and mother blamed each other for imposing discipline on Ariel in the wrong way or at the wrong time.

So much parental ignorance, ambivalence, and misunderstanding of Ariel's intentions and behaviors cannot but have left her in confusion about the rights and wrongs in her actions. She had had to make wild attempts to govern her parents and excuse her ways—a mutual endeavor, unfortunately. While she tried to project her failings on them, she could not avoid being hampered by acute fears and self-denigration. There were few signs of her having made any adaptive identifications, and her observable behavior and thoughts reflected the presence of all of the classic anxieties of childhood. Fear of object loss and abandonment transpired in her brooding about something bad happening to mother. Fear of loss of the object's love appeared in her dread of her parents' disapproval and rejection. Castration anxiety was clear in her impaired self representation and fantasies of body damage (the vomiting, the belly aches). And fear of punishment for her aggressive wishes against her parents came through in her fears of being alone. The latter wishes were continually reinforced by the parents' ongoing censure and corporal discipline, which reinforced her silent feelings of guilt, sadness, and despair. Her capacity for a development of normal superego strength and sound ego ideals was quite obstructed.

Ages 4 to 6: Observed Behavior in Nursery School and Kindergarten

In nursery school Ariel (age 4.5) presented a worrisome picture. Most of the time an angry scowl was present on her face. As she worked with paper and paste she became fretful when meeting a difficulty, whined, made faces, blamed the material she was using, and whimpered as if on the verge of tears. With children, she was bossy, highly competitive, boastful, intrusive, and domineering, or she was excited and silly. With teachers, in contrast, she complained, begged, tried bribing to get what she wanted, and pretended to cry. Constant throughout the morning were her manipulative efforts to gain a position of importance. In kindergarten (age 5.2) her shows of self-assurance were less prominent, but she continued to look disgruntled and listless. Often she made a grim face when her picture did not turn out as she intended, even when it was better than those of her classmates. When she became involved in play near other children, within a short time she was in shrewish dispute with them. Her social encounters were marked by whim, rudeness, arrogance, self-aggrandizement, and verbal cruelty—extensions of her behavior the year before. She gave signs of developing a severe character disorder along with her neurotic anxieties.

Summary of Intelligence Test Results, Ages 3 to 7

Age 3.0: Merrill-Palmer Preschool Scale of Intelligence IQ: 127
Age 4.0: Stanford-Binet, Revised Form L-M IQ: 137
Age 5.0: Wechsler Primary and Preschool Scale of Intelligence (WPPSI) IQ: 129
Age 6.0: Wechsler Intelligence Scale for Children (WISC; see footnote 4, p. 62)

On the Verbal Scale she reached a Superior level; on the Performance Scale she ranked well below Average.

Age 7.0: WISC Verbal IQ: 123
Performance IQ: 120
Full Scale IQ: 123

The disturbances in Ariel's capacity to develop sound object relations and to invest energy in work and play at appropriate age levels had risen with each annual diagnostic test session. At 3 she set out with alacrity to complete more and more tasks, but as soon as she faced one that was difficult for her she protested that she had done it already or she rejected it. She acted as if compelled to try to command the situation, but lacked the resilience necessary to contemplate any other than this fixed way to manage stress. At 4, she came with mother carrying her blanket for her, again quickly performed tasks that pleased her, was even lively and coquettish. But given a task that looked difficult she refused it or made up a quick answer, or was silent, or gave way to regressive speech; or with finger in mouth, she fidgeted, whined, and had to be held on the examiner's lap to complete the test. At 5 she was again restricted in speech, thought, and action, tried to manipulate procedures, denied errors, asserted equality if not superiority to the examiner, and bragged about her abilities. Although she was physically attractive, her hair was dirty and disheveled and her teeth were not clean. She must have succeeded in refusing to be groomed. Often she puckered her lips petulantly so that her face assumed a hostile glare. As she drew pictures of members of her family, she repeatedly showed confusion as to which one she was drawing, which suggested intense ambivalence in her relation to each (see pp. 144–150) for her drawings at ages 4 and 5).

The pattern of Ariel's behavior was the same in following years. At 6, in spite of increased social sophistication, and ability to give perfect responses, she showed more palpable anxiety than before, avoiding tasks, scratching her neck, stamping her feet, staring at the floor or into space, or looking at the ceiling (as seen when at age 6 weeks she restricted her visual field, as if blocking out sight of the person next to her). Or she was didactic toward and scornful of the examiner. It seemed necessary for her to take a rigid stand against whatever question she perceived as an unfair assault on her capacities. She showed no intellectual curiosity. At the end of the session she slyly defeated mother's pleas to leave our offices and as in previous years mother was helpless to act effectively. At 7 Ariel began the test compliantly, spoke intelligently and rapidly when she knew an answer, and seemed to be in good charge of herself until confronted with a task that looked difficult. Then she answered slowly, or offered quick associations, flailed her hands, shook her head, or was silent. Or she avoided the task by physical distractions: pressing her fingers against her cheek, screwing up her face, biting her nails, picking on her skin, clearing her throat, or laying her head down on the table tiredly. (This was done in the same way as at age 1, as seen in Film 5, Case 3 [Brody and Axelrad, 1970a].)

The outstanding theme of her CAT stories was a wish to maintain affectlessness, to escape from personal involvements, and to maintain an empty compliance with parents who were emotionally unavailable. In her view, adults are accusative and unsympathetic, she must sneak for opportunities to be with them, and she knows how to escape their punishment. Presented with the last picture (a parent and child in a bathroom), Ariel's intense negativism suddenly breaks through; she rejects the picture absolutely. It may have threatened an arousal of disturbing anal fantasies that she would have perceived as an unbearable injury to her precarious narcissism. So it was that in each successive year Ariel showed increased distress along with intense efforts to maintain a bold stance. As if to help herself out of her immediate plight of insufficiency, she abruptly volunteered that she disliked Alex but got into his bed and slept with him every night. The severity of her emotional distress, especially shown in her oscillation between excessive, haughty speech and her regressive behaviors, was dismaying.

Summary: Birth to Early Latency

Much unhappiness had been fomented in Ariel's infancy and toddlerhood. There were the delayed, interrupted, and forced feedings, the hours of being alone, the screaming, the physical restrictions, the breath-holding that angered mother, the impulsive acts that were erratically permitted or forbidden, the too early start of toilet training that caused a frightening fall off the toilet seat, and the frightening medical care after the accident in the playground. The harrowing quality of these experiences was hardly alleviated in her second year, when toilet training became something of a disciplinary issue, mother was irritable and tired during her pregnancy, and Ariel was entirely unprepared for mother's sudden departure and sudden return with a boy baby. By the age of 2 Ariel was a child with a battered self representation and a severely hampered freedom for positive object relatedness. Then came the loss of her bed to Alex, the fears and fights about going to bed at night, the demands for particular foods, the fears of leaving mother for school in the morning, and the need to hold onto her blanket most of the time. At school she was impulse-ridden and preoccupied with her social position. At home her "disobedience" brought punitive deprivations, extreme temper tantrums, clinging to mother, and crying herself to sleep. At the end of early childhood she was forlorn, angry, and surely bewildered by her parents' assaults on her for the impulsive behavior they never had been able to help her control.

The psychological injuries to Ariel's ego and superego became known, year after year, as she grew from an irritable, overactive, and unsatisfied infant to a child with discordant attachments to each member of her family, and an inability to form positive relationships with other children. More signs of her internal conflicts were manifest in her eating and sleeping disorders, her sadomasochistic relationship with her parents, her accusative behaviors, her extreme intolerance of any threat to her false air of invulnerability, and her somatic complaints. A capacity for sublimation had not appeared, in spite of her superior intelligence and longing for prestige. By the age of 7 she was burdened with intense preoedipal and oedipal conflicts that placed her character development in jeopardy.

Age 18: Interview with Ariel

Ariel matched my greeting solemnly and guardedly. She became more accessible as she told about her school history—a safe topic. School was all right though unimportant, she said, until she suffered a sharp social downturn at age 10. She was "picked on" and excluded by classmates until the end of elementary school, for no reason she could think of. Probably she knew better than she wished to tell. Later on in high school she got caught up in social activities again, neglected her work, and was graduated with a low B average, which satisfied her. Team sports, dancing, and jazz were her only interests outside of school. Menses began when she was 12 or 13, without any preparation by anyone as far as she could remember. It had not troubled her at all. During the past few years she had had a few part-time jobs in local shops, all "boring." Now she was taking a prelaw course in a small college near home, disliked it because the college was for girls only, and hoped to transfer to a very large university where there would be lots of people. She wanted to be involved with law that had to do with people, like domestic or divorce law. These interests may have been prompted by a longing to achieve justice vis-à-vis her parents.

She spoke with certainty about her many friends, male and female, a few of them intimate, and until a week ago, a steady boy friend. She loved going to parties or to movies, driving to places, shopping, and especially dancing, all indicating a relentless hunger for fast physical activity, as if to obliterate feelings and thoughts. She "loathed" reading. It was "boring." Reading requires a capacity to be alone and to bear tension, a state too hard for Ariel to accept. The only book she had ever finished was a children's book, she said, with a bit of pride or defiance. She supposed that in law school she would just have to read. Reading for her may have been equated unconsciously with eating, a threat to her stand against taking something in. Then she admitted regretfully that what happened when she was 10 was now happening again. She wanted to have friends but didn't trust people. I had the impression she was only vaguely aware of people unless she could be sure of commanding them.

Until age 12 she had been so afraid to be alone at any time that every night she left her room and went to sleep in her parents' bed. Afterward they moved her back to her own. She had to be watchful all of the time she was awake, she said, alert to anything that might happen, and when she fell asleep it was always in a rigid position, with her hands stiff beside her body and her legs outstretched. At some time between ages 4 and 6, according to her memory, she had been plagued by a repeated bad dream in which she felt herself to be old, with a long nose (A witch? A frightening phallus? A lying Pinocchio?); she was being manipulated by puppet-dwarves (parents?), utterly helpless, and in mortal danger. The two memories, the first of keeping her body rigid, and the second of being old, ugly, and helpless, told in sequence, suggested intense castration anxiety and a terror of punishment for masturbatory fantasies or acts. Each time she had the dream she fell off her bed, she said, and on waking would cry and scream for a long time in vain. (This matched mother's telling about Ariel's night terrors.) She also used to be afraid of murderers and robbers, and still now had fears of midgets, cripples, or anyone with something strange about his or her body. The symbolizations contained in these memories testified again to Ariel's longstanding castration anxiety and feelings of helplessness.

She went on to tell of her bad moods. She got very irritated with people who did not try new things; she was driven crazy when she was dead sure of something and people did not agree with her. She lost her temper when her parents did not allow her to do something—once she yelled at them and in her anger hit a wall and broke two fingers. She also got very upset when someone left her. She might cry for weeks.

To my question as to what she might do at home if she were alone with no radio, television, phonograph, or telephone available (in 1983 personal computers were not common), she replied that she would do her nails or her hair or glance at a fashion magazine (Helen, in response to this question, said she would draw or paint). The worst thing would be a loss of the telephone; next worst would be the loss of her blow dryer. Actually, she would be waiting impatiently to get into her car, pick up some friends, and drive to a movie or go shopping somewhere, anywhere. She used to take riding lessons, but gave them up after she began to get stomach aches lasting the whole day before the lessons, she was so afraid of them—an echo of the morning belly aches at ages 3, 6, and 7 that were related to her dread of being apart from mother. Chronic stomach pains when she was 16 brought a diagnosis of peptic ulcer, just a result of bad eating habits, she thought. She felt terrible about her excessive weight (125 lbs., height 5'4") because she was vain and wanted to look fashionable. She had managed to lose weight over about a year by not eating and by making herself vomit. She no longer did this, but ate no breakfast or lunch, had a regular dinner, and a snack at bedtime. Now she was 10 pounds underweight and wanted to stay that way. She did not bother to follow her physician's advice about diet and medicine—maybe she would if the pain got very bad. From time to time she was also having migraine headaches; about them, too, she had no concern. Menses were not interrupted. She had seen a psychiatrist a few times because mother had worried about her weight loss and her vomiting. The sessions did not help, she had no interest in them.

Father thought he was great, but really he was hot-tempered and if provoked he would hit her. Only two years ago he smacked her face, and once he punched her arm. "I drive him crazy," she said. I could not tell if she was taking blame or credit for making him "crazy." Her threats to leave home always stopped him. Of course he was "fantastic" if she needed anything; for example, after she had an accident in the car that she did not like, he bought her a new one that she liked. That was fine. Mother was quieter, she didn't get mad easily, but she was old-fashioned, too critical of Ariel's clothing and makeup. Punishment by both mother and father had always consisted of depriving her of television or what was more painful, sending her to her room. She always fought discipline, and as they said, she was bright but did not apply herself, and was moody. Anyway, now that she was older her parents did not interfere in her life so much. Nor did she appear to be interested in theirs. A bareness of family communication was patent in her not knowing the denomination of the church her parents attended, and whether there was a difference between being Protestant or Catholic. Her account of the family's occupations left me with the impression that the family was more cohesive when they were on vacation, skiing, sailing, or traveling, than at home.

She especially liked about herself that she was adventurous, that she could try things that other people were afraid of, like skiing or jumping over distances (shows of physical freedom?), and that she could make people be close to her if she wanted them to be (a boast? a denial of loneliness?). Her temper was what she most disliked about herself. She felt terrible if she hurt anyone, because she had a strict conscience. She was happiest when she could get out of the house and drive places. *She could never be still.* She wished she could be happier, could stop being fresh and fighting so much. What, I asked, could she think of that would bring her the greatest happiness in the future? "Fame!" she replied brightly, "to be a model, or someone signing autographs and being seen on television," then quietly she added, "or having a great family and getting along with people." Her ultimate happiness, she thus said, would be to stand in the limelight—and in a revealing afterthought, to have satisfying intimate relationships. The wish to be admired by *many* must have been a signifier of her old longing to be loved and appreciated by her two parents.

Age 18: Psychological Test Findings[3]

The scatter in Ariel's WAIS-R subtest scores (Verbal Scale: 112; Performance Scale: 117; Full Scale IQ: 115) does not present any surprising disparities, but qualitatively they show much to be concerned about. She does not think with the precision of a budding lawyer. Her knowledge about the world is superficial. She grabs at the first answers that come to mind, and although she is self-critical she cannot tolerate recognizing any mistakes. Her indiscriminate responses are related to an impulsiveness that becomes apparent when her hostility is aroused. Her Rorschach protocol reveals oppositional behavior, demands for control, possibly to avoid abandonment, and naked, unresolved oedipal conflict. Rage and hostile excitement arouse anxiety and lead to disorganized thinking. Many of her fabulized responses indicate poor reality testing and unrealistic rationalization. With father, she is "skating on thin ice"; father spells danger; and men are dangerous. Paranoid ideation is present. In the Sentence Completion test she adds to: A mother: "can be your best friend or your worst enemy."

Her TAT stories reflect a preoccupation with visual functions (primal scenes? watching parents' toilet functions?

[3] Administered by Carolyn Feigelson.

overstimulated by her sleeping with parents in their bed? or with Alex in his bed?). She hides, but also aims to take charge by being facile and manipulative. She shows a bitter opposition to and rage against her mother. "Mother or the maid" is a nuisance and is not listened to. An air of bitterness pervades parent–child contacts, emotion and human contact are to be shunted off, and responsibility for bad behavior is to be avoided. Her hostile view of marital relations suggests that there is much unpleasantness in the household. Fights occur, yelling is frequent, family members do not listen to each other and are blind to each other's needs. Play turns to angry struggle and sadness, sibling rivalry is unending, no one wins (the doll rips), and the parents can offer no solution (at the end the children cry). Darkness, depression, fear of abandonment, and a foreboding of death appear. Body damage ends in catastrophe. Retreat is to loneliness. All of Ariel's fantasies involve struggle within the family, with the central character in a regressive psychological position, exposed to danger. She can save herself only by running away.

Ariel left no time during the test session to do the Family Drawings, promised to send them to me, but never did. Her poor capacity for commitment had transpired when she had forgotten to keep a previous appointment for the interview and test sessions. Her parents scolded her for her remissness, saying that this sort of forgetting was not at all unusual (once mother, too, had forgotten an appointment for her interview with us.) Ariel's IQ had gone from very superior when she was a child to high average at age 18. So far, little of her intellectual potential had been realized.

Diagnostic Impression: Borderline State, with Unreliable Reality Testing, Rage, Projection, and deep Hostility toward Primary Objects.

Age 18: Clinical Impression

Near the end of her adolescence, because of her very somber facial expression, Ariel looked far less attractive than she had once looked. The information she gave was sparse, and the insouciance she tried to display about her difficulties signified the presence of numerous defenses, among which denial, regression, identification with the aggressor, projection, and turning against the self were prominent. Evidently her main felt need had long been to surround herself with people and to keep continually active with them. She seemed to be aware of the vein of self-destructiveness in her way of life, and of a need to gainsay that awareness as quickly as possible. Several times during our talk, her façade of being carefree was broken by a sad telling of childhood fears and recurrent fights with her parents.

Age 22

Mother, whom I reached first, by telephone, told me that Ariel had graduated from college, had majored in Communications, and intended to become a lawyer. Her health had not been so good. She was troubled by gastritis (mother's complaint years before), for which she took antacids. "She has learned to live with it," said mother. She had been bulimic "for a time," saw a psychiatrist "for a time," and was well again, but now was having skin problems, which mother clearly did not want to describe. She had also suffered from food poisoning several times, a result of eating food in foreign cities. Mother's reticence was patent. Ariel phoned me on the next day, cheerfully ready to explain that her stomach pain had been caused by an ulcer (previously denied), that she had refused medication for a time, then accepted it, was better but not really well. She had had bad eating habits, she said, eating too much or eating the wrong foods. During the past year she had had bouts of stomach virus and severe headaches, but she was not bulimic.

Three years later, when Ariel was 25, I learned in a brief telephone call that she was doing clerical work at a bank. She hated it because it was "boring," but needed the money for law school, which she loved. She had lots of friends there. She was living at home with her parents. This information was given hurriedly—it was not something to dwell on.

Age 27

I tried to reach Ariel at her parents' home. I reached mother, who said Ariel was very well, had no eating problem, dieted moderately but sometimes slipped back, worrying about her weight. As to Ariel's stomach pains, she said, "She'll always have stomach trouble," with an indifference that took me aback, although it was in the same detached manner that she had said, a few years ago, that Ariel was learning to live with the stomach pain. She was proud of Ariel's having passed the bar examination and of her plan to devote herself to criminal law.

Ariel promptly returned my call. She was cordial and glad to tell me more than we already knew about her adolescent eating problems. She had begun to not eat simply because it was the "in thing" to do in high school. At the time she was under stress about social problems (which meant that they had not ended at 14, as she had said when she was 18). She did not vomit anymore, had no ulcer, and no longer had eating problems, all told with cheerful nonchalance.

Recently she had had a difficult break-up with a young man, now had a new fiancé with whom she spent lots of time, and all was well. I gathered that she had had a series of brief relationships with several young men, and felt sure that the present one was the right one. At 18 she had asked me what was in our records about her behavior in childhood; now, at 27, she asked me about the information we had about her at 18. Did she recall any part of the letter I had sent to her about her test performance at 18 (a letter I sent to each subject with similar information)? She had no memory of it, so I mentioned a few of the remarks it contained. Agreeing with my thought that she had appeared to lack self-esteem, she asked, "What would make a person with such a feeling act as if she were always right, even be bossy?" I offered that one might wish to be spared painful feeling, to show the opposite of what one might feel inside oneself. This was an entirely new idea to her, she said, and abruptly closed the subject.[4]

Age: 29

Dr. Massie reached Ariel by telephone. Her tone was clipped, he said, and her voice was like that of a little girl, impatient and guarded, and especially apprehensive about being videotaped, although she was told it was not essential. She said she was too busy to meet him, but would answer his questions on the phone. She was now a deputy district attorney in a city near her parents' home, where she still lived. At work

---

[4]Of the 91 subjects interviewed and given psychological tests at age 18, Ariel was the only one who asked to know what was in our records about her, yet she could not allow herself to contemplate the information I offered.

her only problem was that she became too emotionally involved in legal cases. Outside of work she was interested in exercising, cooking, and watching television sitcoms. She was not married, though all of her friends were. Recently she had received psychotherapy because of problems in separating from unsuitable boy friends.

She recalled that during her childhood her parents argued constantly, although they loved each other and showed physical affection for each other. They did not understand her needs. They meant to be constructive, but were too critical, too harsh, and so they hurt her self-esteem even up to the present. Now she was having trouble making decisions about important things, like leaving people who treated her badly. She had had several two- to three-year relationships with men, but they always broke up because she picked men who were too controlling or too oppositional (a projection?). She had never lived with a man, never been pregnant, and had no areas of discomfort or anxiety in her sexual relations with men. She had anxiety attacks, however, in the form of feeling overwhelmed by breakups with boy friends, the last one about three years ago. She had not used drugs, alcohol, or tobacco, and said she had no manic, paranoid, compulsive, or sleeping symptoms. In college she had suffered from bulimia, throwing up a lot, but did not think she had binged. At that time she was also a fanatical exerciser.

Her earliest memory was that one day when she was about age 3, mother left the house with brown hair and came home with blonde hair. She was scared that this woman was not her mother. Then she recalled the very frightening childhood nightmare: she was lying in bed in a trance. Her body was stiff as a board . . . she was lying on a bed with 12 holes . . . her body bounced stiffly off the bed. (This dream was probably the same as the one she had reported at age 18, or a variant of it.) Her typical mood nowadays was "pretty much okay," but she was hard on herself. She had a strict conscience. Her greatest sadness lay in thinking of her brother's possibly moving far away, and of her parents' arguments. Her greatest worry in life was of being 70 years old and single. Currently, her psychotherapy dealt with the strictness of her parents, her difficulty making decisions, and her troubles with men, yet if she were to relive her life she would not do anything differently (a curious effort to assert self-satisfaction). She had no strong feelings about any social issues—maybe she would have wished to get away from her family because she was too dependent on her parents. She would like to be known for doing something for children. Consciously, at least, she had come far from aspiring mostly to fame and for signing her autograph for admirers.

Ariel's demeanor in the telephone interview, as described by Dr. Massie, was unchanging and rigid. She was reserved, sober, hard to draw out. There was a rote accommodation and stiffness in her voice. She waited passively for questions, and the information she gave was sparse and superficial. As at previous meetings, she expressed most worry about her continuing failures with men. Defensiveness was evidenced in avoidance and denial (saying family relations were good and close), identification with the aggressor (as a lawyer who would like to litigate in court), reaction formation (in the avowed concern for the welfare of children), and probably turning passive to active (in the desire to be a judge). She saw her eating disorder as a past issue.

Age: 30

Numerous telephone calls to Ariel from Dr. Massie and from his associate went unanswered, so I left a voice message for her. She called me on the next day, with the same eagerness for contact she had shown in previous years, to say she was calling because she did not want to "let me down," and so promised to be available for another interview when her immediate official tasks were done. All my further efforts to reach her were unsuccessful. She may indeed have had a presentiment that she would let me down; she had a history of letting her parents down. I could only guess that the possibility of speaking to someone who expressed interest in the events of her everyday life had aroused more anxiety than she could countenance. Months later I telephoned her home once more to learn where she might be and whether there was still a chance of my speaking with her. Mother explained curtly that Ariel did not want to take part in the study any longer, that she watched her weight all of the time but was not too thin. A week ago, however, she had such acute stomach pain after a menstrual period that mother rushed her to the emergency room of a nearby hospital. The doctor found nothing wrong. He said she just had a "nervous stomach." This may have been a recrudescence of the belly aches in Ariel's childhood that had made her reluctant to go to school, the chronic stomach pains at age 16, the ulcer at 18, and the gastritis at 22. Ariel had had her own apartment for a time, then had returned to live with her parents. She was working as a lawyer in a village court and had many boy friends, none whom she wanted to marry. It appeared to me likely that her mother's reporting that Ariel no longer wanted to participate in our study reflected mother's wish to break contact with us.

Chapter 6

Helen and Ariel: A Few Comparisons

All through their childhoods Helen and Ariel clung to their mothers fearfully, then to their blankets. They had little chance to develop the quiet gratifying relationship that a dedicated mother could have allowed them. They must have longed to be embraced with affection by someone on whom they could rely to ensure their physical and emotional security. They did not go so far in their self-starvation that their survival was in question, but after the adolescent phase of their illness, for which they received no diagnosis or treatment, they were left with serious neurotic and somatic symptoms. From their histories we can assume that their self representations could not have been so firm as those of infants whose bodies are held, touched, stroked, and soothed, and who are smiled at, listened to, and talked to, and also allowed to be at peace alone at intervals. To the contrary, the indications are that both experienced faults in their feelings of body intactness beginning in their first weeks and months.

Similarities of experience during infancy lay in the extended time they lay awake and alone, their solitude interrupted by long periods of fretful hunger, crying, and screaming, and too little or too much feeding. Both mothers had little or no knowledge of infant needs, and took it for granted that their scant attention to their infants was sufficient. For both children toilet training was accompanied by their mothers' anger and scolding, and both had toilet regressions after supposedly achieving control at age $2^{1}/_{2}$. Both were overexposed to their parents' sexuality (nakedness of Helen's parents, Ariel's parents having her in their bed). By age 3, both were having severe temper tantrums in response to their parents' insensitive care, reprimands, and frequent threats of banishment to their rooms, which the children usually fought off. Both girls adapted poorly in nursery school. Helen was a wanderer, given to immature and disordered excitement, and was remote from the other children; though when free to make use of her superior ability to draw, she was proficient and contented. Ariel was impulse-ridden, preoccupied with her social status, and at all times peevish, testy, and discontented. During later childhood and early adolescence both girls were in continual and serious dispute with their parents, and there was no sign of the parents ever making an effort to speak sympathetically with the children about their troubling behavior and frank anxieties. Both sets of parents seemed sure that their absences from home made for no problems for their daughters, and both were unable to express simple affection. From their reporting one could gather that the parents had adapted to each other's needs with resignation and little optimism, and had bare interest in their children's emotional and intellectual development.

Helen's second year was marked by physical lags, loneliness, tantrums, aggressive responses to mother, and panic attacks. Problems with food increased. So did mother's scoldings for Helen's picky eating and unruly behavior, and father's excessive teasing, complaints about her misbehavior, and disrespect for her feelings. Mother's abdication from an affective relationship to her left Helen in low spirits.

Ariel's second year brought a string of painful events: an increasing dread of physical restraint; the fall off the toilet seat; the frightful excitement surrounding the injury to her forehead; the mother's irritability during pregnancy; the sudden appearance of a baby brother without any explanations or reassurances; and the loss of her bed to him. Before Ariel was 2, her extreme fears of being alone set in, especially at night, aggravated by the bedtime struggles; then came the painful clinging to mother, with much exchange of recriminations, and no emotional relief. During early childhood Ariel suffered more than Helen because of her demands, defiance, physical aggression, and crossness. She was much more fearful than Helen, and provoked more punishment and ostracism. Gathering tensions between her and her parents, their reprimands and corporal punishments, and their open dissension can have promoted Ariel's readiness, well before latency, to project and externalize her deficiencies. There was no remission from her terror of being alone, and her frequent and severe temper tantrums. Her parents took serious notice of her behavior only when it disturbed their peace. Mother scolded, but submitted to her demands. Father was both overindulgent and overcritical. Passionate conflicts with mother were followed by tearful remorse, wishes and fears about losing mother, and crying herself to sleep. Feelings of shame and guilt for her transgressions were manifested in periodic sadness that she acknowledged but could not explain or shake off. Her somatic symptoms began to appear in her fourth year, with belly aches, and brought her to resist going to school before first grade. Thereafter she was never free of stomach problems.

Helen had another kind of experience, not matched for Ariel, in that from about age 8 her parents often left her and Harry alone in the evenings to go out to enjoy dinner by themselves. When the children were left alone and frightened, Harry would keep maternal grandmother on the phone until the parents came home. In Helen's senior high school year, when Harry was away at college, her parents left her to live alone while they lived elsewhere, assuming that she could manage on her own. While she accepted their relinquishment of care as a relief from their presence, she could not escape feelings of bitterness toward them, as they were literally out of touch and out of sight in ways that echoed her loneliness in early life. Over time the quality of the parents' marriage had declined: father was obdurate in his views, and mother had passively accepted them, but family tension prevailed.

Ariel's parents, in contrast, were regularly at home with her during her childhood and adolescence, but failed to concern themselves with her fears, her excessive need for social activity, and her somatic symptoms. Physically, they were present; emotionally they were far away. Communication between them, and between them and Ariel, was poor. Either they submitted to her demands or they quarreled with her about her self-centeredness. In comparison to Helen, Ariel's anxieties were more disabling, her parents were more tense and inaccessible, and there was no sign of their ever having talked with her about her troubling behavior.

In a few additional ways the histories of Helen and Ariel differed. Helen's parents were unempathic, often verbally mean, and more prone to neglect than to punish her. They appeared never to have taken her seriously; sometimes they treated her with amusement and sometimes as a nuisance.

Helen was able to separate herself, at least literally, from her parents, to revive a measured capacity to work, and to find a husband whom she trusted. Her positive feeling for him was mainly related to gratitude for his encouragement of her painting. Like her mother, she had a personal relationship only with her husband. She developed a range of weak defenses, and a variety of somatic ills.

Ariel's parents took notice of her, but mainly to restrict or scold, were harsh in their expectations of her, and physically punitive. Ariel developed many more frank anxieties than Helen did, with the result that her capacities to manage her loneliness and to struggle toward positive achievement were limited. She appeared never to have had a solid friendship. During adolescence she fled from her disabling affects into fast-moving social and physical activities (some too frightening, like the riding lessons in her childhood) that defensively masked her yearning for close protection. Her social busyness had the quality of a juvenile kind of mania. Her love of fast physical action, including dancing, takes us again to Schilder (1935, p. 208): "Dancing," he said, "is . . . a method of changing of body image and loosening its rigid shape . . . Motion . . . influences the body image to a change in the psychic attitude." The ardor that Ariel expressed for continuous activity must have given her that "increased feeling of freedom concerning gravity and the cohesion of the postural model of the body" that Schilder described. In addition, Ariel showed numerous character faults and gave no sign of developing any age-appropriate ego ideals. Her adult decision in favor of criminal law, and a wish to help children in some way, may have been motivated by a reparative wish to mete justice to the mental representation of herself as both the aggressor, the would-be destroyer of her parents, and/or their victim. At 30 she still lived with her parents.

While Helen had drifted toward a willing isolation and agitated sadness, Ariel had drifted toward social excitements and anxious isolation of affect and of thought. Each in her own way had struggled with feelings of anguish brought on by their mothers' unwitting neglect and/or negative, perhaps jealous attitudes toward their daughters, and their fathers' disinterest and trivialization of their feelings.

After the onset of anorexia, and in Ariel a period of bulimia as well, both adolescents went into adulthood seriously troubled by explicit anxieties and chronic psychosomatic symptoms for which no relief was in sight. Helen was trying hard for artistic achievement. Ariel was trying to do work for a social purpose. Her intelligence probably made her aware that something like a repetition compulsion was governing her social failures. The passing bulimia may have represented, among other unhappy irresolutions, an unconscious wish to reverse her oral–aggressive behavior that at first appeared in her biting, vomiting, hostile speech, and later in the conflict about eating, with its tangled roots that were entrenched in her infancy. Much more than Helen, Ariel was caged in extreme ambivalence about attaining emotional freedom for herself. She might have said, like Byron's *Prisoner of Chillon,*

> My very chains and I grew friends
> So much a long communion tends
> To make us what we are; even I
> Regained my freedom with a sigh.

Sours (1974) reported an absence of oedipal phenomena in developmental histories of anorexic patients, which only means that the reporting parents had not made relevant observations. My data have not emerged from clinical sessions, but they allow for clear inferences about acute oedipal conflicts in Helen and Ariel. Even setting aside their known rivalries with their mothers and the oppressive attitudes of their fathers, we keep in mind the sexual exhibitionism of Helen's parents, and the exposure of Ariel to her parents' bodies in their bed, every night, year after year. For both children, oedipal fantasies, conscious and unconscious, libidinal and aggressive, were probably omnipresent and burdensome in view of the psychic energy they must have consumed. The girls' childish narcissism had never been trained down to a natural degree, and for the most part their adolescent narcissism came to be expressed in perverse and self-destructive ways. But Helen seemed to be less injured by her history in that she had resigned herself to her disturbances, and appeared to feel less humiliation than Ariel. One reason may be that consciously, she gave up the struggle with her parents. She saw herself as a victim of fate. She had said, at 18, that she was a fatalist. It was simply her fate to have parents who could not love.

Chapter 7

Mother and Infant: Four Variations in Their Quality of Engagement with Additional Notes about Both Parents

As my purpose in this book has been to trace the origins of anorexia in Helen and Ariel, it is necessary to look further to find out what conditions may have precipitated the eating disorder of anorexia in just those two, and no others in the sample who had eating disorders in childhood.

Among the 41 female subjects[1] retained in the sample at age 18, 10 had a variety of eating disorders. Three of the 10 were obese; two of them, Helen and Ariel, are included in the other nine. As the basis of their internal conflicts were seen to stem from their early strained relationships to their mothers, we have to examine in what ways their experiences in infancy differed from those of the other nine infants. The

---

[1] The original sample studied through their first year contained 66 female and 65 male infants.

index of those relationships that I have found helpful has been the quality of communication among all 131 dyads in the course of the infants' first year, the period of our most frequent observations of their interaction, and of our interviews with their mothers.

The development of communication between infant and mother has been a subject of considerable research in recent years (Stern, 1971, 1974, 1985; Trevarthan, 1977; Tronick, Als, and Adamson, 1978; Field, Wheedon, Greenberg, and Cohen, 1982). My observations of infants in the care of their mothers described in my publications from 1956 to 1992, and my clinical practice with infants, children, adolescents and their parents have led me to think of a normal psychological experience of the infant that facilitates their emotional communication. It involves an infant's move from physiological anxiety to normal preparedness for psychological anxiety, in keeping with Freud's concept of the protective shield (1920). Although Freud indicated that the receptive function of the shield was almost its more important aspect, as discussed before (Brody and Axelrad, 1970b), writings about the shield have usually referred to its protective function, probably because "shield" implies protection. We considered that the innate wish for comfort is less noisy in the young infant, and much harder to observe, than the need for protection from disagreeable stimuli; therefore, a reinforcement of the infant's emotional investment in external objects, and the receiving of agreeable stimuli may be its more important function. Yet the receiving of disturbing stimuli, with accompanying efforts to ward them off, may be seen as preparing the infant for the experience of psychological anxiety. That preparedness Freud (1926) called signal anxiety. Previously (1915) he had described the discovery of qualitative differences between inner and outer stimuli as "a first distinction and a first orientation" (p. 119) of an infant organism, and an impressive achievement in very early life. In this regard we wrote, "The quality and quantity of the infant's perceptual work leads him toward the psychological experience of being a unit and being alone, and toward the realization that an object that has only recently become cathected is missing" (Brody and Axelrad, 1970b, p. 47).

The success of an infant's longing for an affectionate and reliable person to satisfy his or her needs and to grant pleasure depends on the infant's and mother's mutual capacities for emotional and cognitive investments. Or we might refer to their capacities for connectedness, in the sense of E. M. Forster's (1910) imperative, "Only connect!" Forster was writing about a solid citizen who cared only about utilitarian matters. He seemed to have no conception of feelings in himself or in others. That he should "only connect the prose and the passion" is the whole "sermon" that his new wife wishes him to comprehend. She fails to accomplish this, not having realized his obtuseness. "He simply did not notice things, and there was no more to be said" (pp. 172–173). In just this way unempathic parents may enact only the prose of infant care, protecting the baby's health and physical safety, yet not noticing that the baby has sensations, feelings, and bits of thought that will in time be assembled about a surrounding reality. Such parents cannot invest their prose care with the passion that can help the baby, and later the child, to know that his or her uncontrolled impulses need not frighten the parents or threaten the children's feeling of safety.

Connectedness is one way to describe the quality of the early instinctual investment that is essential for the positive involvement, later for the love between mother and infant. A better way to refer to the investment, one that connotes an affective tie, is *engagement*. I define engagement here as a subjective freedom for an ongoing libidinal and aggressive cathexis of another person who can provide mutual intimacy, pleasure, and trust. It is given play, at first, by liberal sensory contacts that one person (here, mother or infant) initiates and to which the other person (mother or infant) willingly responds. So the infant begins to build a capacity for positive investments in objects, beginning with a human presence. *Ideally that first presence is a mother whose psychic energy is reliably channeled into engagement with her infant.* My interest here is in the quality of the mutual emotional involvements that I could discern in the 131 dyads during the infants' first year.

Accordingly, I have estimated the levels of engagement that I could discern in each of the 41 mothers and their female infants in our sample who were available for study, at least up to age 18. My purpose is to make some ready comparisons between the affective experiences of the 41 infants, as they fell into four groups.[1] The principal criteria I have used to assess the engagement within each dyad derive from direct observations of their interaction during the infants' first year of life only,[2] as follows:

[1]Tables 1–3 show the principal symptomatic behaviors related to orality that were present in the 41 female subjects at ages 1, 7, and 18 (pp. 130–132).
[2]This is a more particular assessment than was made of the mothers' feeding behavior at intervals through that first year (N = 131; Brody and Axelrad, 1970b). The present classification does not correspond with the maternal types previously described there or later (Brody and Siegel, 1992). The one used here has been based on direct observations of all aspects of the mothers' behavior and attitudes at the same intervals in the infants' first year of life. Of the 15 mothers included in group I that follows here, 13 were classified as belonging in the original type A, those originally observed to be among the "more adequate" rather than the "less adequate" mothers in the sample.

I. *Engagement is rich and reliable.* Mother and infant show qualities of mutual intimacy. Mother enjoys holding the infant in positions comfortable for both, allows for the infant's full body contact with her body, protectively and affectionately,[4] and allows as well the infant's smooth movement away from that physical closeness. She is free to caress or to touch the infant's body tenderly, and the infant is free to reach out to her tenderly, to touch or stroke her face or any reachable part of her body. Visual and vocal responsiveness to each other is easy and frequent. Pleasure in such reciprocal activities, in being in each other's presence, and trust in each other's intentions are usually visible, yet each may comfortably turn her attention elsewhere (N = 15).

II. *Engagement is positive but limited.* From time to time mother holds the infant, mainly when the infant is distressed, but she does not encourage body contact with the infant. Her touch of any part of the infant's body is pleasant but scanty. The infant makes occasional overtures to her in body or limb movements or in tactile gestures, which mother accepts with mild interest. They maintain a friendly, respectful distance from each other. Mother's attention is usually divided between the infant and other persons or things in the near environment. A slight formality or self-effacement in her, and mild tension in her and/or the infant may hinder their visual and vocal accommodation to each other. Between the two few distinct signs of pleasure or displeasure are seen. Occasionally the infant shows mild signs of anxiety (N = 10).

---

[4]As may be seen in Mary Cassatt's "Baby's First Caress" (1891; Pastel, New Britain Museum of American Art), the nude baby lies slightly aslant across mother's lap, as they gaze intently at each other. His left hand has a firm hold of her chin, she holds his left leg in her left hand. Her right arm surrounds his body, and her right hand gently covers his right hand.

III. *Engagement is excessive, so that harmony between mother and infant is irregular.* Mother holds the infant and caresses the infant's face and limbs often and with much animation. The infant makes reciprocal gestures and enjoys playful interchanges with her. Her urgent need to arouse the infant's responsiveness, her overeager handling of the infant's body, and her overly mobile facial expressions may lead to overexcitement in the infant, sometimes followed by mother's brief withdrawal. The infant's spontaneous wishes are often not discerned by mother because she is neither free to act on her own impulses nor to be physically quiet. The infant often shows intense excitement, occasionally mixed with signs of anxiety or withdrawal ($N = 4$).

IV. *Engagement is poor or faulty.* The infant spends a large part of her day inactive and alone in her crib, baby tender, or playpen. Mother is confident in her belief that infants should not be picked up or held, especially not when they cry. She avoids answering to the infant's cries, handles the infant's body mainly for cleaning or dressing, withholds affect, and shows little or no curiosity about the infant's states, which may vary from stillness to acute restlessness, with loud complaints. She minimizes the infant's needs and wishes, but expects the infant to comply with her (mother's) needs and wishes. Often she attributes her fatigue or querulousness to the burden of having to attend to the infant. Her detachment suggests that anxiety prompts her to isolate herself from emotional involvement with her infant. Signs of her uneasiness are continually present, and periods of irritability, sadness, or withdrawal are frequent. In general, both mother and infant are subdued ($N = 12$).

Helen and Ariel and their mothers belong to group IV. As their first year proceeded both infants were observed to have given up or lost their natural wishes to be looked at, touched, held affectionately, and addressed fondly. Both grew to be familiar with feelings of unpleasure in the forms of tension, loneliness, helplessness, and marked displeasure in the forms of hunger, anger, withdrawal, screaming, and sadness. Eight other subjects in group IV had varied kinds of eating problems during infancy, childhood, and adolescence, as shown in Tables 7.1 to 7.3; none became bulimic or anorexic. Some, like Helen and Ariel, had been emotionally neglected, some had experienced erratic deprivations and gratifications, or painful disappointments in their parents, and some, aside from receiving physical care, had been merely lived with. Little parental thought was given to their emotional or social well-being, or their cognitive development. They had rarely been played with.

The frequency of specific signs of unfavorable development in the four groups of infants at age 1 appears in Table 7.1.

Not surprisingly, Helen and Ariel show the highest number of signs of unfavorable development. I may reiterate that the division of the mother–infant dyads into four levels of engagement was based solely on direct and filmed observations, and on verbalizations of the mothers during the infants' first year of life. Table 7.2 shows the frequency of observed signs of unfavorable development in the four groups of subjects at age 7. Again Helen and Ariel lead all the rest.

Both Tables 7.1 and 7.2 are intended to compare the conditions of the subjects in groups I, II, and III, with those of group IV. These tables omit references to a small number of unfavorable developments observed and/or reported in the first three groups, but not in group IV. For example, enuresis was present in two cases, one in group I and one in group III. The two tables reveal that the early appearing signs of emotional distress shown at age 1 did not pass away with time, as is often assumed by pediatricians and mental

TABLE 7.1
Age 1: Signs of Unfavorable Development Observed and/or Reported in Four Groups

	1 (N = 15)	2 (N = 10)	3 (N = 4)	4 (N = 11)
Appetite Poor, Erratic, or Excessive	1	2	1	$10^{a,b}$
Attention Span, Short	0	2	3	$10^{a,b}$
Frustration Tolerance Low	1	4	4	9^b
Stereotypic Behaviors^d	0	1	1	$13^{b,d}$
Resistance to Standing; Late Walking^c	0	2	1	8^a
Irritability High	0	3	3	7^a
Angry Crying, Screaming, Moaning	1	2	3	6^a
Activity Excessive; Impulsivity	1	1	3	4^b
Inactivity Excessive; with Flat Affect	0	5	1	4^a
Physical Aggression High	1	0	2	1^b
Expressive Behavior Low^f	0	2	4	2^a
Expressive Behavior Excessive	0	0	2	0
Breath-holding^g	0	0	0	1^b

^{a}includes Helen
^{b}includes Ariel
^{c}15 to 20 months
^{d}includes self-rocking, self-rolling, head-banging, head-wagging, body-thrusting
^{e}Overlap in three cases
^{f}Vocal, visual, gestural
^{g}Also present in three male infants

health workers as well as by the general population. With the passage of time, the early behavioral signs of distress, if pronounced, are more likely to change their form or the degree of their severity than to disappear. For example, impulsivity at age 1 can manifest itself indirectly, in poor social

TABLE 7.2
Age 7: Symptomatic Behaviors Observed and/or Reported in Four Groups

	I (N = 15)	II (N = 10)	III (N = 4)	IV (N = 12)
Appetite Poor, Erratic, or Excessive	1	0	1	$10^{a,b}$
Frustration Tolerance Low	0	1	4	$9^{a,b}$
Speech Excessive	0	1	0	$5^{a,b}$
Speech Withheld	1	5	2	$5^{a,b}$
Resistance to Routines, Restrictions	0	1	0	$10^{a,b}$
Crying, Whining, Excessive	0	1	0	$6^{a,b}$
Temper Tantrums Frequent	0	0	1	7^b
Social Judgment Poor	0	1	1	$8^{a,b}$
Self-esteem Low; Shyness Excessive	0	2	1	6^a
Activity Excessive; Impulsivity	0	0	4	8^b
Expressive Behavior Excessive	2	2	1	0
Expressive Behavior Low	0	2	4	1
Transitional Object	4	0	1	4

^{a}includes Helen
^{b}includes Ariel

judgment at age 7, or later; an overactive infant may be a loner at age 7, or later.

Table 7.3 shows the frequency of principal symptomatic behaviors related to orality that were continuous from ages 1 to 7, as observed and/or reported for the same 41 subjects at age 18.[5]

[5]Other symptomatic behaviors that appeared among the 41 female subjects at age 18 are omitted from Table 7.3 because their relevance to eating disorders can only be speculative.

TABLE 7.3
Age 18: Principal Diagnoses in Four Groups

	I	II	III	IV
Eating Disorder[c]	1	0	0	10[b]
Depression, Mild	4	4	1	2
Depression, Severe	1	0	1	6[a,b]
Dysphoric States	2	2	0	7[a]
Self-Esteem, Low	0	1	2	6[a,b]
Speech Excessive	2	2	1	5[a,b]
Speech Withheld	0	3	1	5[a,b]
Personality Disorders[d]	3	5	1	3
Borderline States	1	1	0	5[a,b]
No Disorder	7	3	0	1

[a]includes Helen
[b]includes Ariel
[c]Included here is one subject who maintained an idiosyncratic diet because of a "weak stomach"; one who ate only "junk foods"; one who called herself "a health fanatic" about food; one who ate irregularly and said that she occasionally "pigs out and then starves"; and one who loved to prepare foods for others but did not like to eat them. Three subjects, one in Group I and two in Group IV, were obese; two of them made suicide attempts in midadolescence.
[d]narcissistic, hysteric, paranoid, immature

One subject in group IV at age 18 showed none of the disorders listed in Table 7.3. At the time of recruitment, her mother had agreed to abide by our regular requirement that she would have full care of her baby (her third), with obvious necessary exceptions. But at the 6-week visit, she told us that most aspects of infant care, especially feeding, were too disagreeable to her; her husband felt as she did. They hired a nurse to be in full charge of the baby, and after a few days the baby was rarely fed by her mother.

Additional Notes about the Parents

The quality of mother–infant engagement in groups I, II, and III ranged from positive to ambivalent, and was poorest in group IV, that in which 10 of the 12 subjects developed eating disorders. A little more needs to be said about the parents of the 10.

The Mothers

The detachment of the eight mothers, aside from those of Helen and Ariel, was manifest in several ways. Two were openly hostile and angry; two were emotionally and intellectually immature; the fifth was didactic and authoritative; the sixth was taciturn, self-satisfied, and controlling; the seventh was depressed and withdrawn; and the eighth was overly nonchalant. None of these characteristics was prominent in the mothers of Helen and Ariel, with a slight exception in the case of Ariel's mother, who suppressed her thoughts and feelings but was not quite taciturn; and she was observed to supervise rather than control her child. I searched for any unique aspect of the poor engagement of the mothers of Helen and Ariel, and at last realized a salient difference between them and the other eight mothers. It resided in my observation that after their first visits to our offices, when Helen was 6, and Ariel was 7 weeks old, the mothers' poor engagements with their infants were qualified by a distinct absence of overtly libidinal or overtly aggressive investment. Toward their daughters, as time went on, we saw that they *never* expressed affection, or pride, or sympathy, or tenderness, or good humor. They could be said to have regarded the infants, and themselves in the role of mothers, as almost barren of needs, wishes, or feelings. Both mothers were restless, dissatisfied women. Their infant care was for the most part managerial. Their affectlessness was undisguised. Helen's parents moved the family's residence at least 10 times in Helen's first 18 years. They repeatedly purchased land with vague prospects of building a new home, reaping only large debts. On day 3 of Helen's life, her mother had already expressed worry about not being able to have enough "outside stimulation." Ariel's mother had had vague intentions of pursuing various careers and dropped all of them. At home she was usually busy with domestic chores, and rarely spent time with Ariel. She loved traveling, finding new restaurants, and outdoor sports. Somewhat like Helen's mother, she sought outside stimulation.

The Fathers

None of the fathers in the sample was accessible for observation or interviews until the children were age 3. It was not feasible to observe them with their children in a standard situation at any time before then. Of those whose wives were in group IV, 2 of the 12 declined our invitations to let them know about or to discuss our thoughts about their daughters' behavior and development. They seemed to feel threatened by our overtures, as if we were asking them to be involved in more than they could or wished to know about. Of the other eight (here excluding those of Helen and Ariel) three were positively concerned about their daughters' well-being and in their activities outside of school, but one of them was constrained, as if he wished to reveal as little as possible about his child or himself. The third was businesslike, and like his wife pedantic and disinterested in his daughter's everyday life; "I don't see much depth in children," he said. The fourth was both harsh and seductive toward his daughter, and condescending to the interviewer. The fifth was grim, angry, and disappointed in his daughter; he said he did not like girls. The seventh and eighth fathers enjoyed trying to fend off our questions with facetious or challenging remarks about their daughters and the research project, and took a sort of mischievous pride in the girls' rebelliousness, yet when pressed both were able to show friendly concern about their development.

The last two fathers, those of Helen and Ariel, showed some similar attitudes, being disinterested, or autocratic, or seductive. They differed from the other eight, however, in being distinctly self-righteous, with a veneer of self-confidence in themselves as parents. They cited plenty of faults in their daughters, then glossed over them as being unimportant. Helen's father tried, with pathetic failure, to present himself as a sophisticated parent. Ariel's father was loud and imperious, and dismissed any thought of inadequacy as a parent. Both men were insensitive regarding the girls' feelings about their bodies, specifically about their buttocks: Helen's father, as told before, liked to embarrass her by repeatedly calling attention to her buttocks as being not round but pear-shaped, a poorly veiled derogation of her sexuality. Ariel's father, like her mother, often spanked her "with her pants down," and in the name of discipline abused and humiliated her. The spankings probably provided both of Ariel's parents with quick escapes from their feelings of desperation about their failures to know how to exercise parental authority. In turn they probably felt provoked to exercise sadistic revenge against their daughters for stirring up their feelings of helplessness. Unequivocally and defensively, these two fathers tried to proclaim that childhood deserved consideration mainly insofar as children needed to be supervised or disciplined. Yet, unlike many fathers of girls and boys in the sample who refused our invitations to speak with us about their children, the fathers of Helen and Ariel came for their interviews annually from their daughters' ages 3 to 7. Perhaps they were persuaded by their wives to be interviewed. Even so, their coming tells us that they wished to be caring and responsible parents, if only they knew how.

The parents of Helen and Ariel were in "bearable" marriages, mutually supportive of each other though frequently in conflict, yet remarkably insensitive to their children's needs, and powerless to act in their favor. Had either father provided the empathic care that his wife could not, each of the girls might have found in her father a love object with whom she could identify positively. Little is recorded about the part played by fathers in the histories of anorexic patients. Bruch (1973) found that the role of the father in eating disorders is not frequently discussed, but that usually he is considered to be weak, passive, and emotionally absent.

Chapter 8

Clinical Signs of Anorexia That Are Known

In the psychiatric and psychoanalytic literature, few direct or indirect causes of eating disorders are mentioned as having been observed during infancy and early childhood. Aside from the cases mentioned in chapter 2, we have mainly Anna Freud's (1946) discussion of infantile feeding disturbances. It deals with problems of early instinctual wishes that make for emotional difficulties between mother and infant and that normally disappear, but which, when severe, may return in adulthood in the form of psychosomatic disorders of the stomach or digestive tract. We now know that many such difficulties, if not treated with psychiatric or psychoanalytic understanding, usually continue through childhood and beyond in a variety of mental and physical ailments. Anorexia or bulimia may appear in adolescence for no clearly known reasons because, with few exceptions, the published accounts of their incidence have been drawn mainly from retrospective accounts given by parents or physicians, or by the patients themselves well after childhood. Certain typical symptoms are referred to most often in the histories of anorexic patients, though none of them is unique for this disorder. With special reference to Helen and Ariel, the well-known symptoms are as follows.

A Disturbed Relationship to the Mother and Father

The mothers of Helen and Ariel attended to the infants' needs and wishes as little as they could in good conscience. Spontaneous communications were rare, as far as they could tell or we could observe. In the children's next years as well, the two mothers rarely expressed awareness of the children's emotional, physical, social, or cognitive development, and were usually insensitive to the signs of distress the children manifested. When difficulties arose in their infant or child care, the mothers turned for help only to their pediatricians, whose training had not provided them with knowledge of how to observe incipient problems in the mother–infant relationship. Or the mothers resorted to uninformed generalizations about infant or child behavior, and carried on their maternal obligations as well as they could. Their investments in the children were shallow, and they appeared to be quite unaware of their aggressive disregard of the children's unhappiness. Sadly for them, they had no understanding of what they could do for their children beyond providing them with food, clothing, and shelter, or of how to take pleasure in the children's emotional or intellectual growth.

I have found no particular references in the literature to the part played by fathers of anorexic patients. Historically, the affective connections of fathers to their infants and children have been limited, with exceptions related to the setting of educational and moral standards especially in the late nineteenth century. As portrayed by certain novelists, a father's giving way to emotion suggested femininity or weakness (Brody, 1982b). Distance and authority were to be sustained by fixed paternal rules, for a variety of social and economic reasons. Thus the paternal attitudes of Helen's and Ariel's fathers, born early in the second third of the twentieth century, are not altogether surprising, but their ambivalent attitudes toward their daughters, patent in their many critical comments about the girls' behavior, and their absence of kindness toward them, reinforced the mothers' patterns of emotional neglect. The children had reason to feel forsaken by both of their parents.

Such feelings were recounted to me by one adolescent and by two women who had been anorexic in late adolescence. Each had stopped eating at some time between the ages of 13 and 23, in determined though vain efforts to win the love of their remote, authoritarian fathers. Their mothers did not provide compensatory affection. Mary, the first of the three, was referred at age 15, after her mother noticed her loss of weight and disinterest in eating. Mary's father, a wealthy bon vivant, had liked to talk to his 12-year-old daughter about his social life, including his sexual affairs before and after his divorce from her mother. At home he enjoyed going about naked in Mary's presence, and joked about her objections to his doing so. When she reached puberty, he began to withdraw from her, perhaps feeling threatened by the sexual arousal stirred up by her maturing body. Not long after, he virtually renounced interest in her. It was then that she began to eat less and less, often complained of feeling cold, made herself remote from friends, and her school grades fell. Her anorexic condition was recognized by her physician. Brief psychoanalytic treatment was effective; although after she was able to eat normally, she succumbed to drug usage for several years, until she received more treatment.

Violet, as a child, was subjected to harsh rebukes by her father, which were seconded by her mother. At 40, Violet was a capable social worker and a concerned, loving mother. She had been depressed since early adolescence, had recovered with the help of medication, but with a renewal of her father's cruel denigration she relapsed into a state of depression, and therefore consulted me. She told me in ample detail of her lifelong feelings of frank rejection by both her parents, their incessant interference with any plan she made for her own pleasure, and their mockery of any interests she mentioned in the hope of eliciting their interest. Even when she was a young child they told her again and again what a difficult, colicky baby she had been, always crying and wanting to be held. During her childhood her father ignored her efforts to please him, and punished her for slight offenses by pulling down her underpants and spanking her. Yet along with his wife he demanded that Violet perform many kinds of tasks for him, tasks befitting a secretary. He never acknowledged her help, and never extended himself to her. She felt like a pariah in her home. At about 16 she began to feel unable to eat. Her larger feeling at that time, as she later remembered, was that it was no longer necessary for her to be a functioning person, or to need her parents. She went about her life believing she could make herself free of them by withdrawing as much as she could. This calmed her. It was as if she had dropped a burden. She felt no need for food anymore because she was already dead. Looking back, it seemed that she had accepted her father's belief that she was not worth bothering with. Strangely, at the same time she felt incredible energy; she could do any amount of physical tasks rapidly and well. Running about by herself, and doing things for other people, including making meals for them but not partaking of them at all, gave her feelings of immense pleasure. During psychiatric treatment, she realized that those bursts of energy had come from a displaced sexual excitement. One day at college, a teacher had told her sympathetically that she looked too pale and thin, and should be eating more. For the first time in her life she felt that someone cared about her. Suddenly, in response to the teacher's kindness, she began to eat lightly, very lightly. Later she realized that in the period when she was anorexic she used to keep her stomach muscles tight, which probably made eating uncomfortable; when she could relax those muscles, she could eat again. At 39 she had a relapse after her father renewed his cruel denigration of her, apparently in jealous rage about her success in the field she had dared to choose for herself. Treatment reduced her fear of eating, but her depressive states continued for years afterward.

The third patient, Laura, was as an infant and young child never allowed to eat near or at the dining room table near her father, but only at a small table in a corner of the dining room out of his view. He refused to tolerate the mess she might make, although she was a quiet and orderly child. He let her know that he had never wanted children, and that her birth had not been welcome. During all of her childhood and adolescence he remained isolated from her daily life. Her mother never intervened on her behalf. At about 16 she began to eat less and less, with the conscious desire to impress her father with her new slender figure, for she had noticed his interest in watching fashionable women. She tried to manage her hunger with a cup of black coffee each morning, and as little food as possible the rest of the day. But he never noticed her disinterest in eating, her loss of weight, and her somber moods; neither did her passive mother. All of Laura's efforts to elicit her father's interest in her were in vain. He continued to make derogatory comments about her, took notice of her artistic aspirations only to trivialize them, and dispatched her paintings to the rubbish can. She contemplated suicide, and held off the impulse only because she knew that her choice of such a fate would be a terrible blow for her mother and sister, who loved her. She appears to have felt that in her father's opinion she, like her paintings, should be dispatched to the rubbish can. In her midtwenties she at last saw the uselessness of her self-starvation. Feeling tense with anger and severely depressed, she underwent psychoanalytic treatment and slowly became able to eat again. She remained slim for her next 50 years, never regaining her preanorexic appetite. She married well, reared a capable and loving daughter, and was able to attain distinction in the artistic endeavors that her father had forbidden. But for as long as she could remember, she was subject to frequent migraine headaches.

I have referred to these three persons who consulted me only to draw attention to the part played by fathers in their development of anorexia, as it appears to have occurred in the early lives of Helen and Ariel. The discord between their parents aggravated the children's grief. They argued a great deal and blamed each other for their ineptitude as parents. Most children are expected to grow up, leave their parents in time, find new persons to love or to live with and new interests to pursue. Then the parents, if unhappy in their marriages, are left alone with each other. Those who are quite dissatisfied, like those of Helen and Ariel, may bind themselves to each other out of feared loneliness and other conflicts about their failed marriages. Helen's parents knew each other only a few weeks before they married, and their marital tensions rose quickly. Ariel's parents appeared to be somewhat better matched, but they were completely lacking in knowledge or imagination about how to rear a child. Wilson's (1983a) observation that parents of anorexic patients set up a united front against their children was borne out by these three sets of parents.

Distortions of Body Image

When at age 18 Helen and Ariel each volunteered that they had been anorexic a few years before, they explained only that they could not bear to be fat, and had to be constantly vigilant against increasing their weight by the smallest iota. Otherwise they felt entirely well, a common assertion of anorexic patients. In the research setting, it would have been intrusive to ask about their thoughts or feelings about their bodies. Some answers may be seen in their projective "Draw-a-Person" test responses at ages 4 and 5, and in Helen's drawings at age 18.

Age 4

Four-year-olds, asked to draw a person, usually draw a circle for the head, and may add two eyes and a mouth. They may add a second large circle for the body, and one or another feature, but are not expected to draw a whole figure. Helen's spontaneous drawing of "a mother" (Figure 8.1) is superior in having an arm, hands, and feet; but the eyes are empty, and the smile vacant. More unusual is the mother's body, made of zigzag slashes, disembodied from the head. It suggests confusion about what the mother represents to Helen: a large person in whom there is detachment between what she feels or says or thinks (the head) and how erratically she acts (the zigzag body). Actually she has no body. The drawing conveys feelings of restlessness, agitation, and anger.

144   CLINICAL SIGNS OF ANOREXIA

Figure 8.1

Ariel, asked to draw a person, at first filled the page with repeated writing of all the letters in her name, in many colors, which suggests that she herself (her name) is all that she could or wished to think of—a cheeky response to the examiner's request. The figure of her mother (Figure 8.2), drawn carelessly, is disturbing: her two eyes are in two different colors, one in light yellow, is not visible in the reproduction. Both are exaggerated in size and shape. Her ears are blotched circles. She does not see or hear rightly, and she

My mother

Figure 8.2

has no benign features. The figure has no coherence; it presents an image of a distraught or unknowable figure.

Age 5

Helen drew all her figures in red, a sign of tightly restrained aggression. The girl (Figure 8.3), small and rigid, has a scarecrow face with an artificial smile and a small, skinny body. Her arms reach out stiffly away from her body, with barely

Figure 8.3

one hand, touching nothing, almost as if she is trying to find her balance. The outstanding quality of this Draw-a-Person is the rigid figure with the scarecrow face. Eerily, the drawing looks like a preview of an anorexic body. Her drawings of mother and father (Figure 8.4) are similar, but their legs have little substance, are barely attached to their bodies, and have no feet. Mother has a crooked sidelong smile, and looks away from the viewer. Is she to be trusted? Father is taller, has a weak, slanting head, and eyes and nose that are aggressive in their darkness. His arms are too small to do anything, and his long, skinny legs look like thin stilts that can bear little weight. He is a weak, ineffectual giant. All three images, of mother, father, and child (Figures 8.1, 8.3, and 8.4), are lusterless and hopeless. They reflect the child's dismal concepts of all three.

Ariel's drawing of a girl (Figure 8.5) has an overly large head and a dramatic hair-do, with a tiny, poorly equipped

CLINICAL SIGNS OF ANOREXIA 147

Figure 8.4

body. It suggests an emphasis on her self-regard that is not convincing, as the girl, with a clownlike nose, looks sad. She has no neck, which suggests a failure of separation between impulse and action; that is, no time for reflection, no tolerance of frustration. The poor show of one hand suggests a poor capacity for positive action. As Ariel drew pictures of

Figure 8.5

CLINICAL SIGNS OF ANOREXIA 149

Figure 8.6

her family, repeatedly she showed confusion as to which one she was drawing, indicating ambivalence in relation to each. Mother and brother are shown together (Figure 8.6). Mother is smaller than Alex, her eyes are cast on something aside from him, and only she has a nose and mouth: this is a weak mother, and a brother with missing facial features. Both were drawn carelessly. In contrast, Ariel and her father (Figure 8.7) are more clearly differentiated sexually. Ariel is taller than her father. He looks self-satisfied and complacent. Ariel's expression has a quality of bliss or victory, as if she

Figure 8.7

had attained something she wanted. They are presented as a happy pair. All members of the family stand on birdlike feet; none has a firm base.

The body images presented by both Helen and Ariel at age 5 show intense desires to be admired and loved: Helen's thin, small girl is a poor, starved figure, appealing for rescue.

Ariel's large girl is brimming with self-approval. Both body images express uneasiness: one looks too poor and weak, the other is too excitedly pleased.

Age 18

Helen's drawings of a female (Figure 8.8), in contrast to the forlorn girl she drew at age 5, is overblown, overdressed, and wears a large picture hat whose brim half covers one eye. The other eye is mostly hidden. She wishes not to see, or not to be seen. She is also unstable, as she stands on very small, laced ballet slippers that are incongruous with the rest of her big costume. Her upper body is tightly separated from the lower part, as in her drawing of the male figure (Figure 8.9). In both drawings the hands are not connected to anything, which hints at feelings of shame. The male is restrained, taut, with very sharp elbows. His eyes are covered by dark glasses, and though his eyes are hidden he looks severe, untouchable. Both figures are excessively shaded, signifying the presence of much troubled feeling about their bodies. The tight belts separating the upper and lower parts of their bodies suggest particular anxiety about the lower body, as if it has to be sealed off. While anorexic persons express intense wishes to change the shape of their bodies from supposed fat to thin, their explicit objections are almost entirely to their abdomens, buttocks, and thighs. We may understand the sexual parts as being silent determinants of the wish to change the part of the body that is at the center of their disliked areas. Helen's drawing of the female, with the tight belt and full but childlike ruffle-bottomed skirt, and hidden or chopped-off hands, brings to the fore her difficulty in acknowledging mature sexuality. It arouses normal anxiety in most adolescents, but usually they do not

Figure 8.8

Figure 8.9

have to deny it so strongly. It is tempting to regard the starved-looking little girl drawn at age 5 as an embodiment of the emotionally impoverished Helen as a child, and her inflated figure of the overly feminine woman at age 18 as being in a quandary as to whether she is a sophisticated adult or an overdressed, wistful child.

In Helen's last picture (Figure 8.10), the boundaries between the family members are sharp. The parents are eating at a table, and though they would seem to be facing each other, their faces are hidden, which implies poor contact with the outer world. They are holding forks that look like pitchforks. Mother regards father with a hesitant smile. Father, with eyes on his food, is stiff. Harry stands alone, drinking straight from a bottle, and Helen, smiling, is speaking on the telephone to someone outside of the family. Her cat, the only figure with two visible eyes, stands apart from her. The cat's tail is not attached to its body.

Ariel at age 18 came late to her test session, did not leave time to draw the human figures, promised to send them, but did not. Perhaps she wished to avoid revealing, even in casual drawings, any thoughts or feelings she had about her family or herself.

The Human Figure Drawings by both girls show considerable tension and dissatisfaction with themselves. Like other anorexic persons, Helen and Ariel expressed intense wishes to change the outer shape of their bodies from fat to thin. I surmise that one reason for these wishes stems more from unconscious ideas about their inner bodies, as I shall discuss below.

Hyperactivity

Helen's physical activity underwent a dramatic change from immobility during most of her first two years to slow, halting

CLINICAL SIGNS OF ANOREXIA

Figure 8.10

movement in the following year or two, and then to restless and disorganized action. In nursery school she appeared to be trying to mask her emotional instability by loose efforts toward hilarity. In adolescence she had a surpassing need to engage in physical activities that amounted to desperate tests of endurance. Ariel, in contrast, was physically overactive by the end of her first year, and continued to be so throughout her childhood. As time went on, both girls showed a need to be in constant flight outward, away from their immediate feelings, thoughts, and surroundings. Thomä (1967) described the anorexic patient's exaggerated show of liveliness as being actually generated by a need for food. He saw the urge to keep moving and the tendency toward kleptomania as responses to the pangs of hunger which take the form of motor activity, in part a displacement of instinctual excitation. Too unwilling to admit their hunger,[1] they still suffer from intense oral envy. It can lead them to an impulsive (displaced) theft, as happened with Helen, and as noted by many clinicians. Abraham (1924b) wrote of the physical restlessness as a compensatory "pleasure of movement." Katz (1986) sees hyperactivity as a secondary symptom in anorexia, one that develops *after* the patient has been extremely active, as in long-distance running. The extreme exercise, he suggests, serves as a trigger for anorexia in persons who are at risk for eating disorders, especially those troubled

---

[1] A dread of being seen in the act of eating was reported by a 13-year-old who explained that if she were seen to be eating, people would not trust her anymore. For this reason she also dared not eat by herself. It appeared that she could not trust herself if she consented to eat, because then she would be in danger of losing control of her dangerous oral–aggressive impulses. At the same time she strongly wished she could eat normally in order to please her mother, so showing that one motive for her food rejection lay in her ambivalence toward mother. I wish to thank Loretta Loeb for this clinical example.

by individual, familial, or sociocultural circumstances. Possibly the trigger is akin to the sexual excitement described by Violet (see pp. 140–141), who believed her bouts of high activity provided a sexual "charge" in her emotionally sterile existence.

The Wish To Be (To Feel) in Control

The most frequently expressed desire of the anorexic patient is to show that she is in complete control of her body and her life. She lives out the desire in her scrupulous watch against eating, which becomes easier in time. It signifies her silent assertion of power to be in complete control of her life, a control that in fact represents a defense against her inner feelings of helplessness. In this silent assertion she also aims to turn the tables and take control of her parents whom she believes (often correctly) have tried to control her way of life. Now she renders them helpless to make her eat. But as long as she is in the grip of her addiction to excessive thinness she is in fact out of control. She may see the addiction as a special form of command over her body's demands, or her thoughts, or her parents, or over instinctual wishes that threaten her, but her inability to eat in spite of extreme hunger has rather the quality of a perverse, grandiose, yet infantile, defiance: "No one can make me eat." The fallacy that she is in control may lead her to hide food, or steal, or tell lies to preserve her aura of autonomy and freedom from a conventional way of life. Abraham (1916) was the first to link the stealing and lying of such patients to cannibalistic fantasies, both stemming from deeply repressed oral–sadistic wishes. The self-starver occupies her mind with her deprived state, and holds on to a hypercathexis of food (with a negative sign) along with a decathexis of almost all else. By means of her keen self-destructive aim, she eases her conscience about the passionate anger she bears against the parents who may once have loved her and whom she had once tried to love. She may hold on to a delusion that it is her choice to be ill (although she firmly denies her illness) rather than to confront her internal conflicts, but such a choice is spurious. It is supported unconsciously by a set of unyielding defensive measures: avoidance (of eating); denial (of hunger); restriction (of normal pursuits); inhibition (social withdrawal), regression (to infantile claims of self-satisfaction, causing others to worry about her); projection (they are wrong—they don't realize how well I feel); and most prominently, isolation of affect (against contemplating the bitter anger and desolation in which she is bound). All these block her capacity to form object relationships. No doubt she wishes desperately to be in control of her life, freed of her parents' (perceived) subjugation, but until she becomes aware of her unconscious fears of losing control of her destructive impulses against them, and against herself, she is barred from achieving a normal degree of impulse control. The severely anorexic patient resorts to pseudocontrols like cathartics, enemas, and excessive physical exercise. The false feeling of being in control misfires.

Asceticism

The anorexic patient is besieged by superego restrictions to forswear normal body pleasure. She seeks alternative gratification in pride for what she believes to be a unique capacity to function ascetically. In the research project, it was not possible to find out how Helen and Ariel satisfied their sexual needs. If we look to their object relationships for their sources of relief from libidinal tensions, we can find nothing because their friendships were always wanting. A prominent anxiety related to sexual arousal in adolescence lies in the aggressive and sexual wishes that are encased in masturbation fantasies. There are few references in the literature to anorexic patients' masturbatory fantasies or practices. Wilson (1983a) mentioned that "the superego of the fasting anorexic can be so strict that she may never have masturbated or permitted sexual fantasies. . . . She is frequently afraid of thoughts and fantasies and only wants to talk about dieting and food" (p. 33). An anorexic patient of Mintz (1983b) reported that she masturbated twice a day in order to increase her metabolism and lose weight. Boris (1984) wrote that "The anorectic knows she looks grotesque to others; she has certainly heard it enough. While her heroics about dieting or, at any rate, weight control are designed to stimulate admiration or, failing that, envy, the body is designed to look asexual and/or sufficiently androgynous as to evoke the most muddled sexual response in both men and women" (pp. 439–440). The pathological need of the anorexic person to feel in perfect control of her impulses neutralizes her freedom for genital pleasure. In early adulthood, Helen's poor sexual satisfaction depended in part on a sadomasochistic sexual practice with her male partner. Ariel had so far not been able to form a lasting positive social or sexual relationship.

The anorexic attitude is also determined by a premium placed on self-denial for the sake of a sometimes perfectionistic higher pleasure in superior intellectual or artistic accomplishment. Self-denial has a long history in religious proscriptions against indulgences of the body, as mentioned above. Self-starvation in its most extreme form did not appear in Helen or Ariel, but their urge toward it was evident in their feeling distinction in a capacity to live on a bare minimum of food. Helen, from early adolescence on, aspired to be a painter. Ariel expressed no aspirations, although as a child she had been intensely competitive and had coveted positions of superiority. Even her wish to be thin was less austere than it was in Helen. The current fashion of being thin has followed a contrary social emphasis, a century before, on plumpness to avoid the danger of tuberculosis ("consumption"). To be thin was heralded in the 1920s by the thin "flappers," and 40 years later by admiration of the skinny British fashion model, Twiggy, a young woman who looked like a sexless young lad. Now we have the Barbie doll, a child-woman, a prized figure that inadvertently does away with (childish) feminine ideas of holding and feeding and caring for a baby. As a slim pubescent doll, Barbie can be grasped in the hand of a child. Moreover, except for her budding breasts, her fancy hair-dos, and her riot of feminine clothing, she has the body of a young, slim adolescent male, and a name resembling that of a boy, Bobby. She has also acquired a matching adolescent boy friend, Ken. Magically, she has skipped over the difficult process of growing up. A central part of her message seems to be that being a child who loves dolls that can be held and cuddled is an old-fashioned, discardable notion. The "in thing" in high school, as Ariel said, was to be admired for being (perfectly) thin.[2] In the present, the implacable wish to be skinny is promoted by professional ballet schools and by Hollywood. It is likely to take a long time before any psychosocial accounting is

---

[2]Mothers and teachers of 9- and 10-year-old girls have told me of the girls' wishing they could look like Barbie, whose figure stirred up the children's determination to begin dieting. In some cases, the impetus for their efforts has been their mothers' inculcation of the value of thinness. Witness the 9-year-old who explained to her teacher that her mother always eats just a few leaves of lettuce for her lunch (as the teacher reported to me).

made of the cost of this extreme endorsement of physical thinness by fashion and the film industry.

Depression

Depression has a major place in anorexia. Helen and Ariel, as their early lives proceeded, were downhearted. As children, they can seldom have felt a capacity to arouse the love of their inattentive parents. That impaired love, experienced by the daughters as disregard, depreciation, and a total absence of empathy, brought on their feelings of hopelessness. At age 18 they tried hard to present themselves (to me) positively, but their moods were heavy. Depression was manifest in their affectlessness, intense disappointment in their parents, loneliness, and low interest in friendships or in learning commensurate with their high native intelligence. Along with their unconscious wishes to destroy their self-centered parents, they felt a pull toward self-effacement as a release from their feelings of guilt for hating the parents, and shame for being unlovable. "The fault, dear Brutus, is not in our stars, but in ourselves, that we are underlings." To little children, parents are stars, stars that in the unconscious are fixed, that may grow dim, but do not disappear. Helen and Ariel, in childhood, felt themselves to be underlings. Moving into adolescence, they became aware of disillusionment with their failed parents, but shrank from a full awareness of their own poorly repressed rage against the fallen stars. It felt safer to find faults in themselves in spite of their assertions of satisfaction with their lives, and to give up desires to live beyond their own small orbits. Notwithstanding their self-absorption, they were left with spare pride in themselves, and with melancholy. It did not matter that their efforts to starve themselves were motivated by identifications with the aggressors, the mothers who did not know how to love them, the fathers who stood by their wives. Szmukler (1987) has emphasized the strong etiological connection between affective disorders and anorexia. It appears that the base of the disorder, when severe, is an incapacity, beginning early in life, to form a positive identification with a love object.

Unless the continuing emotional struggles during the first years of childhood are mitigated during the latency period, or surely before preadolescence, they are liable to have slow-growing pathological effects on mental health, even though they may also foster sublimations. The oedipal conflict does not stand by itself as the core of the infantile neurosis. It rather represents a culmination of a host of internal conflicts of many kinds, degrees, and intensities, experienced in the moves from infancy to childhood and adolescence.

Chapter 9

Clinical Signs of Anorexia That Need Further Study

I wish now to take account of several antecedent conditions in infancy and early childhood that appear to have set roots for the later onset of anorexia in Helen and Ariel. These conditions have not before now been considered to be related to the disorder, no doubt because the state of the infant in actual life has not been sufficiently observed for pathogenic influences on psychological growth. They became known to me as I studied the experiential events in the lives of Helen and Ariel from the time of their birth to adolescence, and in following events up to their age 30.

In the original sample of 131 infants observed at intervals through their first year of life (Brody and Axelrad, 1970b), only Helen and Ariel manifested two behaviors in that year that one might assume to be a part of ordinary infant experience, and not indicative of possible trouble in the present, or ahead. The two behaviors appear to have been significant for the beginnings of their emotional distress and their eating disorders during the oral phase. They were (1) vomiting unrelated to illness or any organic problem, and (2) frequent, intense, and prolonged screaming. Three other forms of behavior that signified unusual stress beginning in the oral phase, though not unique to Helen and Ariel, were (3) stereotypic activities, (4) lingering dejection, and (5) clinging to transitional objects. One more oral sign of their vulnerability, observable after infancy, was (6) unstable uses of speech in early childhood, which reappeared in excessive or rapid speech in adolescence. Direct access to the childhood fantasies of Helen and Ariel about their oral and anal[1] functions was not feasible. I may still propose certain meanings of the several counterproductive behaviors, based on my understanding of relations between instinctual pleasures and displeasures of infancy and early childhood, and the later emergence of anorexia.

Vomiting

For the 131 infants in the sample, a high frequency of vomiting when emotionally distressed was observed and reported only in the cases of Helen and Ariel. Several other infants, like Helen, were seen or said to spit out or refuse foods whose taste or texture displeased them.[2]

---

[1]Toilet training is incomparably more difficult to observe than infant feeding. For an adequate assessment of its course we would need regular interviews, and with the parents' permission, a hidden video camera in the home for extended periods of time, at regular intervals from the beginning to the end of the training. One would wish to observe as well other aspects of the parents' concerns about dirt, messiness, and cleanliness, and parental reactions to the child's genital play in the same general period of time. A large order for some investigators, some day!

[2]Vomiting of mucus was reported of a few other infants when ill or subject to motion sickness, the child of one most inefficient mother

Helen's vomiting was first reported when she was 16 weeks old. Mother said the baby had been having "crying fits" one to two hours long, and sometimes "stimulated herself" to vomit by pushing her finger, or the wooden handle of a small bell, toward her throat. These acts may have been related to unsatisfied hunger, or to a natural wish to bring something into her mouth. "She vomits once a day," mother had said casually, a remark that fitted her loose and often pejorative reporting. She may have been referring to the common "spitting up" of young infants. The next information about Helen's vomiting came before she was 6 months old, on a day when mother left her in the care of maternal grandmother, whereupon Helen screamed inconsolably and vomited. By age 1, according to mother, Helen was getting rid of food by pushing, throwing, or hurling it away, and she had a habit of chewing on a mouthful of food and then spitting it out. A rising anger at mother's erratic ways of feeding may well have been displaced to the food supplied by her. To cast mother away, so to speak, was too frightening. It was easier to cast away the food that she offered, too late and usually too little. From Helen's second year to age 7 there was considerable and lasting tension between her and her parents at mealtimes, but we heard no more about vomiting. Helen herself reported that her decision to reduce her food intake set in shortly before or after menarche, at about age 13. She had shortly before begun to have "gigantic snacks," got frightened of getting fat, and so, she said, her regime of food rejection and overexercise began. At about age 27 she had a frightening dream that began with a big bird vomiting on a train and ended with her own death. At 30 she reported recurrent digestive problems and a chronically poor appetite.

---

gagged occasionally, and one self-righteous mother said that her 6-month-old threw up a lot because she was "such a pig" and ate too much.

Ariel's history of vomiting was more dramatic then Helen's. Her gag reflex, seen at age 3 days, may have indicated an innate disposition to choke up fluid. In the next few weeks, as mother reported, she force-fed milk or baby food, as she believed she should. At 6 weeks, she told us that Ariel regurgitated when mother interrupted her feeding to bathe her, at 26 weeks we saw her gagging when mother was forcing food upon her, and at 54 weeks she cried and vomited after falling off the regular toilet seat where mother had been placing her, in spite of Ariel's protests. At 55 weeks (the postponed 52-week visit) Ariel showed considerable agitation while being fed,[3] leading mother to explain that during the preceding two weeks, while Ariel was cutting her molars, she vomited "numbers of times." Whether this was true vomiting, or regurgitation, or "bubble-vomiting" (food comes up with a bubble of gas), mother could not remember. Ariel's restless response to feedings all through her first year suggests that she was made anxious by the routinely forced feedings given in silence by a tense, fearful, inept mother. At 15 months Ariel vomited after the frightening accident in the playground, where her running was stopped by the blow to her forehead (see chapter 5). Then there were the frightening rides to the physician, to the emergency room of a hospital, followed by isolation from mother while the wound was being sutured. This rapid series of painful events must have been traumatic for a young child as bent as she already was in fighting against any physical restriction.[4] The hospital experience must have been harrowing to her. She spoke of it often in her next years. In those years, which

[3]As seen in Film V, *Maternal Behavior and Object Cathexis in the First Year of Life* (Brody and Axelrad, 1970a).
[4]Her usual struggle against being picked up or held may have represented a defensive reversal of her long-frustrated wish to be picked up and held close by mother or father.

included Alex's sudden appearance on her scene, Ariel's disconcertment about losing her crib to him and being placed in a larger bed without the familiar protective bars involved screaming and vomiting for many weeks, until she was allowed to sleep in her parents' bed. At 4 and 5, she was said to vomit frequently when reproved for disobedience. This may have been the kind of vomiting that young children can learn to induce as a hysterical reaction to emotional stress. She also gagged and vomited after eating chocolate in the evening.[5] Mother's retrospective mention, when Ariel was 4 years old, that she had "upchucked" a lot since her first weeks, may have referred to the regurgitation that occurred when mother interrupted her feeding to bathe her. During all of her childhood Ariel was "a picky eater." Surely it was confusing to her, as a young child, that mother had all along insisted that she eat exactly what she was given, but later allowed or submitted to Ariel's dictating a menu for her meals. Beginning at age 4, and again at 6 and 7, Ariel had chronic belly aches in the morning, gagged at breakfast, and wanted to stay at home with mother, instead of going to school. As far as Ariel could recall at 18, she began to deny herself food at about 14, because it was the fashionable thing to do among her classmates at that time. The information she gave us about her later period of bulimia was scant. She said she maintained it for only a short time, and wished to say no more about it, so that we may note it only as a part of her larger eating disorder. Associations may be seen among the vomiting in infancy and early childhood, the stomach pains in latency, the bulimia, the signs of a stomach ulcer in adolescence, later the gastritis, and at age 30, the "sensitive stomach."

[5]Helen, as noted before (chapter 4), had a fear of eating hollow chocolate figures. Perhaps for both girls anxiety about chocolate was unconsciously perceived as an anal reminder of oral displeasure.

Neither her parents nor the pediatricians, according to the mothers' reports, considered Helen's vomiting and angry food rejection, or Ariel's excessive vomiting and gagging to be of concern.

Screaming

Screaming and enraged crying were habitual throughout Helen's and Ariel's first year. No other infant among the 131 observed through their first year cried or screamed with similar frequency, intensity, or duration. Their screaming sounded like frantic efforts to get away from panic brought on by their angry struggles with their mothers, and their unchanging loneliness. Awareness of their body boundaries (they were rarely held) was likely to have been dulled by other ongoing conditions: the long periods of excessive stillness (Helen) or excessive volatility (Ariel), their continuing uneasiness as seen in their mournful glances, sad states, "freezing" before breaking into poignant crying, sometimes with a brief catching of breath, and at last a weary quietness. The first generation of psychoanalysts, who paid more attention to the vicissitudes of the oral phase than is shown today, had strong interest in the screaming of infants. Their observations may have led, in time, to the rejection of Watson's (1919) famous dictum not to pick up a crying baby. He had regarded overt rage reactions as conditioned responses to fears such as noise and loss of body support, not to any emotional upset. Bernfeld (1929) was the first that I have found,[6] to write descriptively about the anger and the sorrow of a crying infant:

[6]Jones (1929) noted that Freud wrote of the aggressive force that propelled anger in the infant. I have searched for the source of this statement in Freud's works before 1929, in vain.

He cries louder and louder until he gets into paroxysms and finally weeps complainingly, during which his hands and his body are in vigorous but unorganized motion. This ... powerless rage ... is directed not only at the outer world, but has an intention against the whole ego. . . . In it [the feeling of powerlessness] rage, anger, vexation, resignation, and sorrow are united [pp. 279–280].

Jones (1929), referring to an anxiety in early infancy that precedes ideational thought, wrote that

it was experienced as a state of helplessness in the face of intolerable libidinal tension for which no discharge is available, no relief or gratification of it. . . . It ends in exhaustion of the stimulation itself; a hungry man ceases to be hungry when food is unobtainable for long, and fasting experts are presumably men who can tolerate the initial stages of excitation and reach that of gastric anaesthesia better than others can. With the libido ... this would be tantamount to total annihilation ... resulting in a state of aphanisis[7] [pp. 313–314].

In this state of helplessness, the infant runs the risk of oscillating between two reactions, both unfavorable: . . . he may depend too much on the artificial aphanisis of inhibition, and this will, in its turn bring with it the loss of control over the disturbing wishes through losing possession of them, through disappearance of the wishes themselves. On the other hand, he may pursue the easier path of developing in an excessive degree the defensive reactions of fear, hate and guilt [p. 318].

For Helen, one may say that as an infant and young child, the first unfavorable reaction Jones described, the artificial loss of wishes for food and affection, combined with

[7]From the Greek, meaning invisible, unseen. The verb means to make viewless, to obliterate. I wish to thank Lillian Feder for this translation.

her "screaming fits," made primary contributions to her passive surrender of physical and social action. For Ariel, one may say that the second unfavorable reaction, the defensive triad of fear, hate, and (later) guilt, was predominant. In her case, physical and social actions were made bolder, with a dire effect on her capacity for sound object investments. Both girls had discernible longings for signs that they were cherished. Both mothers were so libidinally restricted, and so governed by hidden aggression, that they were quite unable to offer love naturally.

Searl (1933) enlarged on Jones's statement about aphanasis, the meaning he perceived in the infant's "baffled scream of rage, ended only by exhaustion" (p. 193). She suggested that the unsuccessful cry of the child becomes a scream of rage with which to attack the (bad) parent, in a violent effort to overcome pain.

> The first effort seeks to overcome "pain" by love. The second uses hate, but retains an object who may still give some form of relief. . . . When this again accomplishes nothing, there succeeds a third state in which one can say the infant is scarcely more than an embodied scream, in which almost all object-relation is abandoned, the struggle of ambivalence is ended by the complete occlusion of love and desire for relief. . . . This effort failing, there is sometimes a reversal. The child, as if further enraged at this powerless rage itself, holds his breath and there is temporary silence; the climax of rage which is yet an anti-climax. All this time the child is completely inaccessible to all calming, comforting influences. . . . For the child in a blind rage *has*, as far as his own feelings are concerned, killed all that is good in his world, obliterated every trace of a good, helpful parent. It is a situation which provides a basis in experience for belief in the *omnipotence* of infantile death-wishes, rather than their powerlessness [pp. 196–197].

It is to be presumed that Helen and Ariel experienced such feelings of blind rage and terror of annihilation as the several authors described—feelings exemplified in the temper tantrum, which at its end usually leaves a person feeling debilitated. An ensuing attitude of having a special right to vindicate oneself in a retaliatory vengeful act is common in early childhood. It was conspicuous in Helen and Ariel. When a mother's excessive anger provokes her child's wish to retaliate, or if the child's rage provokes her mother's wish to retaliate, the cycle gets to be enacted repeatedly, and neither one will easily be able to extricate herself from their mutual disillusionment. "If we take vengeance for vengeance, then vengeance never dies" (a Hindu proverb).

We have no way but to consider that the prolonged states of screaming of both girls during their infancies did much to shape a fury in them that at times reigned over all other affects, though sometimes in a temporary disguise of impassivity, and that it was followed by remorse and feelings of guilt for the hateful wish to extinguish their faithless primary objects, mother and father. We heard of no happy times during their childhoods. When the girls were adolescent, reaction formations appearing in some efforts to make peace with their parents may have taken hold for a time, although the girls gave no indications that this happened. Even if they did occur, they were abrogated by the girls' turning their destructive aims against themselves in early adolescence. Their self-starvation may be understood in part as an unconscious effort to identify with the aggressors, the needed and hated mothers, the one who withheld food, the other who forced it. We can assume that an important precursor of the eating disorder, in each case, was the unconscious struggle to manage intense ambivalence toward the inhibited, restrictive, and unhappy mother who had rarely, it appeared, been free to assure her daughter that she was dear to her parents.

Prolonged screaming, like the temper tantrum, leaves an infant or young child in a state of physical and emotional exhaustion. When nothing is done to reassure and comfort the frightened infant, her rage may be blunted, but only temporarily. The most dire effects of Helen's and Ariel's repeated inner tempests were instituted by their parents' ineffectual responses. In their perplexity the parents resorted to ignoring the children's distress, or to punishing it.

Stereotypic Behaviors: Self-Rocking, Self-Rolling, Head Wagging

Previous observations (Brody, 1960) led me to propose that normative self-rocking represents an infant's earnest effort to enjoy a rhythmic whole-body movement forward, backward, then again and again forward, leading the infant to experience a form of independent locomotion in place. But repetitious and agitated self-rocking appeared to represent the infant's earnest effort to reestablish a longed-for body contact with mother. I suggested that the gratification supplied by the self-rocking condenses several sensory experiences: a headlong push to get rid of the anxious waiting, the small bridge-journey to the mother, and the passive locomotion felt when in her arms. I wrote that as the infant misses the mother, he acts in a way that makes him feel he is moving toward her, and so he achieves a momentary mental relief. "The gratification of this relief could allow for a hallucinated reunion, oral and tactile in nature, such as normally follows upon satiety [Lewin, 1950], a reunion toward which the contact hungry infant must continue to strive" (p. 487).

CLINICAL SIGNS THAT NEED FURTHER STUDY   173

This view of the tension stirred up by the infant's desire to be physically held and carried may also have been expressed in part in Helen's head wagging and Ariel's self-rocking.

Helen as an infant was discouraged from moving her body. She was inordinately still during most of her infancy except when distressed. At 6 months her affectless head wagging was self-contained, self-distracting, and joyless. For an infant who did not yet have tactile or kinesthetic capacity for communication, her stereotypic body movements can have demonstrated a wish to activate physical nearness, presumably to the mother; that is, to a warm body that has a resemblance to the warmth (body temperature) and security of the womb. The lag in gross motor activity, reported well into her third year, was followed in her next years by a contrasting extreme restlessness. At age 3 she rocked herself as she sat facing the psychologist during the test session. Perhaps by then she was feeling a push toward recapturing the missed pleasurable body excitement, but could do so only in unorganized physical actions, as observed in school. Later on and indirectly that wished-for excitement may have influenced her toward hyperactivity, which came to be entwined with her single conscious aim to be thin. For Ariel, the agitated self-rocking during infancy was followed by excessive physical and pseudosocial activity. She, like Helen, had to do without warm, loving body nearness, but unlike Helen, she acted as if trying to undo her loneliness by eliciting continuous reparative responses from any persons close to her. Whether the responses were positive or negative appeared to be of little consequence. In the long run they intensified the confusion in her object relations, and the instability of her growing ego and superego structures.

For both infants the self-stimulation provided by their stereotypic body movements can have served as substitutes for the lost reception of libidinal nourishment from the outer world in favor of a self-gratifying absorption in their private physical sensations. The hiatus in our project was brought about by the original plan to observe the infants only through their first year. We had not expected to observe them after that, but eventually we did so, at their age 2, 3, or 4, then annually to age 7 and not again until age 18. This means that for a number of subjects we missed first-hand information about their behavior and development in their second and third years; and for all subjects between ages 7 and 18. It is possible that the physical disquiet of both girls in their early childhood was to some extent reduced during the latency period, when classroom attendance and school work provided positive boundaries to the disordered behavior (Helen) and the impulsive behavior (Ariel) observed in their preschool years. Later, when they moved into preadolescence, past inclinations for physical excitement resurged.

The stereotypic acts suggest that as infants Helen and Ariel felt an absence of physical gratification that could have provided a normal relief of tension, and that an ache for whole-body pleasure intensified their need for movements that literally went nowhere.

Dejection

As infants, Helen and Ariel could not yet have turned their aggression inward. They might have been described as low-keyed (Mahler, Pine, and Bergman, 1975), except that their downheartedness was more severe than the term *low-keyed* implies. It is closer to the mark to say that they had lost a capacity for spontaneity. For their enduring low spirits I find *dejection* to be a more fitting name than *depression*. It touches more closely on the woebegone air that invades the moods of neglected infants and children, and omits the self-depreciation characteristic of depression.

There was no sign that Helen's parents ever took serious notice of her unhappiness other than coldly or mockingly. Ariel's mother reported the child's often saying she was sad: mother had no idea why this should be, and expressed no curiosity about it. This is not surprising, as only decades ago depression, which connotes sadness as a diagnostic entity in childhood, was hardly imagined to exist except as known from stories like those of Charles Dickens and Samuel Butler, and of course from fairy tales (probably one reason why those tales of sadness and great fear have been deeply appreciated by children). Still now, common signs of dejection such as social avoidance, frequent need for reassurances, anxiety, moodiness, or readiness to cry or complain, are commonly assumed by many parents to pass with time and to leave no sequel. Melanie Klein (1943–1944) assumed that young infants suffered first from a paranoid position, which she might more simply have described as a state of intense anger against mothers (rather than hatred of the bad breast) who did not offer steady love and care; and second from a depressive position, which she might more simply have described as a state of intense loneliness, of feeling forgotten. I put the issue oversimply, perhaps, but indications of paranoia and depression in the very young infant, as Klein proposed without recourse to documented direct observations, are clinically imaginative but at present untestable. Sadness in the infant and young child became a clinical concept after the impact of early object loss began to be understood through the work of Freud (1905, 1917), Bernfield (1929), Benedek (1938), Spitz (1945, 1946a,b), Brody (1956, 1964, 1982a), Brody and Axelrad (1970b, 1978), Brody and Siegel (1992), Winnicott (1960), Bowlby (1960a), Mahler

(1961), Sperling (1963), A. Freud (1970a,b), Mahler et al. (1975), among others.

Sperling's (1963) statement about loneliness in infancy deserves consideration: "Separation due to loss of the pre-oedipally gratifying mother is of greater importance than castration anxiety" (p. 391). Intense feelings of object loss, when experienced in early infancy and continued in the next two to three years, as they were by Helen and Ariel, may preempt the development of the greater fear of loss of the love of the object, and blur the rise of castration anxiety. As far as I know, we have no empirical data about the timing of the sequence of fear of object loss, fear of loss of the object's love, and the rise of castration anxiety, which includes the fear of punishment. The course in which these intrapsychic phenomena are experienced were outlined by Freud (1905). The sequences and combinations in which they take place in individuals, social groups, and societies constitute large areas of investigation.

Early on, Helen showed an undue physical placidity, interrupted by panic states in which she gave way to excited, angry, prolonged crying. From what we learned about her abiding unhappiness we can infer that she missed reliable pleasure in her body and its functions, and that she was often overcome by feelings of abandonment by parents who deemed it best for her development of independence to be left alone most of the day. The decrement in her physical and emotional life was manifest in her first half-year, and continued in her next two years. In the latter part of her third year her capacity for gross motor activity revived, but by then a large part of her energy was given to repeated contests with mother and father. When at 4 and 5 she gained some freedom to act on her own, as observed in school, outbursts of excitement cut through her sober withdrawals in ways similar to the fluctuations between silence and storm in her infancy. Her libidinal development fell back and her self-esteem was eroding. The combination of excited and inhibited behaviors continued at least up to age 7. Her chronic state of being nearly spent of good feeling through early childhood calls to mind Greenson's (1949) description of the development of a state of apathy that is the end result of deprivation. The apathy he witnessed in prisoners of war was usually preceded by angry rebellion and aggressiveness, and followed by feelings of defeat and humiliation. This series of negative affects is close to Bowlby's (1960a) description of the process of mourning, in which there is a journey from protest, to anger, to grief, as seen in infants and young children bereft of primary care by a familiar and loving person.

Helen's school achievements in the latency period could not extinguish the feelings of despair that had been mounting since her infancy. Her memory, at 18, of feeling so upset at 13 by a friend's reference to her "thunder thighs" that she began to diet suggests that she had displaced the source of her distress from inner, unnameable anxieties to a defective body image. She could not endure her conviction that she was fat. Needless to say, other conscious and unconscious ideas about the forever-lost pleasure-seeking physical body of her childhood and the forever-lost love of her parents must have advanced her misperception of her body as a container of an oppressive enemy.

Ariel had a comparable history of displeasures in infancy and early childhood. Her symptomatic biting, well into her second year, may have had a source in an angry effort to grab and/or destroy something with her teeth, the only weapon an ungratified and enraged infant can use effectively, beside screaming or throwing. The biting can have been unconsciously intended to take in an object that had been loved, and simultaneously to destroy it for its faithlessness. Conceivably, the object was symbolic of one or the other parent, toward whom her ambivalence can only have ben intense. She could not have avoided seeing that they were more involved with each other than either one was with her. When she was only 6 months old mother had said that she kept the radio on so that Ariel would not feel *bored*. This may have been a projection of mother, whose emotions were so hemmed in that she was helpless to stir the baby out of a state that looked to her like boredom. When Ariel was age 1 mother again reported that Ariel was often bored. *Boring*, was the way, years later, Ariel described her schoolwork, *boring* was the way at 18 she described the task of reading, and at 22, her part-time employment. All along the way she had developed few inner resources, felt weary with disappointment in her life, and was at a loss to understand why. She seemed to have lost a capacity for introspection, even of wonder about her sad state. Fenichel (1945) explained boredom as a state of apathy or emptiness of feeling, Greenson (1953), as noted above, linked it to a state of affectlessness, and Bibring (1953) saw it as indicative of a loss of self-esteem that comes from an intense state of helplessness and inhibition of function. All of these definitions apply to the longstanding feelings of listlessness that Ariel tried so hard to cover with hyperactivity, and with a show of self-approval that sometimes rose to a cavalier irresponsibility or a display of arrogance. Early in her adulthood, depression was evident in numerous ways: there were her fears of strange-looking people, somatic symptoms, worry about being fat, the almost lifelong fear of being alone, then of having no stable relationships to men, the limited investment in learning or in work at least up to the time of her pursuing the study of law, and the need at age 30 to go back to live with her parents. Her show of independence was belied by her incessant wish for social busyness. We may assume that the latter need was unconsciously intended to compensate for her surrender of normal wishes to be loved and protected, wishes that might otherwise have been directed toward building an observing ego and an ego ideal. If we accept the reasoning of Schilder (1935) that the body image is never static, we may also assume that Helen's feeling of body intactness, affected by long intervals of lying alone and still, can have been attenuated even while she lay awake. In contrast, Ariel's display of vitality in her rapid physical action can have encouraged her toward ever increased movement during her waking hours, and to feeling a degree of elation that promoted her displays of self-assurance. Freud's (1917) remarks on mania as a diversion from melancholia apply:

> The content of mania is no different from that of melancholia . . . both disorders are wrestling with the same "complex," but . . . probably in melancholia the ego has succumbed to the complex whereas in mania it has mastered it or pushed it aside. . . . We may venture to assert that mania is nothing other than a triumph of this sort (the discharge of joyful emotion and an increased readiness for all kinds of action), only that here again what the ego has surmounted and what it is triumphing over is hidden from it. [p. 254] . . .
>
> The accumulation of cathexis which is at first bound and then, after the work of melancholia is finished, becomes free and makes mania possible must be linked with regression of the libido to narcissism [p. 258].

The dejection observed in Helen and Ariel was first lodged in their profound dissension with their parents, then in their disappointments with themselves. At age 18, Helen recognized this and was moving on in her life, albeit lamely. For Ariel it would seem to have been too self-abasing to recognize feelings of having been bereft of kindness and protection by her parents. She rather identified herself with her mother's blunted affect and her father's overweening display of self-confidence, and remained dependent on them.[9] Among infants with experiences like these, disenchantment with the hope of receiving and giving affection can set in before the end of the first year. The loneliness, the absence of physical, sensory, and affective assurances of love, and the persistent screaming throughout their infancies appear to have been remote causes of their anorexia in adolescence in that they set the stage for the children's feelings of despair. Behind it were the early and unrelieved anxieties of object loss, of loss of the object's love, and of annihilation (the screaming to a state of exhaustion, without relief). During childhood, as their psychic structures matured, they felt the added impediments of the castration complex and of feared punishment for their wrath against their parents. The external sources of their fears lay in their parents' inability to interest themselves in the ways of children, their lack of freedom to create emotional ties to their children, or to hold back their aggressive demands of them.

These four parents had no familial or social support to tide them over common difficulties in childrearing. The children were born in the mid-1960s, still a time when a majority of mothers were virtually cut off from prospects of moving beyond domesticity, and few fathers concerned themselves with the value of communicating with their infants and children or of enriching their wives' self-esteem as

---

[9]About the effects of early disillusionment with parents Jacobson (1946) wrote: "[It] crushes the infantile ego, on one hand, and on the other, may start the super-ego formation at an earlier stage than normally. Thus the super-ego gets endowed with the archaic omnipotence of early parental images, which accounts for the pathological tension arising between an over-powerful super-ego and bent down ego forced to extend itself over its limits" (p. 135).

mothers and as achievers in areas outside of intimate family life. Helen and Ariel became artists, we might say, in denying their affect hunger and all that it connotes by renouncing their hunger for food. Helen's mother saw nothing of her child's unhappiness. Ariel's mother was only baffled by it. Dejection in early life that is unrelieved has the quality of a heavy cloud that needs to burst into a grand rainstorm, but cannot. It can leave a child in a state of flat hopelessness.

Clinging to the Transitional Object

At school age Helen and Ariel still coveted the remnants of their baby blankets. This meant that they had developed a hypercathexis of a thing reminiscent of a private happiness, but still only an inanimate, formless thing to which they clung in ways that interfered with investments in more age-appropriate objects—persons, things, and physical and cognitive skills. Their attachments to the blanket fragments in latency indicated a retention of investment in a part-object (rather than a person), not to be shared by anyone at all, so enhancing their infantile narcissism. Enthusiasm met Winnicott's (1953) discovery of the transitional object. It seemed to describe perfectly the infant's need to cuddle a soft object that revived the positive sensory experience originally provided by loving intimacy with mother. It has been understood as a comfort to allay the infant's feeling alone. It also represents a bridge from mother to a thing, with positive and negative meanings. Several studies (Brody, 1980) have shown that the frequency of dependence on a transitional object is significantly lower among infants who had close physical contact with their mothers, and significantly higher among infants of upper and upper-middle class families than those of middle class. The latter were found to have more direct and frequent physical contact with their infants than those of higher socioeconomic families. Only a few authors (Sperling, 1963; Fintzy, 1971; Dickes, 1978; Brody, 1980; Bourgignon, 1995) have questioned its psychological value when it is retained for more than a few months in latter infancy. The allure of the concepts of the transitional object and transitional phenomena has led to a proliferation of examples that have to do neither with transitions nor with infants (e.g., the mother, the analyst's next patient, a twin, the patient's own body, lullabies, fairy tales, and movies), each considered to be a means of mastering separation anxiety. To the contrary, Sperling (1963), like Wulff (1946), saw the concept as not only fallacious but dangerous because it led to an incorrect assessment of the meaning and function of fetishistic phenomena in childhood, and made for persistence of a part-object relationship, "to specific parts of the mother's body, or to specific qualities of those parts. In essence this means that through the fetish, part-object relationship can be maintained and immediate, unmodified instinctual gratification can be achieved" (Sperling, 1963, pp. 382–383). "The childhood fetish," she said, "represents a pathological defense against separation from mother on the preoedipal (oral and anal) levels" (p. 391) as affording a fantasy of omnipotence. I believe her statements are correct with regard to a child past infancy who, when denied access to the transitional object, becomes anxious until he or she retrieves it, as happened with Helen and Ariel. Sperling wrote that the fetish may be given up without resolving the fetishistic fixation, "with the result that the person treats other people as if they were fetishes . . . and establishes fetishistic relations with them" (p. 385). This statement reminds us that each of Ariel's serial relationships with men ended without gratification. When the baby blanket is held onto uninterruptedly, it can be felt by the older infant or young child almost as a vital body part. This is why it can support an excessive infantile narcissism and reduce interests in social and cognitive interchange. Then the object, rather than being transitional, is valued for its fixedness. Its pull to an infantile investment remains, as it did beyond school age, for Helen and Ariel.[10]

Unstable Uses of Speech

The oral frustrations that marked the infancies of Helen and Ariel may be understood as having been a remote source of the intemperate aggression heard later on in their manners of speech. Helen's vocalizations at the end of her first year were rich, clear, and varied, yet often she dispensed with natural vocalizations and gave way instead to screaming. She could speak more than a dozen words, pronouncing only the first syllable of each, as if holding back from a full investment of language as she did from motor and social action. By the time she was 3 she spoke, during the diagnostic intelligence test sessions, in a low voice or in monosyllables, or she refused to answer questions, preferring to respond by

---

[10]Some of the conceptual difficulties involved in the adjective *transitional* might have been avoided if Stevenson's (1954) name for the object, *the first treasured possession*, had taken priority. She addressed its positive as well as its negative meaning. Of course, Winnicott referred to a transitional period of perhaps a few months. He likely would be taken aback by the now frequent reference to a "transition" that for some children lasts for years. The earliest reference to such a possession that I have found was by Sterba (1941). She described the use of a small bib cherished from early infancy by a 20-month-old. It was first valued for its link to mother and milk, later for its anal odor, both representing objects that the infant must gradually give up.

nodding or shaking her head. In school the next year, she avoided speech and was an isolate. At 4 and 5 she mumbled, had difficulty enunciating several sounds, lifted her shoulders when she could not or wished not to answer questions, and whined instead of speaking. Her social behavior was erratic. At 6 her vocabulary was exceptional and her grammar precise, yet occasionally her words were incomprehensible because she had difficulty enunciating a few sounds and spoke too rapidly. Her responses fluctuated between silence, coyness, jiggling, and agitation. At 7 all of these oral–expressive difficulties remained. She was reluctant to guess answers, shrugged and stared, retreated to long, trancelike pauses or empty smiles, and from time to time manipulated her tongue against her teeth, pursed or pulled at her lips, and sucked her knuckles, amid other oral autoerotic behaviors. Given easy questions, she brightened and gave ready, overlong replies. Overt oral aggression came through when she sharply ordered the examiner not to ask questions. At 18, her speech was clear, but rapid and overabundant.

Ariel at age 1 knew a dozen words and vocalized frequently and cheerfully, but intense oral aggression appeared in her frequent biting and her imperious speech. In the next years she sometimes withheld speech, sometimes was voluble, and sometimes stumbled over her words. She was heard to make "biting remarks" to children at school. At 5 her stratagems of too bold speech or an alternative reticence suggested an excessive need to be watched and listened to by the examiner. At 6 she showed a "sophisticated," know-it-all manner, and spoke impudently to the examiner. At 7 she was loquacious when she knew an answer, otherwise inattentive and withdrawn, and there was a general decline in the maturity of her speech. At age 18 her speech was clear, but her responses to the interviewer were inappropriately long. There are children who keep talking in order to retain an audience, the way some infants, by not swallowing the food in their mouths, keep mother at their side. Ariel's and Helen's urgency to keep talking to a captive listener can have derived in part from an old ungratified longing for their mother's or father's company, and from angry, unrequited wishes to be listened to. Abraham (1924a), as mentioned above, referred to the connection between oral ambivalence and a constant urge to talk. Stone (1961) described speech as a "vehicle of actual object relationship which arises as the more intimate and direct bodily contacts with the mother are drawing to an end, or becoming greatly attenuated" (p. 99). By the other contacts he must have meant the physical, sensory, social, and cognitive experiences that normally usher in the beginnings of speech. Yet for infants whose mothers relate to them poorly, the intimate contacts are likely to be too scanty to recede noticeably. So it was for Helen and Ariel. Nonverbal connections were minimal during their troubled infancies. Soon speaking became their best means of relating, or refusing to relate, to people. They talked too much or too little, without the grace of social skill. The indications are that positive relations exist between intense fears of object loss and loss of the object's love in the oral phase, and later social and intellectual skills.

The inevitable spread of problems that appear or disappear during infancy, childhood, and adolescence complicates the study of their mental health over that span of years. I have presented only observations that can help to explain some significant ways in which early experiences were found to shape psychological states after that precarious period, in order to bring forward information about experiential factors that contributed to the incidence of anorexia in two adolescents.

Data are needed to support the propositions I have offered regarding sources of the anorexia of two subjects that were traceable to their first months of life, from which time they suffered physical, emotional, and social deprivations. In their first year they experienced a scarcity of tactile, kinesthetic, and affective gratification. From then on, they lived through frequent dystonic states of hunger and loneliness, eating in states of distress, vomiting in response to emotional stress, and excessive physical activity or inactivity. During their early childhood they experienced continued absence of oral satisfaction, poor control of urinary and anal functions, poor information about sexual differences, and limited play with persons or things (Brody and Axelrad, 1978, chapter 24). There was no stimulation of curiosity about their environment, frequent physical distance from mother or father, excessive subjection to censure, shaming, and verbal or physical punishment, excessive physical activity or inactivity, and intense social discomfort. During puberty and adolescence they met an array of emotional troubles: continuous friction with parents amid family discord, poor preparation for the demands of adolescence, fear of being fat and the beginning of the obsessional concern with diet, unstable social relationships and social withdrawal, falling off of school grades, limitation of interests, and preoccupation with physical or social activity.

For Helen and Ariel, symptomatic behaviors and states arose in infancy, mounted in childhood, may have remitted in latency, but reappeared in adolescence. The younger the child whose behaviors are noticed as suggestive of disorder, the better the chance that they can be arrested in good time. We could not have marked out the specific dysfunctions that would come to Helen and Ariel in their adolescence. We could have predicted, however, that in Helen's case, her parents' dismissal of her need for physical movement during most of her first two years, unless replaced by their encouragement of physical activity in following months, that is, within the same period of physical growth, was liable to retard her physical development, to lower pleasure and pride in the use of her body and in explorative activities. Or we could have predicted that the distress brought on by the sudden weaning at 3 months, unless moderated by special reassurances and loving care by her parents in following weeks and months, was liable to bring on her poor appetite, diffuse anxiety, and further loss of confidence in her parents' affection. In the case of Ariel we could have predicted, for example, that the low empathic care she received in her first months, unless requited by mother's allowing herself to enhance and enjoy Ariel's perceptual and social experiences in the next months, was liable to bring on her excessive restlessness and/or hyperactivity (insecure body boundaries). And we could have predicted that the loneliness she experienced in those months, unless diminished by mother's play with her to win the child's affection in ensuing weeks and months, was liable to bring on her petulance and sadness.

Disturbing emotional experiences during infancy and toddlerhood are not in themselves pathogenic. They are liable to become so if their negative effects continue through the second and third years, and are observed in struggles with the component (infantile) instincts, which inaugurate and affect the temper of the oedipal demands. On the short way to the normal oedipal phase, the prominent psychological need of the young child is a sureness of being loved by a person who is felt to be kind, steady, and strong, and a security of freedom from an overarching dread of losing that love and the safety it provides. The complex wish for love and the fear of losing it have the longest life, even when in later years they may at times be muted. Logical hypotheses about the relations between psychological conditions in infancy and childhood may be constructed only when the whole context of the infant's and child's continuous and cumulative experiences up to the latency period are knowable in sufficient detail. Then their effects on enlarging object relations, socialization, intellectual growth, defense structure, superego and character development can be taken into account for an assessment of mental health.

We are left with the question why the person who dares not eat is so fixed in her passion to be thin, against all reason, that she places her life in jeopardy; what has led her to be so governed by the single delusion that her body is fat, that her overriding purpose is to lose more and more weight, no matter that this perverse form of self-indulgence can lead to illness or death. She presents a picture of self-love in reverse.

Chapter 10

A Triumph of Rage, and a Surrender

The ingredients of anorexia suffered by the two research subjects were learned about in direct observations of their psychological states from infancy through early childhood, in standard situations, and from parents' reports. During adolescence they had developed few identifications with caring adults, poor resolution of inner conflicts, and unstable defenses, with the most imperative being a repudiation of affect and a turning of rage against the self.

A quick review is in order. For both girls, sensory, physical, and emotional satisfactions in the oral phase were meager, so that during infancy and early childhood their object relations were poorly developed. Helen's mother promoted inactivity in her child, Ariel's mother promoted excessive activity in hers. Helen was too still, Ariel too busy, but for both loneliness, loud crying, and angry screaming characterized their moods throughout most of their first two years, until they developed enough vocal and motor power to express their wishes, but a normal degree of compliance to parental demands never developed. By their third year the two girls sought for means of escape in active defiance of their parents, or passive retreat from them. The investments of both mothers in their children were more aggressive than libidinal, especially as the children's rebelliousness increased in their early years. Their unrest was aggravated in their oedipal periods; it may have receded during latency, when they attended school and were less open to continuous parental criticism. In early adolescence the differing effects on their psychological maturation were manifest in the motor hyperactivity of Helen and the social hyperactivity of Ariel.

Helen's unfulfilled oral needs probably contributed to her erratic uses of speech and silence, and her social withdrawal. Ariel's more severe oral distress probably contributed to her considerable vomiting and gagging during infancy, her biting people in late infancy, her "biting" speech, greediness, and arrogance in early childhood. Curiously, she refused sweets–they made her gag, mother said. It is unusual for a young child to refuse sweets, so I wondered whether she might be inhibited by vague feelings of anxiety about enjoying candy. Then I recalled the father's telling us that each evening he brought home candy for her, with the proviso that she must wait until after her supper to eat it, but as she sometimes opened the package of candy before her supper, he took it away from her. Though our record of the interview with him does not say so, I suspect that he soon gave it back to her, because of his extreme leniency; this in spite of his frequent spankings on her bare behind, which usually "got results." Possibly her refusal of sweets was one prologue to her eventual rejection of food.

Our information about events in the children's anal phase, approximately in their second to third years, was minimal (see appendix), but for both girls toilet training necessitated scolding, nagging, bribing, and final submission by the children. Neither one can have experienced pride in taking command of her anal and urinary functions, a nonmastery that repeated their failure to take charge of their oral functions. Both girls had toilet regressions in their next two years. Such battles against parental insistence that the child use the toilet look like prototypes of the rebelliousness of adolescents against the demands of the adult world. Ariel's anal–destructive fantasy emerged on one day at age 3 in her response to an incident involving her parents. Father had asked mother to put another log in the fireplace, which she did in such a way that it almost fell out. Father remarked that she didn't do her job well. Mother asked, well, did he want her to burn herself? Father then to Ariel: "Isn't that silly of Mommy, to think that I wanted her to burn herself?" Ariel just looked at him and said, "Well, maybe you do." Father proudly considered Ariel's response to be very perceptive, which indeed it was.

The quality of emotional health present at the outset of the oedipal phase is normally a resultant of major skirmishes with parents during the previous instinctual phases. Helen's and Ariel's obstinate defiance against toilet training by mother can be understood to have played a part in their later mutiny against accepting the food she supplied and, by extension, almost all food. For both girls, the latter rejections probably were motivated in part by identifications with the aggressor, the one mother who could not enjoy feeding her baby, the other who could not let her baby enjoy being fed. Our knowledge of how oedipal conflicts took shape in Helen and Ariel came from the parents' interviews and from the children's serial diagnostic psychological tests. From their histories, we know of their excessive exposure to their parents' nudity. In Helen's case, her father found it quite all right to go about their apartment unclothed, and mother after some hesitation agreed to the same. This parental behavior was likely to have aroused much anxiety in Helen that she was forced to repress. A few years later mother reported having told Helen the anatomical facts about making babies, but didn't think Helen had understood what she was told. When Helen feared to take showers in the bathtub, mother joined her there, again overstimulating the child's fantasy.[1] In Ariel's case, the nightly bed-sharing was possibly a more provocative exposure to her parents' bodies. Her mother evaded our inquiry about nudity; her father was emphatic about never being undressed in her presence. For her, the sexual exposure may well have evoked fantasies like those that emerged in the disguise of her nightmares and her fears of unnatural-looking people. She received no sexual enlightenment. The high incidence of parental nudity in the histories of anorexic patients has been noted by Wilson (1983b). Both girls' normal curiosity about sexual differences was probably repressed well before their oedipal phase. From all this we can safely deduce that they received little or no appropriate education about sexual differences or sexual development, and that as they entered adolescence they were left with perplexity and with more than usual anxiety about the changes in their bodies. Sours (1974) mentioned an absence of oedipal material in the cases he presented. The likely reason was that the anamnestic information he received from the parents of his patients omitted what the parents had not been educated to observe.

    Symbolic meanings of food that influence the development of anorexia have been discussed by Bliss and Branch

---

[1]Ferenczi (1919) wrote that "in the nursery" and in the unconscious, nakedness may serve to inspire terror. "The as yet inexperienced ego of the child is frightened at the unexpected quantities of libido and at the libidinal possibilities with which it does not yet know what (or what more) to do" (p. 331).

(1960), Wilson (1983c, 1992), and Mintz (1983b), all of whom have reported food phobias that derived from repressed fears of oral aggression. As Mintz (1992) describes the conflict about eating:

> [It] represented a displacement from a more important and overwhelming dilemma about helplessness in dealing with events and people and a feeling of being out of control. Controlling food and weight . . . served as a substitute for the inability to control people. Here we see that not only does the eating serve the aggressive impulse to destroy people, but in addition, by destroying everyone in opposition, the patient regains control over the world of objects [pp. 330–331].

Helen and Ariel had no opportunity to tell me about any symbolic ideas they had about food, so that I cannot add to these remarks about possible symbolic meanings of food for them, but I assume that conflicts in the anorexic patient about food intake mean that for her, hunger has been libidinized. If so, her addictive pursuit of thinness is a mark of her capacity to hold down her libidinal needs and at the same time to satisfy her aggressive impulses against the parents who want her to eat.

I suggest that a series of unconscious aims arise in the anorexic adolescent: the first is to reach a state of perfect thinness. The second is to satisfy regressive aims. The third is to commit herself to certain social values that have developed in the course of the twentieth century.

1. The insistent pursuit of thinness implies, according to primary-process thinking, that the anorexic adolescent aims to make herself thinner and thinner so as to reduce the space inside of her body which, according to her unconscious fantasy, engrosses the hostile parental introjects. She

hopes in this way to make her body (herself) free of them. There should no longer be room for their representations in her mind or body. Inherent in this wish would be a sharp instinctual defusion in that mainly aggression, with a demand to sustain narcissistic aims, dominates. The patient is charged with the idea that when she is thin enough she will prevail over the naysayers, her body will look just right, and she will like herself and be loved by others. She does not believe that, in this process, she may die. Zerbe (1993) described the eating-disorder patient as trying to starve her body by killing off the maternal object, "the mother within . . . the persecutory object" (p. 167). This seems to me near right; but unless unconscious paranoid ideas are known to be present in the anorexic patient at age 18, I find it simpler to refer back to the addiction to excessive thinness. Only Ariel's test results suggested the presence of mild paranoid thinking. I suggest that the addiction contains a wish to shrink the body so that the hostile introjects (displaced to the hated body fatness) will gradually waste away. Simultaneously the patient wishes to atone for her yearning to rid herself of the mental representations of her hated parental objects. We would need clinical evidence to justify the idea, which dates from Melanie Klein's (1943–1944) propositions, that the introjects are felt by the infant to be persecutory. They might as well, as in Helen's case, be perceived as delinquent or seriously neglectful. Or, in Ariel's case, to be manipulative, or abandoning. An inference may be made that the perfectionistic wish of the anorexic patient to look thin derives from an unconscious idea about the inside of her body, not the outward form she emphasizes.

The self-starving patient cannot or is not willing to recognize that she can succeed in slaying the introjected enemies only by slaying herself. Or if that is the only course, so be it—except that she is enthralled by a belief that only with the destruction of those mental representations can she attain her desired state of (bodily) perfection. In extreme cases, her disavowal of illness borders on a state of psychotic denial of reality: she insists that she feels well and is not ill, which in accordance with her unconscious denial, is true. What others forewarn is pointless, for she is certain that she can risk inanition with impunity. This denial of danger is beyond adolescent rebelliousness. It indicates a level of magical thinking that sustains a delusion of power. Her relinquishment of a normal biological need for food implies the presence of a wish for a secret glorification of her capacity for suffering. Outwardly she surrenders to feelings of desolation. Inwardly she savors her special condition, perversely, for she sees her rage as turning into a triumph over the hated introjects. It might be said that she prepares for the kind of silent instinctual storm that is sometimes known to take place among those who prepare to commit suicide.

The psychological setting is yet more complex. The clinical data indicate that the patient detects the unconscious destructive aims of her parents against her. Their behavior and attitudes, as appeared in the cases of Helen and Ariel, suggest that the parents, too, are trapped in their destructive wishes. Helen, at age 30, said her parents should never have had children because they cared only about their wishes for themselves. Ariel's mother saw her daughter's somatic troubles as givens that would always be with her, so nothing need be done about them. One has to consider that both girls, in profound obedience to their mothers, unconsciously perceived the mothers' unconscious death wishes against them. This reasoning requires the support of much more clinical data than have so far been gathered. Had Helen and Ariel been patients in psychoanalytic treatment instead of subjects in a clinical research effort with necessarily restricted purposes, then reports of their affective states, their fantasies, and their dreams would have provided the kinds of information required to help support or refute the proposition I have brought forward.

2. The regressive aims: The second unconscious aim of the anorexic person, that I suggest, attaches to the first aim to crowd out the mental representations of the hated introjects, but is more regressive. Several authors have noted a wish of the anorexic to stop time, to stop the body from growing older, to go back to childhood and an imagined freedom from present anxieties. Keiser (1958), for example, referred to a patient who explicitly described a wish to return to the womb as "a yearning for a state in which a mouth was unnecessary. In the womb he would be fed by the absorption of maternal fluids" (p. 360). My reasoning follows from Lewin's (1950) proposition concerning the oral triad of wishes: to devour (to eat), to be devoured (to be eaten—to enjoy a yielding relaxation), and to go to sleep. Certain elements characteristic of sleep gain representation in the manic state: "Sleep is rejected in favor of elated overactivity. If mania, by an extension of definition, is a special form or equivalent of sleep, it is certainly a very vigilant one. . ." (p. 37). Considering this paradox, Lewin described a state of ecstasy as the fulfillment of the oral triad that ends in the wish to relax and be devoured in happy sleep:

> An easy transition leads from the rapt, inwardly attentive ecstatic states to the trance and to states more nearly resembling sleep. Indeed, the words *trance* and *ecstasy* were [in his clinical cases] often used interchangeably. Trances, transports, and ecstasies have been called dreamlike, and all three words suggest a type of partial sleep or somnambulic equivalent. . . . The predormescent state of yielding to relaxation, with its ideational content to be swallowed and join the mother, can lead to heaven or to nirvana [p. 150].

We need to go back to ask again what unconscious force impels the anorexic person to risk her life with outward calm. I have referred to the beliefs of religious zealots in the Middle Ages and the Renaissance who aspired to a state of purification by vowing a renunciation of earthly pleasures (Bemporad, 1996). Their asceticism brought them to experience feelings of exaltation, sometimes of ecstasy. Hogan (1983b) described the feeling of moral superiority in anorexic patients who take intense pride in their starved, bony figures. Two of his patients, in this mood, displayed transient identifications with Christ (pp. 138–139). In the eighteenth and nineteenth centuries, some of the young women who starved themselves for religious reasons found ways to pretend they were existing without benefit of any food, until their pretenses were undone, and their dishonesties shamed them (Brumberg, 1988). We have a comparable historic account (Brown, 1986) of a dramatic failure of abstinence in the story of one Benedetta Carlini, a religious mystic in Renaissance Italy. Unusual in her story is the available knowledge of her childhood. At her birth in 1590 to a family of high social standing, she was not expected to live. Her devout father prayed earnestly for her life, and when she indeed survived, in gratitude he at once dedicated her to a religious life. Benedetta, unlike most girls of that time, was as a young child given a strict religious education in Christian doctrine. Soon she began to have strange experiences (for example, a black dog threatened her—was he a devil in disguise?). More uncanny events that she experienced privately were assumed to have come from preternatural sources. Why did God choose her to help fight the devil? Perhaps because she was chosen to embrace the world of God. At age 9 she made a long journey to a convent far from home. Her behavior there was exemplary until she began to tell about more strange visions. The nuns at first assumed that the visions derived from the devotional literature she had been reading and the religious paintings and sculptures in her present environment. Probably the visions were hallucinatory, part of a psychological state not understood in her time. Questions arose among her superiors.

> The problem was not whether the visions were real or not, but whether they were diabolical or heavenly in origin.... Upon hearing Jesus tell her that he would always be with her, "she felt fear . . . and then terror. . . ." Yet the fear . . . always gave way gradually to feelings of great happiness and contentment . . . and she felt in love with Jesus [pp. 48–49].

She must have reached a psychotic state, as is made clearer when after more time she showed miraculous stigmata on her body, like those of Christ. The stories she told about her sublime experiences were regarded with so much awe that at an early age she rose to the position of abbess. And yet, her accounts of stories she experienced in her "trances" were at odds with religious and realistic beliefs. As new doubts arose about them, she was pressed to explain them but could not. Then she began to complain of numerous somatic problems too obscure to be understood medically. On the advice of her confessor, she tried to suppress her visions, for they appeared to be an outrage of God's grace. Her physical symptoms increased. "The deep sense of conflict between her natural inclination to give in to ecstatic experiences and her desire to follow the advice of her confessor weighed very heavily on her mind. . . . . She wanted desperately to believe that her visions were good, that they were of divine origin and that they exalted her" (p. 53). Her continuing accounts of dramatic conversations with Christ, and of exchanging her heart with his, perhaps a metaphor for a fantasied sexual encounter, brought such fright to her superiors that they assigned a younger woman to watch over her at all times. Then she reached a too strange state of exhilaration about her coming marriage to Christ. The marriage, she averred, meant he had to protect her from all vice, so he ordered her not to eat meat, eggs, and milk products, and not to drink anything but water, and he appointed an angel to help her maintain spiritual purity. When once she tried to eat one of the forbidden foods, she choked and vomited what she had eaten. After her trancelike vision of a splendid marriage to Christ, she immediately returned to her normal senses as if nothing unusual had happened. This led to a fresh wave of skepticism about her strange stories. A series of investigations disclosed that all her accounts of mystical experiences were fabricated. Her worst undoing came to light in the disclosure by her guardian of a long-standing sexual relationship between them, at Benedetta's demand. Female homosexual acts, in that time and place, constituted the worst imaginable sexual transgression. Benedetta was forced to surrender to the truth, as far as she knew it. She lost her position of abbess, escaped the death penalty for her sins, and spent the rest of her life in prison under tormenting conditions until her death at 71.

The hallucinated marriage to Christ can have represented a psychotic oedipal victory for Benedetta. In line with her father's wish, she believed she owed her life to the church, a belief not shared by her mother until the mother was persuaded by her husband that he was right. Therefore, when the child Benedetta prepared for travel to the convent, her mother had advised her that she must now forsake her real mother and see the Virgin Mary as her true mother. It is imaginable that the child felt abandoned by both of her parents to the church, and in a tangled mental state tried to construe her position with imaginings about who she really was, an ordinary religious girl, or one destined miraculously to be mothered by the Virgin and married to Christ.

In confusion about her sexual impulses in adolescence and after, she felt invested by erotic "commands" to find a psychical connection to Christ in whatever form possible in her environment. She may have believed that the guardian was placed with her to provide satisfaction in a unity with the most holy figures she knew of, the Virgin representing her mother, later Christ representing her father. While the self-starvation of religious ascetics stemmed from an ideal altogether different from that of the modern anorexic adolescent, this true story of Benedetta who gave up mother and father for her union with holiness and for a way back to an infantile security, has a psychological relevance to anorexic young women in the present who have acute longings to be loved, perhaps even adored, by parents who actually and endlessly frustrated these longings, with little or no awareness of doing so.

Our interest here is in the exaltation that Benedetta experienced during her trances of received miracles. It seems that in her imagined conversations with Christ and imagined marriage to him she felt ecstasy in a belief that she had achieved a special state of spiritual grace. Such feelings of elevation, though far less intense, can have been present in Helen and Ariel, as in some other anorexic patients who feel immense pride in being able to control their hunger, thus to be in full command of their other instinctual impulses as well. Among patients more severely anorexic than Helen and Ariel, the abstinence probably is felt to bestow a unique strength even when they honestly protest that they feel no hunger and cannot possibly eat. The presumptive unconscious fantasy, as I have suggested above, is that self-starvation will bring freedom from the hated introjects. If death were the main intention of the patient, she could find easier ways to achieve it. But in keeping with her ambivalence toward her parents and toward her own longing to rid herself of their mental representations, she aims to destroy the representations, slowly, acting upon a grim wish to destroy them. For this deed she is ready to pay the painful price of starvation. It may be presumed that Benedetta experienced her miracles in altered states of consciousness, years before she stopped eating adequately; and that the mixture of religious abstinence and instinctual excitements of adolescence brought her to an uncanny state, leading her to believe that she had attained the higher plane of living assigned to her at her birth. A related unconscious wish may exist in those who "willingly" starve themselves so as to reach a state of supreme liberation and bliss, a state of Nirvana, which brings an end of suffering, and simultaneously an end of desires. The bad dream Helen reported at age 30 (chapter 4) appeared to contain such a wish for rebirth. The self-destructive behaviors and isolated affects of both Helen and Ariel suggest the presence of wishes to achieve a perfect (infantile) freedom from devastating inner conflicts.

3. Social change: A third contribution to the prevalence of adolescent anorexia, at least in the United States, appears to have emerged from changes of mores in probably all socioeconomic classes. The indirect result has been an increasing demand for freedom for promiscuous aggressiveness in speech and action, presently observable in age groups from early childhood through the first four or five decades of life. Some of these social changes appeared in the 1920s, in a period when a rudimentary knowledge of psychoanalytic theory promoted a popular fascination with self-knowledge. Many groups placed a high value on self-understanding (Benjamin and Dixon, 1996), and in the next decades a deep misunderstanding of psychoanalytic ideas took shape in our culture. It began with a wishful and naive idea that since neurotic problems resulted from repression of sexual

and aggressive instinctual wishes, repression was bad. Therefore, if children's energies were going to be freed for productive and happy lives, strict methods of child rearing and child education had to be renounced. A wave of progressive education enlarged our knowledge of children's emotional needs, but the importance of freedom for personal expression of personal wishes and ideas was adopted too rapidly, with insufficient awareness of the pace with which new ideas can be safely and thoughtfully exercised. In the 1930s and 1940s many parents and educators, with the best intentions, mistakenly equated permissiveness and individual freedom with personal growth (Olden, 1952). By the end of the twentieth century we saw the effects of a long epidemic of overstimulation and overgratification of infantile desires, in offerings of pacifiers (of all sorts) to children, adolescents, and young adults. At the same time there has been a complementary dismissal of historically valued social mores that in the past were expressed in civil courtesies and the work ethic. One of the results has been an artificial aggrandizement of self-esteem among many whose emotional and intellectual development is still in flux, and whose ego ideals are loose, narrow, or immature.

But in this too liberal social setting, the "superego" does not sit by idly. When parents have been remiss, knowingly or not, in not setting limits to their child's free speech and action, the conscience of the normal child is overwhelmed. When the adolescent is not or does not feel protected from asocial feelings and actions, his or her superego demands go out of order: they are too lenient or too harsh or both. Then the adolescent, unless psychotic or psychopathic, can feel a degree of remorse that can hardly be verbalized, but demands reparation. In good circumstances the healing is attained in improved personal conduct and in achievements that strengthen the ego. In bad circumstances, the adolescent unconsciously experiences excessive guilt about past rage and aggression against those adults who have, or seemed to have, failed the child or adolescent. Then he or she resorts to harsher means of setting his or her self-esteem aright by some form of self-punishment. When other circumstances, such as those described in previous chapters, are present, self-punishment by starvation has a fair chance of becoming a symptom of choice to quell intolerable feelings of guilt. The convictions of guilt, worthlessness, and deficiency can be all-enveloping, bringing about the patient's wholly negative self-image and the surrender of hope.

Early on, Helen and Ariel lost their capacities to feel pleasure in their bodies, or to reach out for gratification from being with people and from higher learning. By the beginning of adolescence, they who had long longed to be in control could not govern their accumulated self-accusations for having screamed too much, demanded too much, complained too much, and rebelled too much. By midadolescence, it appears, a rising sense of reality rendered them unable to simply blame their parents for their unhappiness. Their aggression recoiled against themselves, in their sadomasochistic conviction that they had lost their chance to be loved. They might as well show the world—their parents—that they no longer cared, an exquisite identification with the aggressor. They could dramatize their unlovability by starving themselves, with an aggressive bonus in worrying their parents, a libidinal bonus in feeling proud of their unearthly self-control, and an infantile grandiosity in assuming that the hostility residing in their self-starvation cannot invoke punishment.

Self-starvation, Boris (1984) wrote, "is a wonderful antidote for guilt and reparation—witness Lent and Yom Kippur and the taboo of foods in other cultures. So is purgation; the vomiting and exercise of the bulimic is not solely to evacuate calories; they are a means of disgorging guilt" (p. 438). The control that the anorexic patient exercises over her hunger is specious. It expresses a bravado about her sadomasochistic compromise, and a hiding of her intense guilt and need for punishment (Mintz, 1992), as noted above. As Helen and Ariel were leaving adolescence and perceiving the futility of their demands of their parents, they could also recognize their parents' failings with more tolerance than before. They could say to themselves: "Enough of this anger and demand for revenge! Enough of this need to reject them and hate them! Stop, and just give up!" And they did give up some of their conscious hatred, but also their expectations that they could ever love and be loved. An important base for the anorexic syndrome appears to lie in so great an incapacity to contain aggressive demands and to be relieved of oppressive guilt that they must seek redemption in slow self-destruction.The anorexia of Helen and Ariel was not so severe that they were in immediate mortal danger, but at age 30 they were still oppressed by severe anxieties and somatic symptoms.

I have offered the idea that the self-starvation of anorexic persons is motivated by three unconscious wishes. The first is to destroy the internalized mental representations of the hated introjects; the second is to achieve a Nirvana-like peace; the third is to accept punishment by the superego in order to allay a consuming guilt for indulgences partly determined by social change.[2] The anorexic patient

---

[2] *New York Times,* December 9, 1999: "Once a country of catastrophic famines. . . . [China] is becoming obsessed with thin. . . . While some are shedding pounds for health, most are pursuing a new notion of beauty. . . . Cases of anorexia and bulimia, once virtually unknown in China, have multiplied dramatically in the last five years. . . . [Dr. Zhang] said that her patients tend to be well-off and educated urban girls in their middle to late teens. . . . She attributes the girls' problems to a combina-

abstains from more than food. She narrows down her corporal needs. Helen and Ariel, in their colorless lives, lost their appetites for staying alive and well. Helen could enjoy only a bizarre kind of painting that expressed something ominous and inscrutable. As she described the recently finished picture, it must have looked like a formless fecal mass, symbolizing a preoccupation with destructive wishes, a hostile display of feelings of worthlessness—and yet a certain vanity. One would hope that this kind of painting represented for her a desirable transition to other forms of artistic endeavor. What were Ariel's aims? She expressed no aspirations other than for fame and marriage until in her late twenties she began to interest herself in law. In her case, one might hope that she could in time sublimate an old wish to address the unjust emotional wounds she had suffered and to quiet her retributive anger.

The explanations I have suggested for the development of anorexia in two adolescents have derived from a reliance on clinical and theoretical knowledge of instinctual processes, unconscious fantasies, defense structures, and compromise formations that emerge and diversify from early infancy to adolescence. My intention has been to enlarge our reasoning about the origins of the disorder. To learn more about those origins and their outcomes, we shall need empirical data that can reveal the ongoing psychological conditions that spark the development of specific unconscious conflicts abiding in anorexia.

---

tion of the intense academic competition in Chinese high schools and the growing social pressure to be beautiful as well. A study in West Malaysia (Goh, Ong, and Subramanian) found that nine out of 15 subjects with eating disorders had body image disturbances.

Chapter 11

The Present Problem

The *The American Journal of Psychiatry Supplement* (2000) states: The percentage of individuals with anorexia nervosa who *fully* recover is modest. Although some patients improve symptomatically over time, a substantial proportion continue to have disturbances with body image, disordered eating, and other psychiatric difficulties. . . . Over all, about two-thirds of patients continue to have enduring morbid food and weight preoccupation, and up to 40 percent have bulimic symptoms [p. 6]. . . . In many other countries, there appears to be an overall increase in eating disorders, even in cultures in which the disorder is rare [p. 7].

For the parents of an anorexic child or adolescent the disorder is unnerving. It seems to have arrived without any immediate cause. The remote cause most frequently named is a disturbed relation to the mother in the patient's infancy, but many psychiatric disorders are attributable to that cause, and no unique form of the disturbance has been identified as being at the root of eating disorders. Anorexia, because of its most usual appearance in adolescence, is often attributed to the adolescents' declaration of freedom from parental control, or their presumption of invulnerability. These explanations are not incorrect but too general. Other conditions that over time have been named as relevant to the disorder are also not distinctive for it. For example, prolonged subdued states, or excessive fussiness or crying, early forerunners of depressive vulnerability, may appear in the first months of life. Hyperactivity, and an immature demand to be in control, which is prominent in adolescent anorexia, may be manifest in the second year of life, in a variety of forms. Conflicts about body image may arise during the latency period and especially in prepuberty without being a prelude to an eating disorder. Asceticism and depression usually appear later, in early to midadolescence, and may be associated with obsessional symptoms more than with an eating disorder. I have referred to a number of other behaviors that appear to set an early base for the later anorexic condition, in particular the misery of the screaming infant who must vomit or throw away the food that has been given without love. That misery leaves the infant and young child sad and anxious to find any possible substitute satisfaction. Some relief of tension may be found in repetitive activities (part or whole-body pleasurable excitement), or in prolonged clinging to formless objects like blankets; the latter being a sole reminder of feeling the pleasure of the mother's soft, warm, enveloping arms, however brief that pleasure may have been.

For Helen and Ariel we have seen cumulative psychological insults experienced during infancy and early childhood, a rise of disturbances as childhood proceeded, in open conflicts with parents, psychosomatic symptoms, and social withdrawal or discord in later childhood and early adolescence. In those years and through adolescence Helen and Ariel suffered periods of pervasive loneliness, aggravated by their parents' affectlessness. How did it happen that these mothers and fathers, believing themselves to be caring and responsible parents, were so relentlessly inaccessible, so unable to experience pleasure in their children's behavior and activities, that the girls were left to feel increasing states of desperation, and to surrender to self-destructive impulses? The outstanding reason that emerged in their histories appears to have lain in their parents' abdication from responsiveness to the children's emotional states, their incapacity to stir positive responses from the children, and their primary absorption in (misguided) efforts to retrieve some dignity for themselves. The children's presence was recognized, but as they grew from infancy to early childhood, we observed no fond glances between the parents and the children, no signs of good humor, no kinds of play, certainly no laughter, no praise for achievements like beginning to speak words or to walk, no glad references to birthdays (Ariel's mother once forgot the date of her son's birthday), and as far as our observations and the parents' reports could tell, never any delight in the children's presence; and no expressions of sympathy when the children were not well. Ariel's mother expressed no concern about the child's fright during or after her accident at 15 months; to other people in following years, however, Ariel often called attention to the scar on her forehead.

The narcissistic self-containment of the parents was presumably determined in large part by the unempathic climate in which they themselves had been reared (poor relationships with their families of origin). The bareness of their positive affect may also have been fixed by their marital disappointments, and their failure to develop any ego ideals or earnest aspirations. Helen's mother was ever eager for something new to do outside of home and family. As Helen put it, mother always wants her own way, her own wishes always come first. This mother appeared to place no value on human relationships beyond her bondage to her husband. Ariel's mother showed more self-sufficiency than Helen's mother, but was hemmed in by her compulsive need to satisfy herself in diversions of home care, cooking, finding new restaurants, and traveling. She saw Ariel as being bored, possibly a projection of her own inner state. As she thus withdrew from her child, she was not disposed to be aware of the child's growing emptiness of positive affect, even though Ariel often spoke of feeling sad. Later on Ariel, like her mother, referred to various activities as boring. This feeling of ennui came to be unhappily balanced by an aggressive stance, demands for immediate gratifications, and an almost hopeless relinquishment of finding pleasure in human relations or in an inquiring mind. Her mother considered Ariel's somatic problems as givens. "She'll always have stomach problems," mother said dryly, as if such problems were outside of her domain. In contrast, mother was ever ready during Ariel's infancy and childhood to describe her own physical troubles, which made attending to Ariel so difficult for her.

The core of these parents' reluctance to care for their children with competence and affection lay in their stark inability to regard their children as persons in their own right. They expected the children to fit into the parents' patterns of living. It was enough for these parents to know that the children existed and to assume, tacitly, that they would grow by themselves. They took little or no note of the children's fears, hopes, desires, and preoccupations. Helen, calling herself a fatalist, must have felt destined to fall into a pattern set for her by her parents. Only her artistic abilities could save her. As noted above, when as a young adult she was asked why she often returned to visit with her parents for whom she had no feeling, she said resignedly, "You go back to the only thing you know."

It is no wonder that these over- and undercontrolled girls gave way to pathological measures to take absolute control of their appetites, with sadomasochistic efforts to control their parents. They had come to recognize the ignorance, insensitivity, and self-interest that governed their parents' parental behaviors, and that would not change. Had the fathers been able to provide some of the empathy, tact, and good humor that the mothers lacked, the two girls might have been saved from the mothers' indifference. But with both parents emotionally inaccessible, Helen and Ariel had no relief from a realization of their unimportance in their parents' eyes. It appears that in unconscious identification with their parents, both girls stifled the libidinal investments they had once made in those parents. Yet they retained their poorly hidden depression.[1]

I have found no general discussions of conditions that before puberty may lead to the advent of anorexia, in spite of the clinical understanding that the original causative factor is a disturbed relationship between the infant or young child and the mother. The great majority of publications on the subject are devoted to epidemiology, and to treatment of the disorder after it makes its appearance in puberty or adolescence. The consequent assumption that it stems from emotional conflict mostly in those years, has obscured the need to look for precursors other than the troubled early relationship to the mother. A pervasive error has lain in a general assumption that the problem is one of adolescence,

---

[1]Among the 50 male subjects willing to be interviewed in detail at age 18, none reported a serious eating disorder, but self-destructive symptoms were present in 14, as shown in severe depression, hyperactivity, tendencies toward delinquency, dangerous risk-taking, and regressive behaviors.

even though we have learned from psychoanalytic theory and practice that adolescence often stirs up a recrudescence of early childhood dilemmas. The observational data I have gathered about the mothers' maternal behavior and their attitudes toward Helen and Ariel, and about the girls' development from birth to late adolescence, has enabled me to search for premonitory signs of their eating disorders.

For the most part, investigations of anorexia nervosa have been the province of medicine and psychiatry, according to its diagnosis in 1873 as a nervous illness. Its study belongs as well as to pediatrics and psychology. Anorexia has turned out to be one form of pathology that takes a surreptitious start in the first years of life. All that I have read and thought about it indicates that it represents a distressful consummation of a process that has its onset in infancy, with a possibility of lasting psychosocial and psychosomatic illness. In a limited number of cases, psychiatric or psychoanalytic treatment deflects the force of the illness. Or the patient musters sufficient inner strength to take realistic control of the aberration that has thrived on self-destructive impulses, a loss of libido, and inexpressible yearnings for atonement and peace.

Infants and toddlers have limited capacities to express unrest. Aside from crying out, screaming, biting, hitting, and pushing or hurling things away, or social and physical withdrawal, or excessive sleep, they have no means of escape from indifferent care. Helen's mother had no idea of her baby's joylessness when she said, "She's happy whenever anyone talks to her," as if Helen's threshold for happiness was ever-present, only waiting to be tapped by anyone at all. It is a melancholy fact that in our culture and society so many parents expect to rear their young with minimal understanding of the infant's, or child's, or adolescent's continuing needs for consistent love, protection, and containment. Parents bring their own emotional needs to their task of child care, and often require more help to rear a child than they ever dared to imagine. The pain of admitting this can be unbearable. Then their only relief may be in passive neglect or active hostility to the child, attitudes they may hardly be aware of.

Training of students in the healing professions to observe aspects of parental behaviors and attitudes, and their short- and long-term effects, from earliest infancy on and ideally through their fourth and fifth years, is much to ask for, but the rewards in broadening a child's capacities for sustained pleasure and for productive living can be huge. The twentieth century was called the century of the child, and immense progress has been made. Present public education about loving and protective care of infants and young children is increasing. One aim of this book is to direct attention to the psychological desolation that may be avoided by our taking time to become kindly engaged with a young life, to take notice, look at, listen to, and respond to an infant's smiles and cries even when they are silent.

Afterword

Franz Kafka perceives the hidden aggressive wishes of the hunger artist. The man is not simply a lamentable figure who never received the love he longed for. That may be true, but it is also true that he is obstinate in his demand for an audience to witness and to pity his slow wasting away. Should he not be admired for his fortitude in not compromising? Yet he equivocates: "But you shouldn't admire me," as if he is not sure that his wish for the right food is justified. Then again, the wish is beyond his control, he cannot help it. He has been in despair for a long, long time, and has never been able to get rid of his agitation or his grievance. And so with his very last breaths he must try to stir awe, in any remaining listener, for his stoic readiness to die for his conviction that hunger has been his vital experience.

Appendix

The Longitudinal Study: Phase 1

The original research data about mother-infant interaction were drawn from The Infancy Research Project, a larger, horizontal study of individual differences among infants in Topeka, Kansas (N = 128). Sixteen infants at each of eight age levels (four to 32 weeks) and their mothers were observed in one session of approximately four hours (Escalona and Leitch, 1952). Each mother was interviewed once, during the session when her infant was observed and tested (Gesell Developmental Schedules). I was an assistant investigator in that project for one year, from 1949 to 1950. In order to study relations between maternal behavior and infant development, I selected 32 of the dyads, that is, eight infants at each of four age levels (4, 12, 20, and 28 weeks) and their mothers. For the eight 4-week-old infants, it appears that oral satisfaction was secondary to the very young infants' need for whole body comfort and security. For the other 24 (older) infants, the need for oral satisfaction appeared to be primary, as had been previously assumed by psychoanalytic investigators for all infants. I inferred, provisionally, that the young infant's first need was for kinesthetic and tactile feelings of safe body balance and security. (Bowlby, as indicated in chapter 1, apparently had not noticed my prior finding [1956] about the infant's first need for body security, quickly followed by the need for oral satisfaction. He proposed that the oral drive was secondary to a primal biological need for proximity to the mother. His argument has led to the present flourishing of attachment theory. My pilot study constituted the first direct observational study of normal infants living at home with both parents and cared for by their mothers (Brody, 1956). It allowed for a provisional classification of maternal behavior with infants up to the age of 28 weeks.

I renewed my studies with a larger population in New York City to find out whether my first classifications of maternal behavior would show consistency at several intervals through the infants' first year (at age 3 days, 6, 26, and 52 weeks) with a larger sample (N = 131). If so, we might be able to construct a provisional typology of maternal behavior in order to see how it might be related to the infants' development at one year. Each mother's maternal behavior with her infant was observed directly and in 16mm films of entire feeding episodes, and rated according to her empathy, competence, and consistency while feeding her infant. My hypothesis, that the mother's activity of feeding her infant was the best single index of a mother's overall conduct with that infant, was supported. The 131 mothers, first classified in eight groups, were reclassified into two, A and B, for statistical purposes. Group A (N = 42) consisted of the mothers who were empathic and/or consistent (Types I and VI) in their mothering. They were later referred to as the "more adequate" mothers. Group B (N = 89) consisted of the mothers whose infant care was found to be restrained (Type II), or aggressive (Type III), or harsh (Type IV), or withdrawn (Type V), or timid (Type VII), or a few who could not be classified with any of the others (Type VIII); these were later included in the group of "less adequate" mothers.

At age 1, the infants of the Group A mothers were found to show, cumulatively over the year, significantly more Signs of Favorable Development and significantly fewer Signs of Disturbance than the infants of Group B (Brody and Axelrad, 1970b).

The Longitudinal Study: Phase 2

The first follow-up study enabled us to observe aspects of early mental health and character development in the children up to age 7 (N = 121). Because of the hiatus in the study between the children's age 1 and age 2 or 3, we missed gathering observations and reports of their toilet training, speech, and motor development in those important years. Our hypothesis in this second phase of the research, setting aside trauma or very unusual events in the child's or the family's life, that maternal behavior and attitudes are characterized by an enduring pattern observable from the child's infancy until the beginning of latency proper, was supported (Brody and Axelrad, 1978). We found significant and consistent differences between the development of the children of Group A and Group B in their first year of life, and again at ages 3, 6, and 7.

We were at first surprised that at ages 4 and 5 differences in the development of Group A and Group B children, in nursery school and in kindergarten, and in the maturity of their object relations, were not statistically significant. Our explanation was that the failure of significance between the two groups at ages 4 and 5 reflected many clinical findings that these are the years in childhood when the oedipal conflict is most intense. Most children at these ages show more troubled behaviors than during their previous or their subsequent years of childhood. The essential differences between the children of the more or the less adequate mothers that were seen at ages 1 and 3 reappeared, however, at age 6, at the beginning of latency; and again more strongly at age 7 (Brody and Axelrad, 1978). According to the data provided by our successive interviews with mothers and fathers over the years, we found no notable changes in their characteristic attitudes toward their children or their modes of child rearing. On the whole, the children's familial and environmental conditions did not change appreciably. No subject had a serious illness or accident; there was one death of an infant sibling; and one severe accident of a younger sibling. There were seven divorces and/or legal separations of parents in the period covering the first follow-up study (up to the children's age 7), from 1968 to 1973.

The Longitudinal Study: Phase 3

The third phase of the project dealt with the psychological status and the character of the subjects (those originally observed through their first year with their mothers) at age 18. Funding was private, because foundation personnel believed it would not be possible to find the subjects after a hiatus of approximately ten years. From among the 118 adolescent subjects believed to be traceable, I found 98 (computers that might have traced more were not yet available). Of these, 91 were able to continue their participation in the research. Each was interviewed at length by me, and received a battery of diagnostic psychological tests by clinical psychologists who had no previous contact with the subjects or their parents. The findings appeared in Brody and Siegel (1992). At their age 30, 76 subjects were seen by Henry Massie, who videotaped his interviews with them. An account of his findings is in preparation.

References

Abraham, K. (1916), The first pregenital stage of the libido. In: *Selected Papers of Karl Abraham.* London: Hogarth Press, 1948, pp. 248–279.
——— (1924a), The influence of oral erotism on character formation. In: *Selected Papers of Karl Abraham.* London: Hogarth Press, 1948, pp. 393–406.
——— (1924b), A short history of the development of the libido, viewed in the light of mental disorders. In: *Selected Papers of Karl Abraham.* London: Hogarth Press, 1948, pp. 418–501.
Ainsworth, M. D. S., & Wittig, B. (1969), Attachment and exploratory behavior of one-year-olds in a strange situation. In: *Determinants of Infant Behavior,* Vol. 4, ed. B. M. Foss. New York: Barnes & Noble, pp. 111–136.
American Psychiatric Association (1994), *Diagnostic and Statistical Manual of Mental Disorders,* 4th ed. (DSM IV). Washington, DC: American Psychiatric Press.
American Psychiatric Association (2000) Practice guideline. For the treatment of patients with eating disorders, revised. *Amer. J. Psychiat.,* 157 (Suppl):1.
Baumrind, D. (1993), The average expectable environment is not good enough: A response to S. Scarr. *Child Develop.,* 64:1299–1317.
Bemporad, J. R. (1996), Self-starvation through the ages. *Internat. J. Eating Disord.,* 19:217–237.
Benedek, T. (1938), Adaptation to reality in early infancy. *Psychoanal. Quart.,* 7:200–215.

Benjamin, L. T., & Dixon, D. N. (1996), Dream analysis by mail: An American woman seeks Freud's advice. *Amer. Psychologist,* 51:461–468.

Bernfeld, S. (1929), *The Psychology of the Infant.* London: Kegan Paul, Trench, Trubner.

Bibring, E. (1953), The mechanism of depression. In: *Affective Disorders,* ed. P. Greenacre. New York: International Universities Press, pp. 13–48.

Bliss, E. L., & Branch, C. H. Hardin (1960), *Anorexia Nervosa: Its History, Psychology, and Biology.* New York: Paul Hoeber.

Boris, H. N. (1984), On the treatment of anorexia nervosa. *Internat. J. Psycho-Anal.,* 65:435–442.

Bourgignon, O. (1995), L'objet transitionel n'est pas une étage normale du development. *L'Evolution Psychiatrique,* 60:267–284.

Bowlby, J. (1940), The influence of early environment, neurosis and neurotic character. *Internat. J. Psycho-Anal.,* 21:154-178.

——— (1944), Forty-four juvenile thieves: Their character and home life. *Internat. J. Psycho-Anal.,* 25:19–52, 107–127.

——— (1951), *Maternal Care and Mental Health.* Geneva, WHO. New York: Columbia University Press.

——— (1958), The nature of the child's tie to the mother. *Internat. J. Psycho-Anal.,* 39:350–373.

——— (1960a), Grief and mourning in infancy and childhood. *The Psychoanalytic Study of the Child,* 15:9–52. New York: International Universities Press.

——— (1960b), Separation anxiety. *Internat. J. Psycho-Anal.,* 41:89–113.

——— (1969), *Attachment and Loss,* Vol. 1. London: Hogarth Press.

——— (1973), *Attachment and Loss,* Vol. 2. New York: Basic Books.

Brazelton, T. B., & Als, H. (1979), Four early stages in the development of mother-infant interaction. *The Psychoanalytic Study of the Child,* 34:349–369. New Haven, CT: Yale University Press.

——— Tronick, E., Adamson, L., Als, H., & Wise, S. (1975), Early mother-infant reciprocity. In: *Parent-Infant Interaction.* Ciba Foundation Symposium 33. Amsterdam: Elsevier, pp. 137–154.

Brenman, M., & Knight, R. P. (1945), Self-starvation and compulsive hopping with paradoxical reaction to hypnosis. *Amer. J. Orthopsychiatry*, 15:65–71.

Breuer, J., & Freud, S. (1893–1895), Studies on Hysteria. *Standard Edition*, 2. London: Hogarth Press, 1955.

Brody, S. (1956), *Patterns of Mothering*. New York: International Universities Press.

——— (1960), Self-rocking in infancy. *J. Amer. Psychoanal. Assn.*, 8:464–491.

——— (1964), Formation of the body image. In: *Passivity: A Study of Its Development and Expression in Boys*. New York: International Universities Press, pp. 73–82.

——— (1975), Comments, in a Panel Report, Parenthood as a developmental phase, reported by H. Parens. *J. Amer. Psychoanal. Assn.* 23:158–160.

——— (1980), Transitional objects: Idealization of a phenomenon. *Psychoanal. Quart.*, 49:561–605.

——— (1981), The concepts of attachment and bonding. *Internat. J. Psycho-Anal.*, 29:815–829.

——— (1982a), Psychoanalytic theories of infant development and its disturbances: A critical evaluation. *Psychoanal. Quart.*, 51:526–597.

——— (1982b), Fathers in nineteenth century novels: Some portrayal of unconscious conflict in paternal attitudes and behaviors. In: *Father and Child: Developmental and Clinical Perspectives*, ed. S. H. Cath, A. R. Gurwitt, & J. M. Ross. Boston: Little Brown, pp. 399–416.

——— Axelrad, S. (1970a), Film 5: Maternal behavior and object cathexis in the first year of life. *Maternal Behavior and Infant Development: Six Films of Mother–Infant Interaction*. Univ. California Extension Media Center, Berkeley, CA.

——— ——— (1970b), *Anxiety and Ego Formation in Infancy*. New York: International Universities Press.

——— ——— (1978), *Mothers, Fathers, and Children. Explorations in the Formation of Character in the First Seven Years*. New York: International Universities Press.

——— Siegel, M. (1992), The rise of the superego. In: *The Evolution of Character, Birth to 18 Years. A Longitudinal Study.* New York: International Universities Press, pp. 469–476.

Brown, J. C. (1986), *Immodest Acts. The Life of a Lesbian Nun.* New York: Oxford University Press.

Bruch, H. (1965), Anorexia and its differential diagnosis. *J. Nerv. & Ment. Dis.,* 141:555–566.

——— (1973), *Eating Disorders: Obesity, Anorexia, and the Person Within.* New York: Basic Books.

——— (1978), *The Golden Cage. The Enigma of Anorexia Nervosa.* Cambridge, MA: Harvard University Press.

Brumberg, J. J. (1982), Chlorotic Girls, 1870–1920: A historical perspective on female adolescence. *Child Develop.,* 53:1468–1477.

——— (1988), *Fasting Girls: The Emergence of Anorexia Nervosa as a Modern Disease.* Cambridge, MA: Harvard University Press.

Bynum, C. W. (1985), Fast, feast, and flesh. The religious significance of food to medieval women. *Representations,* 11:1–25.

Candland, D. K. (1993), *Feral Children and Clever Animals.* New York: Oxford University Press.

Carmichael, L. (1946), *Manual of Child Psychology.* New York: John Wiley.

Cassatt, M. (1891), Maternal caress. In: *Mother and Child in Modern Art,* Plate 13. The Baltimore Museum of Art, Baltimore, MD, ed. B. Hooton & N. N. Kaiden. New York: Duell, Sloan and Pierce.

Chatoor, I., Hirsh, R., Ganiban, J., Persinger, M., & Hamburg, E. (1998), Diagnosing infantile anorexia: The observations of interactions. *J. Amer. Acad. Child & Adol. Psychiatry,* 37:959–967.

Darwin, E. (1796), *Zoonomia, or The Laws of Organic Life.* London.

Deutsch, H. (1944), *The Psychology of Woman. A Psychoanalytic Interpretation,* Vol. 1. New York: Grune & Stratton, pp. 129–130.

Diamond, E. (1998), Hunger artists and holy men: Asceticism in rabbinical law and lore. Paper presented at the Jewish Theological Seminary Lehrhaus, New York City, March 24.

Dickes, R. (1978), Parents, transitional objects, and childhood fetishes. In: *Between Fantasy and Reality: Transitional Objects and Phenomena*, ed. S. Grolnick, L. Barkin, & W. Muensterberger. New York: Jason Aronson, pp. 307–331.
Edelson, M. (1986), Causal explanation in science and in psychoanalysis: Implications for writing a case history. *The Psychoanalytic Study of the Child*, 41:89–128. New Haven, CT: Yale University Press.
Eissler, K. (1943), Some psychiatric aspects of anorexia nervosa. *Psychoanal. Rev.*, 30:121–145.
Ellenberger, H. F. (1970), *The Discovery of the Unconscious. The History and Evolution of Dynamic Psychiatry*. New York: Basic Books.
Emde, R. N. (1983), The prerepresentational self and its affective core. *The Psychoanalytic Study of the Child*, 38:165–192. New Haven, CT: Yale University Press.
────── Gaensbauer, T. J., & Harmon, R. J. (1976), *Emotional Expression in Infancy: A Biobehavioral Study*. New York: International Universities Press.
Escalona, S., & Leitch, M. (1952), Early phases of personality development: A non-normative study of infant behavior. *Mon. Soc. Res. in Child Develop.*, 17.
Fenichel, O. (1945), *The Psychoanalytic Theory of Neurosis*. New York: W. W. Norton.
Ferenczi, S. (1913), Stages in the development of the sense of reality. In: *First Contributions to Psychoanalysis*. New York: Brunner/Mazel, 1980, pp. 213–239.
────── (1916–1917), Silence is golden. In: *Further Contributions to the Theory and Technique of Psycho-Analysis*. London: Hogarth Press, 1926, p. 250.
────── (1919), Nakedness as a means of inspiring terror. In: *Further Contributions to the Theory and Technique of Psycho-Analysis*. London: Hogarth Press, 1950, pp. 329–332.
────── (1929), The unwelcome child and the death instinct. In: *Final Contributions to the Theory and Technique of Psycho-Analysis*. London: Hogarth Press, 1950, pp. 102–107.

Field, T. M., Wheedon, R., Greenberg, R., & Cohen, D. (1982), Discrimination and imitation of facial expressions by neonates. *Science*, 218:79–81.
——— Schanberg, S. M., Scafidi, F., Bauer, C. R., Vega-Lahr, N., Garcia, R., Nystrom, J., & Kuhn, C. M. (1986), Tactile/kinesthetic stimulation effects on preterm neonates. *Pediatrics*, 77:654–658.
Fintzy, R. T. (1971), Vicissitudes of the transitional object in a borderline child. *Internat. J. Psycho-Anal.*, 52:107–114.
Forster, E. M. (1910), *Howard's End*. London: The Folio Society, 1973.
Freud, A. (1936), The ego and the mechanisms of defense. *Writings of Anna Freud*, Vol. 2. New York: International Universities Press.
——— (1946), The psychoanalytic study of infantile feeding disturbances. *The Psychoanalytic Study of the Child*, 2:119–132. New York: International Universities Press.
——— (1960), Discussion of Dr. John Bowlby's paper, Grief and mourning in infancy and early childhood. *The Psychoanalytic Study of the Child*, 15:53–62. New York: International Universities Press.
——— (1965), *Normality and Pathology in Childhood*. New York: International Universities Press, pp. 62–107.
——— (1970a), The symptomatology of childhood: A preliminary attempt at classification. *The Writings of Anna Freud*, Vol. 7. New York: International Universities Press, pp. 157–188.
——— (1970b), The infantile neurosis: Genetic and dynamic considerations. *The Writings of Anna Freud*, Vol. 7. New York: International Universities Press, pp. 189–203.
——— Burlingham, D. (1943), *War and Children*. New York: Medical War Books.
Freud, S. (1892–1899), Extracts from the Fliess papers. *Standard Edition*, 1:173–280. London: Hogarth Press, 1966.
——— (1905), Three Essays on the Theory of Sexuality. *Standard Edition*, 7:123–243. London: Hogarth Press, 1953.
——— (1914), On narcissism: An introduction. *Standard Edition*, 14:67–102. London: Hogarth Press, 1957.

——— (1915), Instincts and their vicissitudes. *Standard Edition*, 14:109–140. London: Hogarth Press, 1957.
——— (1917), Mourning and melancholia. *Standard Edition*, 14:237–258. London: Hogarth Press, 1957.
——— (1920), Beyond the pleasure principle. *Standard Edition*, 18:1–64. London: Hogarth Press, 1955.
——— (1923), The Ego and the Id. *Standard Edition*, 19:1–59. London: Hogarth Press, 1961.
——— (1926), Inhibitions, symptoms, and anxiety. *Standard Edition*, 20:75–175. London: Hogarth Press, 1959.
——— (1938), An outline of psychoanalysis. *Standard Edition*, 23:141–207. London: Hogarth Press, 1964.
Friedman, M. (1985), Survivor guilt in the pathogenesis of anorexia. *Psychiatry*, 48:25–39.
Fritz, G. K., Fritsch, S., & Hagino, O. (1997), Somatoform disorders in children and adolescents: A review of the past 10 years. *J. Amer. Child & Adolescent Psychiatry*, 3:1329–1338.
Furman, E. (1982), Mothers have to be there to be left. *The Psychoanalytic Study of the Child*, 37:15–28. New Haven, CT: Yale University Press.
Gesell, A. (1928), *Infancy and Human Growth*. New York: Macmillan.
Goh, S. E., Ong, S. B., & Subramanian, M. (1993), Eating disorders in Hong Kong. *Brit. J. Psychiatry*, 162:276–277.
Goldberg, S., Muir, R., & Kerr, J. (1995), *Attachment Theory: Social, Developmental, and Clinical Perspectives*. Hillsdale, NJ: Analytic Press.
Greenacre, P. (1953), Certain relationships between fetishism and faulty body image. *The Psychoanalytic Study of the Child*, 8:75–98. New York: International Universities Press.
Greenson, R. R. (1949), The psychology of apathy. *Psychoanal. Quart.*, 18:290–302.
——— (1953), On boredom. *J. Amer. Psychoanal. Assn.*, 1:7–21.
Gull, W. W. (1873), Anorexia (apepsia, anorexia, hysterica). In: *Evaluation of Psychosomatic Concepts. Anorexia Nervosa: A Paradigm*, ed. M. R. Kaufman & M. Heiman. New York: International Universities Press 1964, pp. 132–138.

Hanly, C. (1978), A critical consideration of Bowlby's ethological theory of anxiety. *Psychoanal. Quart.*, 47:364–380.

Harlow, H. F. (1961), The development of affectional patterns in infant monkeys. In: *Determinants of Infant Behaviour*, Vol. 1, ed. B. M. Foss. New York: John Wiley, pp. 75–80.

——— Zimmerman, R. R. (1959), The development of affectional responses in the infant monkey. *Science*, 130, 421.

Hartmann, H. (1939), *Ego Psychology and the Problem of Adaptation*. New York: International Universities Press, 1958.

Hildanus, F. (1646), *Proceedings of the Amer. Philosophical Society*, 102:507–509.

Hitchcock, J. (1992), The importance of aggression in the early development of children with eating disorders. In: *Psychodynamic Technique in the Treatment of Eating Disorders*, ed. C. P. Wilson, C. C. Hogan, & I. L. Mintz. Northvale, NJ: Jason Aronson, pp. 223–236.

Hogan, C. C. (1983a), Psychodynamics. In: *Fear of Being Fat. The Treatment of Anorexia Nervosa and Bulimia*, ed. C. P. Wilson, C. C. Hogan, & I. L. Mintz. New York: Jason Aronson, pp. 115–128.

——— (1983b), Object relations. In: *Fear of Being Fat. The Treatment of Anorexia Nervosa and Bulimia*, ed. C. P. Wilson, C. C. Hogan, & I. L. Mintz. New York: Jason Aronson, pp. 129–149.

——— (1983c), Technical problems in psychoanalytic treatment. In: *Fear of Being Fat. The Treatment of Anorexia Nervosa and Bulimia*, ed. C. P. Wilson, C. C. Hogan, & I. L. Mintz. New York: Jason Aronson, pp. 197–215.

——— (1992), The adolescent crisis in anorexia nervosa. In: *Psychodynamic Technique in the Treatment of Eating Disorders*, ed. C. P. Wilson, C. C. Hogan, & I. L. Mintz. New York: Jason Aronson, pp. 111–127.

Hug-Hellmuth, H. von (1919), A study of the mental life of the child. *Nervous & Mental Diseases Monograph*. Washington, DC: Nervous & Mental Diseases.

Jacobson, E. (1946), The effect of disappointment on ego and superego formation in normal and depressive development. *Psychoanal. Rev.*, 33:120–147.

Janet, P. (1907), *The Major Symptoms of Hysteria.* New York: The Macmillan Co.

Jones, E. (1929), Fear, guilt and hate. In: *Papers on Psychoanalysis.* London: Ballière, Tindall, & Cox, 1948, pp. 304–319.

Kafka, F. (1926), A hunger artist. In: *Franz Kafka: The Complete Stories,* ed. N. N. Glazer. New York: Schocken, 1971.

Katz, J. L. (1986), Long-distance running, anorexia nervosa, and bulimia: A report of two cases. *Compreh. Psychiatry,* 27:74–78.

Kaufman, M. R., & Heiman, M. (1964), *Evaluation of Psychosomatic Concepts.* New York: International Universities Press, 1964, pp. 141–155.

Keiser, S. (1958), Disturbances in abstract thinking and body-image formation. *J. Amer. Psychoanal. Assn.,* 6:628–652.

Klein, M. (1928), Early stages of the oedipal conflict. In: *Love, Guilt, and Reparation and Other Works, 1921–1945.* London: Hogarth Press, 1975, pp. 186–198.

—————— (1935), A contribution to the psychogenesis of manic–depressive states. In: *Love, Guilt, and Reparation and Other Works, 1921–1945.* London: Hogarth Press, 1975, pp. 236–247.

—————— (1936), Weaning. In: *Love, Guilt, and Reparation and Other Works, 1921–1945.* New York: Delacorte Press, 1975, pp. 290–305.

—————— (1937), Love, Guilt, and Reparation. In: *Love, Guilt, and Reparation and Other Works, 1921–1945.* London: Hogarth Press, 1975, pp. 306–343.

—————— (1940), Mourning and its relation to manic-depressive states. In: *Love, Guilt, and Reparation and Other Works, 1921–1945.* London: Hogarth Press, 1975, pp. 344–369.

—————— (1943–1944), Some theoretical conclusions regarding the emotional life of the infant. In: *Developments in Psycho-Analysis,* ed. J. Riviere. London: Hogarth Press, 1952, pp. 198–236.

—————— (1950), On observing the behaviour of infants. In: *Envy, Gratitude, and Other Works, 1946–1963.* London: Hogarth Press, 1975, pp. 94–121.

—————— (1952a), Some theoretical conclusions regarding the emotional life of the infant. In: *Envy, Gratitude, and Other Works, 1946–1963.* London: Hogarth Press, 1975, pp. 61–93.

——— (1952b), On observing the behaviour of young infants. In: *Envy, Gratitude, and Other Works, 1946–1963*. London: Hogarth Press, 1975, pp. 94–121.

Lasègue, C. (1873), On hysterical anorexia. *Medical Times and Gazette*, 368.

Lewin, B. D. (1950), *The Psychoanalysis of Elation*. New York: W. W. Norton.

Linn, B. D. (1955), Some developmental aspects of the body image. *Internat. J. Psycho-Anal.*, 36:36–42.

Lorand, S. (1943), Anorexia nervosa. *Psychosom. Med.*, 5:282–292.

Lorenz, K. Z. (1935), Companionship in bird life. Fellow members of the species as releasers of social behavior. In: *Instinctive Behavior*, ed. C. H. Schiller. New York: International Universities Press, 1957, pp. 83–128.

MacCulloch, J. A. (1912), Fasting. In: *Encyclopedia of Religion and Ethics*, Vol. 5:759–765, ed. J. Hastings. New York: Scribner's Sons.

Mahler, M. S. (1961), On sadness and grief in infancy and childhood. Loss and restitution of the symbiotic love object. *The Psychoanalytic Study of the Child*, 16:332–351. New York: International Universities Press.

——— Pine, F., & Bergman, A. (1975), *The Psychological Birth of the Human Infant*. New York: Basic Books.

Main, M. (1995), Recent studies in attachment. Overview, with selected implications for clinical work. In: *Attachment Theory: Social, Developmental, and Clinical Perspectives*, ed. S. Goldberg, R. Muir, & J. Kerr. Hillsdale, NJ: Analytic Press, pp. 407–474.

Marchi, M., & Cohen, P. (1990), Early eating behaviors and adolescent eating disorders. *J. Amer. Acad. Child & Adol. Psychiatry*, 29:114–117.

Masserman, J. H. (1941), Psychodynamisms in anorexia nervosa and neurotic vomiting. *Psychoanal. Quart.*, 10:211–242.

Massie, H. N., & Szajnberg, N. (in preparation), *Lives across Time*.

Mintz, I. (1983a), Psychoanalytic description: The clinical picture of anorexia nervosa and bulimia. In: *Fear of Being Fat. The*

Treatment of Anorexia Nervosa and Bulimia, ed. C. P. Wilson, C. C. Hogan, & I. L. Mintz. New York: Jason Aronson, pp. 83–114.

——— (1983b), Anorexia and bulimia in males. In: *Fear of Being Fat. The Treatment of Anorexia Nervosa and Bulimia,* ed. C. H. Wilson, C. H. Hogan, & I. L. Mintz. New York: Jason Aronson, pp. 263–301.

——— (1992), The unconscious role of teeth in anorexia and bulimia. The lizard phenomenon. In: *Psychodynamic Technique in the Treatment of Eating Disorders.* Northvale, NJ: Jason Aronson, pp. 311–354.

Minuchin, S., Rosman, B. L., & Baker, L. (1978), *Psychosomatic Families: Anorexia in Context.* Cambridge, MA: Harvard University Press.

Mogul, S. L. (1980), Asceticism in adolescence and anorexia. *The Psychoanalytic Study of the Child,* 35:155–175. New Haven, CT: Yale University Press.

Montagu, A. (1971), *Touching.* New York: Harper & Row.

Morton, R. (1689), *Pathisologica, or A Treatise on Consumption.* London: Smith & Waldford.

Mushatt, C. (1992), Anorexia as an expression of ego-defective development. In: *Fear of Being Fat. The Treatment of Anorexia Nervosa and Bulimia,* ed. C. P. Wilson, C. C. Hogan, & I. L. Mintz. New York: Jason Aronson, pp. 301–309.

Olden, C. (1952), Notes on child rearing in America. *The Psychoanalytic Study of the Child,* 7:387–392. New York: International Universities Press.

Oppenheim, J. (1991), *Shattered Nerves, Doctors, Patients, and Depression.* New York: Oxford University Press.

Palaez-Nogueras, M., Field, T. M., Hossain, Z., & Pickens, J. (1996), Depressed mothers' touching increases infants' positive affect and attention in still-face interactions. *Child Develop.,* 67:1780–1792.

Piaget, J. (1937), *The Construction of Reality in the Child.* New York: Basic Books, 1954.

Prodromidis, M., Field, T. M., Arendt, R., Singer, L., Yando, R., & Bendell, D. (1995), Mothers' touching newborns: A comparison of rooming-in versus minimal contact. *Birth,* 22:4.

Provence, S., & Lipton, R. (1962), *Infants in Institutions*. New York: International Universities Press.

Putnam, M. C., Rank, B., & Kaplan, S. (1951), Notes on John, I: A case of primal depression in an infant. *The Psychoanalytic Study of the Child*, 6:38–60. New York: International Universities Press.

Rado, S. (1928), The problem of melancholia. *Internat. J. Psycho-Anal.*, 9:420–438.

Rangell, L. (1955), On the psychoanalytic theory of anxiety: A statement of a unitary theory. *J. Amer. Psychoanal. Assn.*, 3:389–414.

Rampling, D. L. (1980), Abnormal mothering in the genesis of anorexia nervosa. *J. Nerv. Ment. Dis.*, 168:501–504.

Ribble, M. (1943), *The Rights of Infants*. New York: Columbia University Press.

Ritvo, S. (1984), The image and uses of the body in psychic conflict: With special reference to eating disorders in adolescence. *The Psychoanalytic Study of the Child*, 39:449–469. New Haven, CT: Yale University Press.

Rose, J. A. (1943), Eating inhibition in children in relation to anorexia. *Psychosom. Med.*, 5:117–124.

Sandler, J. (1960), The background of safety. *Internat. J. Psycho-Anal.*, 41:352–356.

Schilder, P. (1935), *The Image and Appearance of the Human Body*. New York: International Universities Press, 1950.

Schur, M. (1960), Discussion of Dr. John Bowlby's paper, Grief and Mourning in infancy and early childhood. In: *The Psychoanalytic Study of the Child*, 15:63–84. New York: International Universities Press.

Searl, M. N. (1933), The psychology of screaming. *Internat. J. Psycho-Anal.*, 14:193–205.

Skrabanek, P. (1983), Notes toward the history of anorexia nervosa. *Janus*, 70:109–128.

Sours, J. P. (1974), The anorexia nervosa syndrome. *Internat. J. Psycho-Anal.*, 55:567–576.

——— (1980), *Starving to Death in a Sea of Objects: The Anorexia Syndrome*. New York: Jason Aronson.

Sperling, M. (1963), Fetishism in children. *Psychoanal. Quart.*, 32:374–392.
——— (1978), Anorexia. In: *Psychosomatic Disorders of Childhood*, ed. O. Sperling. New York: Jason Aronson, pp. 129–173.
——— (1983), A reevaluation of classification, concepts, and treatment. In: *Fear of Being Fat. The Treatment of Anorexia and Bulimia*, ed. C. P. Wilson, C. C. Hogan, & I. L. Mintz. New York: Jason Aronson, pp. 51–82.
Spitz, R. A. (1945), Hospitalism: An inquiry into the genesis of psychiatric conditions in early childhood. *The Psychoanalytic Study of the Child*, 1:53–74. New York: International Universities Press.
——— (1946a), Hospitalism: A follow-up report. *The Psychoanalytic Study of the Child*, 2:113–117. New York: International Universities Press.
——— (1946b), Anaclitic depression. *The Psychoanalytic Study of the Child*, 2:313–342. New York: International Universities Press.
——— (1960), Discussion of Dr. John Bowlby's paper, Grief and mourning in infancy and early childhood. *The Psychoanalytic Study of the Child*, 15:85–94. New York: International Universities Press.
Sroufe, L. A., & Fleeson, J. (1986), Attachment and construction of relationships. In: *Relationship and Development*, ed. W. Hartup & Z. Rubin. Hillsdale, NJ: Erlbaum, pp. 51–72.
Stayton, D., & Ainsworth, M. D. S. (1973), Development of separation behavior in the first year of life. *Develop. Psychol.*, 9:226–235.
Steiner, H., & Lock, J. (1998), Anorexia and bulimia in children and adolescents: A review of the past 10 years. *J. Amer. Acad. Child & Adol. Psychiatry*, 37:352–359.
Steinhausen, H. C., Ed. (1995), *Eating Disorders in Adolescence: Anorexia and Bulimia*. New York: De Gruyter.
Sterba, E. (1941), An important factor in eating disturbances of childhood. *Psychoanal. Quart.*, 10:365–372.
Stern, D. N. (1971), A micro-analysis of mother–infant interaction: Behaviors regulating social contact between a mother and

her three-and-a-half-month-old twins. *J. Amer. Acad. Child & Adol. Psychiatry*, 10:501–517.

——— (1974), Mother and infant at play: The dyadic interaction involving facial, vocal, and gaze behaviors. In: *The Effect of the Infant on Its Caregiver*, ed. M. Lewis & L. A. Rosenblum. New York: John Wiley.

——— (1985), Affect attunement. In: *Frontiers of Infant Psychiatry*, Vol. 2, ed. J. D. Call & R. L. Tyson. New York: Basic Books.

Stevenson, O. (1954), The first treasured possession. A study of the part played by specially loved objects and toys in the lives of certain children. *The Psychoanalytic Study of the Child*, 9:199–217. New York: International Universities Press.

Stone, L. (1961), *The Psychoanalytic Situation*. New York: International Universities Press.

Sylvester, E. (1945), Analysis of psychogenic anorexia and vomiting in a four-year-old child. *The Psychoanalytic Study of the Child*, 1:167–187. New York: International Universities Press.

Szmukler, G. I. (1987), Some comments on the link between anorexia nervosa and affective disorder. *Internat. J. Eat. Disord.*, 62:181–189.

Thöma, H. (1967), *Anorexia Nervosa*. New York: International Universities Press.

Tinbergen, N. (1951), *The Study of Instinct*. London: Oxford University Press.

Trevarthan, C. (1977), Descriptive analysis of infant communication behavior. In: *Studies in Mother-Infant Interaction*, ed. H. R. Schaffer. London: Academic Press, pp. 227–270.

——— (1979), Communication and cooperation in early infancy: A description of primary intersubjectivity. In: *Before Speech: The Beginning of Interpersonal Communication*, ed. M. M. Bullowa. Cambridge, U.K.: Cambridge University Press, pp. 321–347.

Tronick, E. Z. (1997), Doctor's orders. *Natural History*, 10:46–47.

——— Als, H., & Adamson, (1978), Structure of early face-to-face communicative interaction. In: *Before Speech: The Beginning of Interpersonal Communication*, ed. M. M. Bullowa. Cambridge, UK: Cambridge University Press, pp. 349–372.

——— ——— ——— Wise, S., & Brazelton, T. B. (1978), The infant's response to entrapment between contradictory messages in face-to-face interaction. *J. Amer. Acad. Child Adol. Psychiat.*, 17:1–3.
Tyson, P. (1989), Two approaches to infant research: A review and integration. In: *The Significance of Infant Observational Research for Clinical Work with Children, Adolescents, and Adults.* Workshop of the Amer. Psychoanal. Assn., ed. S. Dowling & A. Rothstein. Madison, CT: International Universities Press, pp. 3–23.
——— Tyson, R. L. (1990), *Psychoanalytic Theories of Development: An Introduction.* New Haven, CT: Yale University Press.
Waelder, R. (1976), Review of Sigmund Freud, Inhibitions, Symptoms and Anxiety. In: *Psychoanalysis: Observation, Theory, and Application: Selected Papers of Robert Waelder.* New York: International Universities Press, pp. 57–67.
Watson, J. B. (1919), *Psychology from the Standpoint of a Behaviorist.* New York: J. B. Lippincott.
Weber, M. (1921), *The Theory of Social and Economic Organization.* New York: Oxford University Press, 1947.
Welsh, H. K. (1983), Psychoanalytic therapy: The case of Martin. In: *Fear of Being Fat. The Treatment of Anorexia and Bulimia,* ed. C. P. Wilson, C. C. Hogan, & I. L. Mintz. New York: Jason Aronson, pp. 305–314.
Werner, H. (1940), *Comparative Psychology of Mental Development.* New York: International Universities Press, 1957.
Wheedon, A., Scafidi, F. A., Field, T. M., Ironson, G., Valdeon, C., & Bandstra, E. (1993), Massage effects on cocaine-exposed preterm neonates. *Develop. & Behav. Ped.,* 14:318–322.
Wilson, C. P. (1982), Abstaining and bulimic anorexics. *Primary Care,* 9:517–530.
——— (1983a), The fear of being fat in female psychology. In: *Fear of Being Fat. The Treatment of Anorexia and Bulimia,* ed. C. P. Wilson, C. C. Hogan, & I. L. Mintz. New York: Jason Aronson, pp. 9–28.
——— (1983b), The family psychological profile and its therapeutic implications. In: *Fear of Being Fat. The Treatment of Anorexia*

and Bulimia, ed. C. P. Wilson, C. C. Hogan, & I. L. Mintz. New York: Jason Aronson, pp. 29–47.

——— (1983c), Dream interpretation. In: *Fear of Being Fat. The Treatment of Anorexia and Bulimia,* ed. C. P. Wilson, C. C. Hogan, & I. L. Mintz. New York: Jason Aronson, pp. 245–254.

——— (1992), Ego functioning and technique. In: *Psychodynamic Technique in the Treatment of the Eating Disorders,* ed. C. P. Wilson, C. C. Hogan, & I. L. Mintz. Northvale, NJ: Jason Aronson, pp. 19–23.

——— Hogan, C. C., & Mintz, I. L., Eds. (1983), *Fear of Being Fat.* New York: Jason Aronson.

——— ——— ——— Eds. (1992), *Psychodynamic Technique in the Treatment of the Eating Disorders.* Northvale, NJ: Jason Aronson.

Winnicott, D. W. (1936), Appetite and emotional disorder. In: *Through Paediatrics to Psycho-Analysis.* London: Hogarth Press, 1975, pp. 33–51.

——— (1941), The observation of infants in a set situation. In: *Through Paediatrics to Psycho-Analysis.* London: Hogarth Press, 1975, pp. 52–69.

——— (1945), Primitive emotional development. In: *Through Paediatics to Psycho-analysis.* London: Hogarth Press, 1975, pp. 145–156.

——— (1953), Transitional objects and transitional phenomena. A study of the first not-me possession. *Internat. J. Psycho-Anal.,* 34:89–97.

——— (1957), *Mother and Child. A Primer of First Relationships.* New York: Basic Books.

——— (1958), The capacity to be alone. In: *The Maturational Processes and the Facilitating Environment.* New York: International Universities Press, pp. 29–36.

——— (1960), Ego distortion in terms of true and false self. In: *The Maturational Processes and the Facilitating Environment.* New York: International Universities Press, 1965, pp. 140–152.

——— (1962), Ego integration in child development. In: *The Maturational Processes and the Facilitating Environment.* New York: International Universities Press, pp. 56–63.

———— (1963), The development of the capacity for concern. In: *The Maturational Processes and the Facilitating Environment.* New York: International Universities Press, pp. 73–82.

Wulff, M. (1946), Fetishism and object choice in early childhood. *Psychoanal. Quart.,* 15:450–471.

Zerbe, K. J. (1993), Whose body is it anyway? Understanding and treating psychosomatic aspects of early eating disorders. *Bull. Menninger Clinic,* 57:161–177.

Zetzel, E. (1935), The concept of anxiety in relation to the development of psychoanalysis. *J. Amer. Psychoanal. Assn.,* 3:369–388.

———— (1953), The depressive position. In: *Affective Disorders,* ed. P. Greenacre. New York: International Universities Press, pp. 84–116.

Name Index

Abraham, K., 24–25, 33, 156, 157, 185
Adamson, L., 11, 124
Ainsworth, M. D. S., 9, 10
Als, H., 11, 124
Arendt, R., 14n
Axelrad, S., xiv, 10, 13, 16, 40, 85, 99, 124–125, 126n, 163, 166n, 175, 186, 219–220
Azarian, M., x

Baker, L., 27
Bandstra, E., 14n
Bauer, C. R., 14n
Baumrind, D., xv–xvi
Bemporad, J. R., 20, 197
Bendell, D., 14n
Benedek, T., 175
Benjamin, L. T., 201
Bergman, A., 29, 174, 175–176
Bernfeld, S., 2, 168–169, 175
Bibring, E., 178
Bliss, E. L., 19, 26–27, 35, 192–193
Boris, H. N., 159, 203–204
Bourgignon, O., 182
Bowlby, J., 5–7, 8–9, 11, 175, 177, 217–218
Branch, C. H., 19, 26–27, 35, 192–193
Brazelton, T. B., 11
Brenman, M., 26
Breuer, J., 23
Brody, S., xiv, 2, 4–5, 6, 7, 10, 13, 15, 16, 29, 40, 57–58n, 85, 99, 124–125, 126n, 139, 163, 166n, 172, 175, 181, 182, 186, 218–220
Brown, J. C., 197–198
Bruch, H., 27, 31–32, 136
Brumberg, J. J., 20, 21, 22, 23, 24, 36–37, 197
Bynum, C. W., 20
Byron, G., 120

Candland, D. K., 13
Carmichael, L., 2
Cassatt, M., 127n
Chatoor, I., 34
Cohen, D., 124
Cohen, P., 33

Darwin, E., 21
Deutsch, H., 35
Deutsch, J., x
Diamond, E., 19
Dickes, R., 182

Dixon, D. N., 201

Edelson, M., 40
Eissler, K., 25, 26
Ellenberger, H. F., 24
Emde, R. N., 11
Emery, M., x
Escalona, S., xiii, 217

Feder, L., ix, 169n
Feigelson, C., 106n
Fenichel, O., 26, 178
Ferenczi, S., 2, 192n
Field, T. M., 14n, 124
Fintzy, R. T., 182
Fleeson, J., 10
Fliess, J., 23
Forster, E. M., 125
Freud, A., 7, 8, 13, 137, 175–176
Freud, S., 2, 3, 5, 7, 8, 13, 23, 24, 26, 124–125, 168n, 175, 176, 179
Fritsch, S., 93n
Fritz, G. K., 93n
Furman, E., 2

Gaensbauer, T. J., 11
Ganiban, J., 34
Garcia, R., 14n
Geizrals, J., ix
Gesell, A., 2
Goh, S. E., 204–205n
Goldberg, S., 10
Greenacre, P., 13
Greenberg, R., 124
Greene, M., ix
Greenson, R. R., 177, 178
Gull, W. W., 21
Guttman, I., x

Hagino, O., 93n
Hamburg, E., 34
Hanly, C., 8–9
Harlow, H. F., 5
Harmon, R. J., 11
Hartmann, H., xv
Hildanus, F., 20
Hirsch, R., 34
Hitchcock, J., 33
Hogan, C. C., ix, 11, 29, 30–31, 34–35, 197
Hossain, Z., 14n
Hug-Hellmuth, H. von, 2

Ironson, G., 14n

Jacobson, E., 180n
Janet, P., 24
Jones, E., ix–x, 168n, 169–170

Kafka, F., xi, 215
Kaplan, S., 32–33
Katz, J. L., 27–28, 156–157
Keiser, S., 196
Kerr, J., 10
Klein, M., 2–3, 175, 194
Knight, R. P., 26
Kuhn, C. M., 14n
Kurtz, J., x

Lasègue, C., 21–22
Leitch, M., xiii, 217
Lewin, B. D., 172, 196
Linn, B. D., 13
Lock, J., 33–34
Loeb, F., ix
Loeb, L., ix
Lorand, S., 25, 26
Lorenz, K. Z., 5

NAME INDEX

Luckom-Nurnberg, F., 71n

MacCulloch, J. A., 19
Mahler, M. S., 29, 174, 175–176
Main, M., 9
Marchi, M., 33
Masserman, J. H., 25
Massie, H. N., 39n, 73–74n, 75n, 112–113, 220
McKannay, L., x
Mintz, I. L., ix, 11, 29, 30–31, 32, 34, 35–36, 159, 192–193, 204
Minuchin, S., 27
Mogul, S. L., 27, 28
Montagu, A., 13
Morton, R., 20
Muir, R., 10
Mushatt, C., 29

Nachman, P., ix
Nystrom, J., 14n

Olden, C., 202
Ong, S. B., 204–205n
Oppenheim, J., 21

Palaez-Nogueras, M., 14n
Persinger, M., 34
Piaget, J., 13
Pickens, J., 14n
Pine, F., 29, 174, 175–176
Prodromidis, M., 14n
Putnam, M. C., 32–33

Rado, S., 33
Rampling, D. L., 28
Rank, B., 32–33
Ribble, M., 12

Ritvo, S., 33
Rose, J. A., 25–26
Rosman, B. L., 27

Sandler, J., 14
Scafidi, F., 14n
Schilder, P., 11–12, 25, 119, 179
Schur, M., 7
Schyanberg, S. M., 14n
Searl, M. N., 170
Siegel, M., xiv, 10, 29, 57–58n, 126n, 175, 220
Simon, A., x
Singer, L., 14n
Skrabanek, P., 20
Sours, J. P., 27, 28–29, 30, 120, 192
Sperling, M., 27, 28, 29, 31, 175–176, 182
Spitz, R. A., 7, 175
Sroufe, L. A., 10
Stayton, D., 10
Steiner, H., 33–34
Sterba, E., 32, 183n
Stern, D. N., 11, 124
Stevenson, O., 183n
Stone, L., 185
Subramanian, M., 204–205n
Sylvester, E., 32
Szmukler, G. I., 162

Thöma, H., 20, 27, 156
Tinbergen, N., 5
Trevarthan, C., 124
Tronick, E. Z., 11, 124

Valdeon, C., 14n
Vega-Lahr, N., 14n

Watson, J. B., 168

Weber, M., xv*n*.
Werner, H., 13
Wheedon, A., 14n, 124
Wilson, C. P., ix, 11, 29, 30–31, 34, 143, 159, 192, 193
Winnicott, D. W., xv, 3–4, 17, 175, 181, 183n
Wise, S., 11

Wittig, B., 9
Wulff, M., 182

Yando, R., 14n

Zerbe, K. J., 194
Zetzel, E., 33, 53
Zimmerman, R. R., 5

Subject Index

Abandonment, fear of, 61, 70, 176–177
Abstinence, 19–20
Achievement, emphasis on, 30
Adaptive behavior, 83–84
  tactile stimulation and, 13
Adolescence
  anorexia appearing in, 22–23, 207–208
  female experience in, 36–37
  libidinal and aggressive excitement in, 24, 26–27
  rapid changes during, 31–32
Affect
  isolation of, 35, 158
  rejection of, 30, 189
Affectionless character, 5–6
Affective disorders
  anorexia and, 161–162
  eating disorders and, 33–34
Affectlessness, 100, 161
  maternal, 133–134
Aggression, tightly restrained, 145–146
Aggressive behavior, 87–88
Aggressor, identification with, 35, 108, 112, 161–162
  self-starvation and, 171–172

Anal-destructive fantasy, 191
Anal phase, 190–191
Androgyny, 159
Annihilation, fear of, 169–171
Anorexia
  categories of, 21
  clinical signs for further study, 163–188
  depression in, 27–28
  history of, 19–37
  known clinical signs of, 137–162
  in males, 35–36
  percentage of individuals recovering from, 207
  precursors of, 211–213
  present problem of, 207–213
  psychogenic sources of, xiv–xv, 26–27
  psychological definition of, 20–21
  psychological events of infancy in, 17
  religious definition of, 19–20
  search for causes of, xvi–xvii
  sociological roots of, 21–23
  studies of, 34, 211–212
Anorexia mirabilis, 20
Anorexia nervosa, 21

243

SUBJECT INDEX

Anorexics
  comparisons of, 115–121
  psychoanalytic cases of in childhood, 32–33
  unconscious aims of, 193–204
Anticipatory anxiety, 11
Anxiety. *See* Castration anxiety; Separation anxiety
  around menarche, 36–37
  childhood, 61
  defenses against, 17
  ego formation and, xiv
  flooding with, 92–93, 95
  infant screaming and, 169
  maternal, 49–51
  origin of, 11
  physiological and signal, 15–16
  psychological sources of, 8
  signal, 15–16, 124–125
Anxious isolation, 120
Apathy, 176–177
Apgar scores, 43, 77
Aphanasis, 169–170
Appetite
  lack of, 58
  loss of, 20, 27
  need to control, 24
As-if personality, 72
Asceticism, 19, 28–29, 158–161, 197–201, 208
Assertive behavior, lack of, 57
Atonement, rites of, 19–20
Attachment
  quality of, 10–11
  theory of, 8–9
Attachment behavior, control theory of, 6
Attachment-seeking, 6
Average expectable environment, xv–xvi

Avoidance, 112

Baby blanket, clinging to, 67–68, 92, 115, 181–183
"Baby's First Caress," 127n
Barbie, ideal of, 160
Bed-sharing, 192
Bedtime struggles, 94, 117
Biting, 177–178, 190
Bliss, achieving state of, 200–201
Bodily perfection, pursuit of, 194–195
Bodily pleasure
  absence of, 57
  capacity for, 203
Body
  dulled boundaries of, 66–67, 168, 187
  fluctuating control of, 63–64
  poor development of, 54–55, 56–57
  rigidity of, 67
Body damage, fear of, 61
Body ego, 7
Body function, instinctual gratifications of, 2
Body image
  anorexia and, 26
  anxiety about, 177
  building up of, 12
  continuing conflicts about, 207, 208
  dancing and, 119
  derogation of, 37
  distortions of, 143–155
  disturbance in, 11–12, 27–28, 34, 35, 67
  tactile stimulation and, 12–14
  uneasiness with, 150–151
  vulnerability of, 36

SUBJECT INDEX

Body integrity
  faults in, 115
  fears about, 24
Body mastery, failure of, 57
Body safety
  infant need for, 5–6
  maternal behaviors and, 6–7
  need for, 14–15
Body weight, overconcern with, 33–34
Borderline state, 72, 107
Boredom, 178
Bottle-feeding, 49, 80–81
Bowel control, 32
Breast
  consciousness of, 2–3
  loss of, 66
Breast feeding
  ambivalence about, 48–49
  rejection of, 79
Bridgman, Laura, sensory experience of, 13
Bulimia, 167
  in males, 35–36
  motivation for, 120
  studies of, 34

Cannibalistic fantasies, 157–158
Cannibalistic stage, 24–25
Carlini, Benedetta, visions of, 197–201
Castration anxiety, 61, 96–97, 103
Catholic church, fasting in, 19–20
Character development, 219–220
  anxiety and, xiv
Character disorder, 97
Childhood
  disturbing emotional experience during, 187–188
  histories of, xiii

painful events of, 117
pathological mourning in, 7–8
stress of, 27–28
Childhood fetish, 182
Children's Apperception Test (CAT), 64–65
  stories in, 100
China, anorexia and bulimia in, 204–205n
Chlorosis, 22
Christ, identification with, 197–201
Christian beliefs, medieval, 19–20
Clinging, 6, 115, 117
  to transitional objects, 67–69, 164, 181–183, 208
Clinical assessment, 108
Clinical data, notes on, 39–41
Clinical evaluation, 73
Clinical signs, 137–162
  needing further study, 163–188
Clumsiness, 62, 65
Cognitive investment, capacity for, 125
Cold personality, 9–10
Communication
  development of, 124–125
  infrequent, 138
  quality of in mother-infant dyad, 124–136
Compromise formations, 26
Connectedness, 125–126
Control, need for, 30–31, 37, 157–158
Crankiness, 54
Crying, 6, 48–49, 52–53, 189
  enraged, 168–172
  vomiting and, 165
Curiosity, lack of, 99, 186

Dancing, 119

Day of Atonement, 20
Death-wishes, omnipotence of, 170
Defenses, 108
   rigid, 35
   strict, 67
   supporting fallacy of control, 158
Dejection, 174–181
   lingering, 164
   signs of, 175
Denial, 108, 112
   gross, 35
   psychotic, 195
   supporting fallacy of control, 158
Depression, 161–162, 174. *See also* Dejection; Melancholia; Sadness
   in anorexia, 26, 27–28, 35
   with changes of adolescence, 31–32
   in early adulthood, 178–179
   primal, 32–33
   self-starvation and, 24–25
Depressive state, 2
Depressive vulnerability, 33, 208
   during infancy, 53
Detachment, maternal, 133–134
Diet, concern with, 23
Dieting, 27
Digestive disorders, psychosomatic, 137
Direct observations, gaps in, 41
Discipline, 46
Disorganized action, 61–62, 80, 156
Displeasure, 129
Disuse atrophy, 63–64
Draw-a-Person exercise
   body image distortions in, 143–155
   rigid figures in, 145–147
Drives, mental representations of, 8

Dynamic psychiatry, 23

Early loss, abiding painful experiences of, 5–6
Eating
   being in control of, 28–29
   dread of being seen, 156n
   as infantile gratification and frustration, 33–34
   primitive taboos against, 19
Eating disorders. *See* Anorexia; Bulimia
   continuing, 207
   disgust with food and, 24
   failure of mother-infant bonding in, 28
   increasing incidence of, 34–35
   infancy and early childhood causes of, 137–138
   personal-historical events in, xiv–xv
   psychoanalytic literature on, 25–26
   psychological events of infancy in, 17
   signs of in oral phase, 163–188
   variety of, 123–124
Eating habits, changing, 69
Ecstasy, 196
Ego
   anxiety and formation of, xiv
   early development of, 17
   fragile, 73
   weak, 73
Emotional communication, infant-mother, 124–125
Emotional freedom, ambivalence about, 120
Emotional investment, capacity for, 125

SUBJECT INDEX

Emotional withdrawal, 84
Engagement
  assessing level of, 126–128
  definition of, 126
  excessive, 128
  poor or faulty, 128–129
  positive but limited, 127
  quality of, 123–136
  rich and reliable, 127
Erotic overstimulation, 60, 61, 191–192
Evolutionary adaptedness, 6
Exercise
  extreme, 156–157
  preoccupation with, 186

Family
  ambivalent relationships in, 149–150
  conflict in, 69–71
  sharp boundaries in, 154–155
Family Drawings, 107
Fantasies, infant, 2
Fasting
  public, xi
  religious, 19–20
Father
  anger of, 104–105
  of anorexic patients, 134–136
  disturbed relationship to, 138–143
  education of, 44–45
  hostile teasing, 65–66
  judgmental, 59–60
  remote, authoritarian, 139–142
  self-righteous, 135
  withdrawn, 83
Fatness, fear of, 23, 29–30, 69
Fear-hate-guilt triad, 170
Fear of Being Fat, 34, 292

Feeding
  assessment of, 126n
  control of, 28–29
  disturbances in, 137, 290
  excessive, 84
  routine of, 80–81
  slow, 52, 53–54
Feeding schedules, 45
  erratic, 66
  problems with, 47–51
  rigid, 85–86
  strict maintenance of, 25–26
Feet, problems with, 74
Female experience, adolescent, 36–37
Female spitefulness, 20–21
Feminine decorum, 20
Feminine delicacy, ideals of, 22
Fine motor skills, 76
Fine motor tasks, 62
  perfectionism in, 63
First treasured possession, 183n
First year, life history in, 43–56, 77–88
Flappers, 23, 160
Fliess papers, Draft F, 23
Following, 6
Food
  anxiety about, 91
  disgust with, 24
  hypercathexis of, 157
  interest in preparation of, 29
  rejection of, 32–33, 34, 55–56, 57, 58, 165, 208
  religious abstinence from, 19–20
  symbolic meanings of, 192–193
Food phobias, 29–30, 193
Force-feeding, 80, 84, 100
Freedom, 202–203
  self-denial and, 26–27

SUBJECT INDEX

Friendships, 102–103
  low interest in, 161
Frustration
  chronic, 57, 61
  of infancy, 3
  intolerance for, 147–148
Function pleasure, absence of, 57

Gagging, vomiting and, 167–168
Gastritis, 108
Gesell Developmental Schedules
  at 6 weeks, 46–47, 79–80
  at 26 weeks, 51–52, 81–82
  at 52 weeks, 54–55, 83–84
Gesell Developmental Tests, Motor
    and Adaptive sectors of, 13
Gratification
  absence of, 66
  from stereotypic behaviors,
    172–174
Gross motor activity
  discouragement of, 67
  independent, 83–84
Gross motor atrophy, 63–64
Guilt, 27–28
  self-starvation for, 203–204

Hallucinatory gratification, 16
Head wagging, 52, 173
Helplessness, 27
  screaming and, 169
Hereditary weakness, 21
Hopelessness, 161
Hostile introjects, killing off,
    193–195
Human Figure Drawing, 143–155
Hunger artist, xi
  hidden aggressive wishes of, 215
Hyperactivity, 28–29, 80, 88,
    154–157, 187, 208

Hypotonia, 57–58
Hysteria, 22
  anorexia as symptom of, 20–21,
    23
Hysterical vomiting, 24

Immobility, 154
Impatience, oral ambivalence and,
    24–25
Impulse control, 35
  failure of, 147–148
  fear of losing, 31
Impulsive behavior, 88, 101
Individual freedom, 202–203
Infancy
  disturbing emotional experience
    during, 187–188
  escaping indifferent care
    during, 212–213
  experiences of, xv–xvi
  histories of, xiii
  importance of, xvi, 1–17
  loneliness in, 176
  negative attachment during,
    9–10
  powerlessness and anxiety of,
    169
  psychoanalytic literature on, 2–3
  refusal of food during, 32–33
  sadistic fantasies during, 2
  solitude during, 116
  sources of disturbance during,
    8–9
  vulnerability of body image
    during, 11–12
Infancy Research Project, xiii–xv,
    217
Infant
  continuity of experiences of, 1
  disturbance in feeding of, 137

SUBJECT INDEX

mother's behavior and attitudes toward, xiii–xv
Infant-mother communication, development of, 124–125
Infanticidal wishes, reaction formation against, 28
Infantile negativism, 27
Infantile security, longing for, 200
Infantile sexuality, 2
Infantile thought, 2
Inhibition, 158
Inner self, getting rid of, 76
Instinctual gratification, renouncing, 28–29
Instinctual wishes, problems with, 137
Intelligence quotients, 62–63
Intelligence tests, 98
  findings in, 71–72
Internal conflicts, unresolved, 162
Intimacy, need for, 5–6

Keller, Helen, sensory experience of, 13
Kindergarten
  behavior in, 61–62
  observed behavior in, 97–100
Kinesthetic gratification, 4–6

Language development, 51, 55
Latency period, continued frustrations in, 60–61
Lent, 20, 203–204
Libidinal pleasures, rejection of, 29–30
Libido
  diminished, 28
  hysterical loss of, 23
Life histories, 23
  at 2-7 years, 57–59, 88–97

at 4-5 years, 59–60
at 4-6 years, 97–100
at 6-7 years, 60–61
at 14 months, 56–57
at 18 years, 68–73, 101–108
at 22 years, 108–109
at 27 years, 109–110
at 29 years, 110–112
at 30 years, 112–113
at birth to early latency, 66–68, 100–101
in early adulthood, 73–76
in first year, 43–56, 77–88
intelligence quotients in, 62–63
in nursery school and kindergarten, 61–62
observed behavior during psychological test sessions in, 63–65
poststudy parent conference in, 65–66
Loneliness, 107, 116, 161, 189
  capacity to manage, 119
  dejection and, 176
  hunger and, 186
  infant screaming and, 168
  pervasive, 208–209
  screaming and, 54
Longitudinal studies, 16
  phase 1, 217–219
  phase 2, 219–220
  phase 3, 220
Love, fear of losing, 3

Magical thinking, 195
Maladaptive eating patterns, 33–34
Mania
  as diversion from melancholia, 179
  sleep rejection and, 196

SUBJECT INDEX

Manipulative behavior, 97, 98–99
Mastery, pleasure of, 2
Masturbatory fantasies, 159
　fear of punishment for, 103
Maternal behaviors
　observation of, 217, 218–219
　showing need for body safety,
　　6–7
Maternal deprivation, 9–10
Maternal object, killing off,
　　193–195
Maternal role, ambivalence about,
　　45–46
Medieval taboos, 19
Melancholia, 23
　mania as diversion from, 179
　oral ambivalence and, 24–25
　self-starvation and, 24–25
Menarche
　anxiety around, 36–37
　conscious food rejection and,
　　165
Menstruation, 36, 102, 104
　ambivalence toward, 69
　stomach pain with, 113
　taboos regarding, 22–23
Mental capacity, of infants, 2
Mental representations, of drives
　　and experience, 8
Merrill-Palmer Preschool Scale of
　　Intelligence, 62, 98
Moral codes, strict, 30
Moral promiscuity, 70–71
Moslem culture, fasting in, 20
Mother
　affectless, 117
　of anorexic patients, 40
　biological need for proximity
　　to, 5–6
　childhood of, 78–79

　clinging to, 115, 117
　conflict with, 117
　detachment of, 133–134
　disturbed relationship to, 138
　early disappointment in, 32
　education of, 44
　emotionally distant, 95–96
　failure to notice child's sadness,
　　180–181
　fears about infant care, 49–51
　ineffective, 82–83, 87–88, 116
　interviews of, 57–59, 88–97
　longing for gratification from,
　　25–26
　managing ambivalence toward,
　　171–172
　need for closeness to, 90, 91–92
　overcontrolling, 31
　postpartum interview of, 43–46,
　　77–79
　preoedipal problems with, 27–28
　rage against, 107
　restrictive, 84–85
　unknowable, 144–145
　wish for physical contact with,
　　172–173
　withdrawal of, 53–54
Mother-child relationship
　difficulties in, 57–59
　early problems in, 35
　libidinal and aggressive, 8–9
　problems in, 40n
　tension in, 84–85, 93–94
Mother-infant bonding,
　failure of, 28
Mother-infant needs, 4–5
Mother-infant relationship
　disturbance in, 138
　level of engagement in, 126–128
　longitudinal research on,

SUBJECT INDEX 251

xiii–xv, 217–220
quality of engagement in,
123–136
Motor development. *See also* Fine
motor activity; Gross motor
activity
restricted, 52–53
tactile stimulation and, 13
Mourning, pathological, 7–8
Movement, pleasure of, 156–157
Mutual intimacy, 127
Mutual withdrawals, 7–8

Nakedness, 191–192
Narcissism
clinging to transitional object
and, 181
perverse and self-destructive, 121
Narcissistic self-containment,
209–210
Needs, mother-infant, 4–5
Negative attachment, 9–10
Nervous disease, 21
psychogenic factors in, 23
Newborns, need for physical
handling, 13–15
Nursery school
behavior in, 61–62, 97–100
poor adaptation to, 116

Object
clinging to, 6
injection of, 33
Object cathexis, low capacity for,
57
Object loss
fear of, 3, 29, 35, 61, 85, 94,
96–97
intense feelings of, 176
Object relations

anorexia as disturbance in, 26
development of, 15–16
disturbance in, 98–99
oral aggression and, 25
Oedipal conflict, 191–192
in anorexics, 120–121
representing internal conflicts,
162
unresolved, 72, 106
Oedipal fantasies, 2
Oral aggression
intense, 184–185
repressed fears of, 193
reversing of, 120
Oral ambivalence, 24–25
Oral autoerotic behaviors, 184
Oral envy, 156
Oral fixation, 26
Oral frustrations, 183–184
Oral gratification, 3
Oral needs, unfulfilled, 190
Oral phase, 2
behaviors of, 3–4
complexity of, 4–5
events in, 16
lack of satisfactions in, 189–190
self-starvation and, 24
signs of emotional distress and
eating disorder during,
163–188
Oral pleasure, rejection of, 91
Oral sadism, 34
Oral-sadistic wishes, 157–158
Oral satisfaction
absence of, 186
need for, 217–218
Oral triad of wishes, 196
Overactivity, 196
food rejection and, 165
Overexcitement, 128

Painting, 75–76
Panic attacks, 57, 116–117
Paranoid thinking, 194
Parent-child relationship,
  sadomasochistic acts in,
  64–65
Parental control, 22
Parental intrusion, 30–31
Parents. *See also* Father; Mother
  abandonment by, 176
  absence of, 118
  ambivalence toward, 99
  of anorexic patients, 40, 132–136
  asocial, 70–71
  conflict with, 116, 186
  defiance of or retreat from, 190
  destructive wishes of, 195–196
  disillusionment with, 161, 180n
  distancing self from, 69–70, 180n
  disturbed relationship to,
    138–143
  emotionally distant, 118, 209
  forming united front against
    child, 142–143
  interviews with, 57–59, 88–97
  nudity of, 191–192
  observing behaviors and
    attitudes of, 213
  oedipal conflicts with, 120–121
  overcontrolling, 31
  pleasureless relationship with, 30
  poststudy conference with, 65–66
  punitive, 119
  rejection of, 75
  relinquishment of care by, 118
  reluctance to care for children,
    209–211
  repeated absences of, 85, 89, 116
  sadomasochistic effort to
    control, 211
  sadomasochistic relationship
    with, 101
  unempathic, 118–119, 125, 161
  unresponsive, 74
Part-object relationship, 182
Perfectionism, 23
  in fine motor tasks, 63
  parental demand for, 31
  self-denial in pursuit of, 159–160
Permissiveness, 202–203
Persecutory object, killing off,
  193–195
Persecutory states, 2
Personal growth, 202–203
Personal-Social development, 51
Phobias, 75
Physical handling, 14–15
Physical lags, 54–55, 56–57, 116
Physical movement, lack of,
  186–187
Physiological anxiety, 124–125
Picky eater, 60–61, 167
Postpartum interview, 43–46,
  77–79
Primates, attachment-seeking
  behavior of, 6
Prisoner of Chillon, 120
Prisoners of war, apathy in, 177
Progressive education, 202–203
Projection, 108
  supporting fallacy of control, 158
Promiscuous aggressiveness,
  freedom for, 201–204
Protective shield, 124
Psychoanalytic theory, 39
  on neurotic eating disorders,
    25–26
*Psychodynamic Technique in the
  Treatment of the Eating
  Disorders*, 34

SUBJECT INDEX

Psychological anxiety, preparation for, 124–125
Psychological disorders, 21
Psychological testing, 220
  findings in, 71–72, 106–107
  observed behavior during, 63–65
Psychopathology, origins of, xiii
Psychosocial factors, 26–27
Punishment, fear of, 61, 96–97, 103
Purgation, 203–204

Rabbinical law, in medieval period, 19
Rage. *See also* Screaming; Temper tantrums
  infant screaming and, 168–172
  retributive, 204–205
  turned against self, 189
Ramadan, fasting during, 20
Reaction formation, 112
  against infanticidal wishes, 28
Regression, 35, 67, 108
  supporting fallacy of control, 158
Regressive aims, 196–201
Relationships, difficulty with, 110, 111
Religious fasting, 197–201
Religious rites, 19
Reparation, self-starvation for, 203–204
Repression, 201–202
Resistant behavior, 89–90
Restlessness, 67, 187
  feeding problems and, 49
  oral ambivalence and, 24–25
Restriction, supporting fallacy of control, 158

Sadistic fantasies, 2
Sadness, 27–28, 53, 76, 117
  early, 32
  parents' failure to notice, 175–176, 180–181
Sainthood, for abstinence, 20
School
  anxiety about, 93
  social experience in, 102
Screaming, 54, 57, 189, 208
  enraged, 168–172
  frequent, intense, and prolonged, 164
  tantrumlike, 80–81
Self-care, discouragement of, 55–56
Self-denial, 19
  perfectionism and, 159–160
Self-esteem
  artificial aggrandizement of, 202
  loss of, 178
  low, 67–68, 110
  self-punishment for, 203
Self representation
  battered, 100–101
  insecure, 115
  object relations and, 15–16
  poor, 73
Self-rocking, 172–173
Self-rolling, 172–173
Self-starvation, 20
  fallacy of control in, 157–158
  for guilt and reparation, 203–204
  identification with aggressor and, 171–172
  to kill off hostile parental introjects, 193–195
Sensorimotor responses, 77
Sensory deprivation, 13–14
Sensory integration, 14–15
Separation anxiety, 7–8, 85, 117
  early, 29
  mastering, 182

Sexual development, confusion about, 192
Sexual excitement, displaced, 140–141
Sexual exhibitionism, 121
Sexual fantasies, restriction of, 159
Sexuality, denial of, 151–154
Signal anxiety, 15–16, 124–125
Skin sensation, 4–5
Sleep, 196
Smiling, 6, 51
Social activity, 186
Social busyness, 119, 178–179
Social change, in adolescent anorexia, 201–204
Social development, 14n
Social excitements, 119–120
Social immaturity, 62
Social mobility, desire for, 40
Social overtures, response to, 57
Social play, lack of, 52–53
Social pressures, 34–35, 109
Social withdrawal, 51, 84
Socialization, 15–16
Sociological roots, 21–23
Speech
  unstable uses of, 164, 183–185
  withheld and rapid, 67, 99
Stanford-Binet, Revised Form L-M, 98
Stanford-Binet Intelligence Scale, Revised Form L-M, 62
Starvation. *See also* Food, rejection of; Self-starvation
  melancholia and, 24–25
Stereotypic behaviors, 164, 172–174
Stomach disorders, 73–74
  psychosomatic, 137
Stomach pain, chronic, 104, 108–109, 113, 117–118, 167, 210
Strange Situation paradigm, 9, 10–11
Strangers, fear of, 57
Sucking, 6
Superego
  early development of, 17
  fragile, 73
  in liberal social setting, 202–203
  restrictions of in asceticism, 158–161
Superego retribution, 61
Sweets, rejection of, 91, 167, 190

Taboos, around menstruation, 22–23
Tactile stimulation, 4–6, 12–14
Talking, constant urge for, 184–185
Teasing, hostile, 65–66
Teething
  difficulty with, 86
  vomiting during, 166
Temper tantrums, 59, 92, 101, 116, 172
Thematic Apperception Test (TAT) stories, 71–72, 106–107
Thinness
  fashionable, 23, 160–161
  insistent pursuit of, 27, 193–196
Toddlerhood, escaping indifferent care during, 212–213
Toilet regressions, 191
Toilet training, 32
  conflict in, 190–191
  difficulty observing, 164n
  problems with, 58, 86–87
  schedule for, 45
  too early, 100–101
  unsuccessful, 90–91

SUBJECT INDEX

Touch
 in infant development, 12–14
 sensation of, 4–5
Transitional objects, 67
 clinging to, 164, 181–183, 208

Unfavorable development
 diagnosis of, 131–132
 signs of, 129–131
 symptomatic behaviors showing, 130–131
Unpleasure, feelings of, 129

Visions, 197–198
Visual functions, preoccupation with, 106–107
Vomiting, 92, 164–168, 186, 208
 daily, 52–53
 for guilt and reparation, 203–204
 hysterical, 24
 with teething, 86
 weight loss and, 104

WAIS-R
 subtest scores, 106
 Verbal Scale, 71

Weaning
 emotional problems related to, 2–3
 problems with, 48–50
 sudden, 187
Wechsler Intelligence Scale for Children (WISC), 62–63, 98
Wechsler Intelligence Scale for Children (WISC) IQ, 63
Wechsler Primary and Preschool Scale of Intelligence (WPPSI), 62, 98
Weight loss, 104
 extreme, 74
Whole-body pleasure, ache for, 172–174
Withdrawal, 55–56
 from unpleasurable surroundings, 58–59
Womb, return to, 196

Yom Kippur, 203–204

Zigzag body, 143–144